Ethics and Politics
Early Childhood E

Early childhood education and care services have become a policy priority for governments and international organisations. The mainstream debate treats these services in a highly instrumental way, as the solution to many economic and social problems. Technical practice, summed up in the question 'what works?', is put foremost.

This book challenges the mainstream debate and explores an alternative approach to early childhood services: putting ethics and politics first, in services that are essentially 'public spaces' full of unpredictable possibilities. The authors offer readers a very different way of thinking about and practising early childhood work. They make accessible important discussions in philosophy, ethics and politics, mostly unheard of in the early childhood field yet highly relevant. These include:

- the work of post-structural thinkers such as Foucault and Deleuze, Derrida and Levinas;
- concepts such as the ethics of an encounter, the ethics of care, a pedagogy of listening, minority politics and Utopia;
- and the ways in which neoliberal capitalism shapes early childhood work.

The authors connect theory to practice by drawing on a wide range of examples of early childhood work in several countries, including the Northern Italian city of Reggio Emilia.

This book presents essential ideas, theories and debates to an international readership, which includes practitioners, trainers, students, researchers, policy makers and anyone with an interest in early childhood education.

Gunilla Dahlberg is Professor at the Stockholm Institute of Education, Sweden. **Peter Moss** is Professor at the Institute of Education, University of London.

Contesting Early Childhood Series
Series Editors: Gunilla Dahlberg and Peter Moss

This ground-breaking series questions the current dominant discourses in early childhood, and offers alternative narratives of an area that is now made up of a multitude of perspectives and debates.

The series examines the possibilities and risks arising from the accelerated development of early childhood services and policies, and illustrates how it has become increasingly steeped in regulation and control. Insightfully, this collection of books will each show how early childhood services can in fact *contribute* to ethical and democratic practices. The authors explore new ideas taken from alternative working practices in both the western and developing world, other academic disciplines in addition to developmental psychology. They also locate theories and practices in relation to the major processes of political, social, economic, cultural and technological change occurring in the world today.

Titles in the series:

Ethics and Politics in Early Childhood Education

Gunilla Dahlberg and Peter Moss

RoutledgeFalmer
Taylor & Francis Group

LONDON AND NEW YORK

First published 2005
by RoutledgeFalmer
2 Park Square, Milton Park, Abingdon, Oxfordshire OX14 4RN

Simultaneously published in the USA and Canada
by RoutledgeFalmer
270 Madison Ave, New York, NY 10016

Reprinted 2005, 2006, 2007

RoutledgeFalmer is an imprint of the Taylor & Francis Group, an informa business

© 2005 Gunilla Dahlberg and Peter Moss

Typeset in 10/12pt Baskerville MT by Graphicraft Limited, Hong Kong
Printed and bound in Great Britain by TJ International Ltd,
Padstow, Cornwall

British Library Cataloguing in Publication Data
A catalogue record for this book is available
from the British Library

Library of Congress Cataloging in Publication Data

Dahlberg, Gunilla, 1945–
    Ethics and politics in early childhood education / Gunilla
Dahlberg and Peter Moss.
        p. cm. – (Contesting early childhood series)
    Includes bibliographical references and index.
        1. Early childhood education – Political aspects. 2. Early
childhood education – Italy – Reggio Emilia. I. Moss, Peter,
1945– II. Title. III. Series.
LB1139.23.D27 2004
372.21–dc22

                                                        2004007061

ISBN 10: 0-415-28041-9 (hbk)
ISBN 10: 0-415-28042-7 (pbk)

ISBN 13: 978-0-415-28041-9 (hbk)
ISBN 13: 978-0-415-28042-6 (pbk)

Contents

Series editors' preface

Early childhood education and care have become a subject of public interest in recent years, in many countries and among influential international organisations. The subject is on the agenda today not only of those who work in the field but also of others who, until recently, have shown little interest, such as politicians, economists and businessmen and businesswomen. This heightened interest has converted into increasing levels of provision in many countries, part of a process of the institutionalisation of childhood.

In our view this expansion of early childhood education and care opens up new possibilities – for children, for families and for communities. We are not nostalgic for a past when early childhood was only lived in families. Institutionalisation of childhood can be a force for good. But, as Foucault reminds us, though not everything is bad everything is dangerous: expansion, therefore, brings new risks. One is that increasing institutionalisation of childhood may lead to greater and more effective governing of children. This may happen in particular when early childhood institutions are understood as enclosures for the effective application of technologies to produce predetermined and standardised outcomes – a very common way of thinking today.

Another related risk is that more provision will be accompanied by more uniformity and normalisation of thought and practice, as the early childhood field is increasingly dominated by one discourse. This discourse is Anglo-American in origin, first spoken in the English language though increasingly spoken in other languages. It is produced in a very specific context: a resurgent economic and political liberalism. It is informed by the discipline of developmental psychology and, more generally, adopts a positivistic and empirical-analytic paradigm.

What we term here the dominant early childhood discourse is inscribed with the assumptions and beliefs of modernity: for example, a desire for objectivity, universality, certainty and mastery, through scientific knowledge. It embodies, too, particular understandings including, for example, of childhood, learning, evaluation and institutions for children (such as the image of the institution as an enclosure for producing outcomes). This discourse offers a regime of truth about early childhood education and care as a technology for ensuring social regulation and economic success, in which the young child is constructed as a redemptive agent who can be programmed to become the future solution to our current problems. The discourse is instrumental in rationality and technical in practice, and seeks closure through searching for the answer to one question: what works?

This discourse may be increasingly dominant and increasingly confident of its own necessity. But there are other discourses in the early childhood field. Some welcome complexity, diversity and otherness. They offer resistance to the dominant discourse, with its embodied values, assumptions and beliefs. They have a variety of sources. They may be produced from local experiences, for example the early childhood work in the Italian city of Reggio Emilia. Or they may be produced by researchers and others in the early childhood field working with non-foundational perspectives – termed by some postmodernism or poststructuralism – and with the ideas of theorists outside the field, such as Foucault, Derrida, Deleuze and Levinas.

The purpose of this series is to problematise what we have termed the dominant early childhood discourse, and to make space where other discourses can be heard. In so doing, the series seeks to reclaim early childhood education and care for ethics and politics by arguing that ethical and political choices face us in many areas: for example, understandings of the child and early childhood institutions; pedagogical theories and practices; and evaluation. There is, in these and other areas, always more than one possibility, more than one answer to any question. This means we have to make choices, choices for which we must take responsibility, choices that will be provisional and contestable.

Three other themes run through this series. First, relations of power, whether between countries of the North and South or the effects of dominant discourses. Second, early childhood is treated as part of the world we live in today; to understand early childhood, we need to make critical analyses of the broad social, technical, political and economic forces that are producing so many changes. Third, while focused on early childhood education, the series often engages with issues of wider educational relevance; indeed, all the volumes speak to schooling and education for older children and young people.

The current volume addresses all of these issues and themes. In particular, it offers a discourse of early childhood institutions as, first and foremost, places of ethical and political practice, demoting technical practices to a subsidiary place. We consider what this discourse would mean for pedagogical work. What might it mean, for example, if pedagogical practice was to embody the ethics of an encounter, treating the alterity of the Other with respect rather than making the Other into the Same? What might the concept of 'minor politics' mean if applied in early childhood institutions? We offer examples of people and places working in ways which we think illustrate the possibilities of this other discourse. Finally, we put forward the case for experimentation and Utopian thought and action, to help us open up to new possibilities and new hope.

Acknowledgement

Material from Rose, N., *Powers of Freedom: Reframing Political Thought* (Cambridge: Cambridge University Press, 1999) is reproduced with permission of Cambridge University Press and the author.

Chapter 1

Opening narrative

From The University in Ruins *by Bill Readings (1996):*

> The Enlightenment proposes education as the site of emancipation, the freeing of the student from all obligations, including that to the teacher. The modern bureaucratic state proposes to reduce the relation to that of development and training of technocrats through the transmission of education. These attempts can be summarised under the rubric of the ideology of autonomy. I want to suggest, however, that pedagogy can also be understood otherwise: other than as the inculcation or revelation of an inherent human autonomy, other than as the production of sovereign subjects . . .
>
> My aim, then, is an anti-modernist rephrasing of teaching and learning as sites of *obligation*, as loci of *ethical practices*, rather than as sites for the transmission of scientific knowledge . . . I want to insist that pedagogy is a *relation, a network of obligation* . . .
>
> The condition of pedagogical practice is, in Blanchot's words, 'an infinite attention to the other' . . . [and] education is this drawing out of the otherness of thought . . . *Listening to Thought* is not the spending of time in the production of the autonomous subject (even an oppositional one) or of an autonomous body of knowledge. Rather, to listen to Thought, think beside each other and beside ourselves, is to explore an open network of obligations that keeps the question of meaning open as a locus of debate. Doing justice to Thought, listening to our interlocutors, means trying to hear that which cannot be said but that which tries to make itself heard. And this is a process incompatible with the production of (even relatively) stable and exchangeable knowledge.
>
> (154, 158, 161–162, 165; original emphasis)

This book is about a possibility for institutions for children and young people. It is a possibility that we have been moving towards in previous writings, both together and with other colleagues (cf. Dahlberg and Åsén, 1994; Moss and Pence, 1994; Dahlberg *et al.*, 1999; Moss and Petrie, 2002). The possibility is that these institutions can be understood, first and foremost, as forums, spaces or sites for ethical and political practice – as 'loci of ethical practices' and 'minor politics'. That these institutions can be places where the Other is not made into the Same, but which open up instead for diversity, difference and otherness, for new possibilities and potentialities. That they can be places where children and adults are governed less, not in the neo-conservative sense of 'smaller government', but through being able to confront dominant discourses that claim to transmit a true body of knowledge, and that seek to manipulate our bodies, mould our subjectivities and govern our souls. That they can be places, too, for confronting injustice, in particular, structural domination and oppression.

We talk of a possibility, because institutions for children and young people are not necessities: there is more than one way in which they can be thought about and exist. They confront us with choices, for which we must take responsibility. It is possible for these institutions to be understood in different ways, with very different consequences. We have just outlined one possibility: the institution as a locus for ethical and political practice. Another possibility, usually discussed as if it was natural and inevitable, is the institution as first and foremost a site for technical practice, seeking the best methods and procedures for delivering predetermined outcomes – a stable, defined and transmittable body of knowledge, but also implicitly a particular subject, today the autonomous and flexible child. The defining question for this possibility is 'What works?': which technical practices will most effectively ensure the desired outcomes?

We are at a historical moment when it has become urgent to raise the question: what are the possibilities for institutions for children and young people? The possibility that we have just termed 'the institution as first and foremost a site for technical practice', a construction with deep historical roots, has gained such dominance that it becomes hard to treat it as an option – not as natural, an inevitability. Large, complex and contestable concepts such as 'the child', 'education' and 'evaluation' are reduced to a small, simplified and technical discourse of classifications, norms and criteria. Our purpose in this book is to denaturalise this often taken-for-granted construction of institutions for children, opening it to scrutiny – and by so doing to return this construction to its rightful place as just one of many possibilities.

At the same time, another historical process, the institutionalisation of childhood, is entering a period of acceleration. With the expansion of preschools[1] and school-age childcare and the lengthening period of schooling, children enter institutions at earlier ages, leave them (as young people) later and spend more of their days in them too. We raise this process not from some nostalgic longing for the days when children spent more time at home or were free to roam their immediate neighbourhoods: the institutionalisation of childhood is not, from our perspective, necessarily a bad thing. But it does demand of us – as adults – to take responsibility for what we have set in motion, in particular to look critically at the conditions for childhood that we are creating. Too often, however, this ethical and political subject – our responsibility for others – is replaced by a technical question: how effective are preschools/schools/school-age childcare in producing certain outcomes?

Our arguments apply, we believe, to all institutions for children, not least the school. But we have taken the preschool as our main case for exploring the themes of this book. This is partly because the preschool has been our particular interest over the years. But also because the preschool has become a growth area, in terms of both the expansion of services and the interest and hopes it arouses among politicians, researchers and others. At such a time, the possibilities that inspire change become very visible – or, we should say *the* possibility, since dominating the process of change is a very particular idea of what the preschool should be. The current situation of preschools, therefore, exemplifies very vividly more general changes in thought and practice, including the way technology, science and management drive out ethics and politics: exploring this process in the preschool, and how it might be reversed, can contribute to a wider debate.

Services as loci of technical practice

Providing services for young children has moved up the policy agenda in many countries. A recent review of 'early childhood education and care' (ECEC) policies by the Organisation for Economic Cooperation and Development (OECD) points out that these services are now 'firmly on the national policy agenda of all 12 countries participating in the thematic review' (OECD, 2001: 45). While such services have had priority for some time in some countries, for example in Scandinavia and France, 'in others, an unprecedented political focus on young children and families has emerged in the last five years' (*ibid.*). Over this period, countries 'with comparatively low public expenditure (such as Portugal, the Netherlands, the UK, the USA) have increased expenditure significantly' (*ibid*.: 86). Even countries with high levels of provision – notably Denmark and Sweden – have in recent years expanded further and introduced entitlements to provision for children from 12 months of age upwards. Overall, OECD concludes, the recent increased policy interest has 'fostered several major developments in the field, including rapid expansion of early childhood provision, increased focus on quality improvement, attention to coherence and integration, and higher levels of public investment in the system as a whole' (*ibid*.: 45).

International organisations have also been paying attention to early childhood services. Article 27 of the Council of Europe's revised Social Charter refers to the need 'to take appropriate measures . . . to develop or promote . . . child daycare services and other childcare arrangements' (Council of Europe, 1996). The European Union has laid out principles for 'childcare services' (cf. the 1992 Council Recommendation on Child Care), and in 2002 member state governments agreed targets for levels of childcare provision (places for 35 per cent of children under 3 years and 90 per cent of children aged 3 to 6 years). The OECD, as already noted, has conducted a detailed review of 'early childhood education and care' in 12 countries (OECD, 2001), and is continuing its work in this field with further national reviews of ECEC and international seminars on particular themes. The United Nations Educational, Scientific and Cultural Organization (UNESCO) has an active programme of publications on early childhood policy (see www.unesco.org), while the World Bank has loaned over £1 billion to support a range of ECEC programmes in the Majority World, maintains a website on Early Childhood Development (see www.worldbank.org/ children), commissions publications and organises regional and global conferences (Penn, 2002).

This increased interest in preschool services by nation states and international bodies is mostly of a very particular kind. It is stirred by the prospect of preschools being sites for producing predefined outcomes, mainly through the application of technical practices to the efficient governing of children. A successful service is defined in terms of its ability to deliver the goods on time, to specification and as cost-effectively as possible. Apart from stimulating women's employment by providing 'childcare', these outcomes are mainly concerned with the future development, educational attainment and employability of the child, in a context of increasing competition and change, as well as with the prevention or amelioration of a range of social ills among children, families and communities. The prize at stake – in particular among those countries that have previously lagged in the provision of services – is to secure both social order and economic success.

The magnitude of the prize can be seen in the policy documents of both international organisations and national governments. The United Nations International Children's Emergency Fund (UNICEF), for example, concludes that increasing government interest in early childhood services is because they offer 'an apparent opportunity to break into the cycle by which disadvantage tends to reproduce itself' and because 'no nation today can afford to ignore opportunities for maximising investments in education in a competitive economic environment increasingly based on knowledge, flexibility and lifelong learning skills' (UNICEF, 2002: 24), while the UK government lists a raft of policy goals to which 'childcare' is presumed to contribute:

> The availability of good quality, affordable childcare is key to achieving some important Government objectives. Childcare can *improve educational outcomes* for children. Childcare enables *parents, particularly mothers, to go out to work*, or increase their hours in work, thereby lifting their families out of poverty. It also plays a key role in *extending choice for women* by enhancing their ability to compete in the labour market on more equal terms . . . Childcare can also play an important role in meeting other top level objectives, for example in *improving health, boosting productivity, improving public services, closing the gender pay gap and reducing crime*. The targets to achieve 70 per cent employment among lone parents by 2010 and to eradicate child poverty by 2020 are those that are most obviously related. Childcare is essential for those objectives to be met.
>
> (Cabinet Office Strategy Unit, 2002: 5; emphasis added)

This particular social construction of preschools – as producers of predetermined outcomes – is constituted within a particular socio-political context. Put another way, it is contingent on certain conditions and assumptions. First, there is the hegemony of a particular *rationality*, that is, a way of thinking about the world and justifying actions in a systematic manner. Santos (1995) describes this hegemonic rationality as the 'cognitive-instrumental performative-utilitarian rationality of science' (23), and argues that the hegemony of this cognitive-instrumental rationality has been achieved at the expense of other rationalities, for example the 'moral-practical' and the 'aesthetic-expressive'. Instrumental rationality is inscribed with a desire to order the world and dominate nature, and an optimism that this is possible (Beck, 1994). It is preoccupied with calculation and quantification: with the relationship between inputs and outputs, with finding the most economical application of means to a given end (Taylor, 1991), with what Lyotard (1984) terms 'performativity'. It is a rationality that cannot imagine any other way to justify and evaluate preschools except in terms of their ability to produce pre-specified outcomes and through the application of measurement techniques that are assumed to be objective and universally valid.

A second condition is *a knowledge* to complement an instrumental rationality, a knowledge which offers a basis for assuring control and performance: scientific or objective knowledge. This is a causal knowledge

> which aims at formulating rules in the light of observed regularities and with a view to foreseeing the future behaviour of phenomena . . . Knowledge that is based on the formulation of laws has as its metatheoretical presupposition the idea of order and stability in the world, the idea that the past repeats itself in the future . . . [O]rder and stability in the world are preconditions for the transformation of reality. Mechanistic determinism provides a clear horizon for a form of knowing that was meant to be utilitarian and functional, acknowledged less for its capacity to understand reality at its deepest level than for its capacity to control and transform it.
>
> (Santos, 1995: 14)

What this means, in effect, is to privilege one form of knowledge over others. This privileged form claims to discover the truth, rather than create particular and provisional understandings. It is based on order, prediction and the control of phenomena. Scientific knowledge is a very appealing prospect to international organisations, governments and corporations pursuing an instrumental agenda and seeking certain and unequivocal answers to the question, 'What works?' But scientific knowledge is 'only capable of knowing by going from chaos to order, the order that we then impose on the objects of our study, be they human humans (social sciences) or human nonhumans (natural sciences). The modern book of nature is thus a book of knowledge-as-regulation' (*ibid.*: 37).

Scientific or objective knowledge, therefore, provides a basis for achieving order. It claims to guarantee predetermined outcomes, ensuring we get what we expect. We know the adult we want the child to become, we know the world in which that adult must live and work.

The challenge is to produce the adult to fit that world, in the most cost-effective way – and with the help of scientific knowledge-as-regulation the challenge can be met.

At present, at least in the English-language world, one discipline makes a dominant claim to provide scientific knowledge in the pre-school field. The scientific discourse of developmental psychology provides a way of understanding children, teachers and their work by representing, classifying and normalising them through its concepts. Scientifically guided principles, based on generalisations that are considered sufficiently reliable, indicate the continuing efforts to find a universal and scientific guide for 'who' the child is and how to govern his or her progress and development. Burman (2001) notes how the 'quasi-scientific status' of developmental norms slips from description to prescription: from a mythic norm (mythic because no one actually 'fits' it) to statements of how people should be: 'whether milestones, gender types, reading ages, cognitive strategies, stages or skills . . . they become enshrined within an apparatus of collective measurement and evaluation that constructs its own world of abstract autonomous babies; of norms, deviation from which is typically only acknowledged in the form of deficit or "problem" ' (5–6).

Today, established notions of development intersect with 'a new normality of the child' – a child who will be flexible, who is developmentally ready for the uncertainties and opportunities of the twenty-first century. We return to this 'new normality' later in the chapter.

The third condition is the availability of knowledge-related *technologies* that can be applied to children and adults in preschools to bring about the required outcomes as certainly as possible. These human technologies, or technologies of government, are pervasive and complex. They consist of:

> an assemblage of forms of practical knowledge, with modes of perception, practices of calculation, vocabularies, types of authority, forms of judgement, architectural forms, human capacities, non-human objects and devices, inscription techniques and so forth . . . [They are] imbued with aspirations for *the shaping of conduct in the hope of achieving certain desired effects and averting certain undesired events.*
>
> (Rose, 1999: 52: emphasis added)

To be more precise, these technologies include practices or methods for *working with children towards agreed ends*, often drawing on scientific

knowledge in particular developmental psychology. An example is the
concept and practice of 'developmental appropriateness'. 'Developmentally appropriate curricula' is a widely applied technique that:

> correlates lesson plans with a sequence of capabilities . . . It appeals
> to developmental psychology for its scientific base, it inscribes
> assumptions of progressive efficiency, and it assumes a behaviourist
> approach to establish educational objectives . . . [This] interweav-
> ing of developmental psychology, efficiency, and behaviourism in
> educational curricula becomes a technology of normalization. I call
> this technology *developmentality* as a way of alluding to Foucault's
> governmentality, and focusing on the self-governing effects of
> developmental discourse in curriculum debates. Developmentality,
> like governmentality, describes a current pattern of power in which
> the self disciplines the self.
>
> (Fendler, 2001: 120; original emphasis)

We shall return to governmentality – its meaning and working – later in
the chapter, and indeed throughout the book, as it plays a central part
in our argument.

Penn (2002) has described in some detail how the World Bank's
intervention in early childhood services is based on 'scientific application of scientifically proven facts', with particular emphasis placed on
the technology of 'developmentally appropriate practice' (DAP). Like
Burman, Penn draws attention to the search for 'the prototypical child
as the developmental subject or the unit of development . . . instead of
diverse children and childhoods' (Burman, 2001: 15). While claiming
scientific objectivity and truth, in practice DAP is inscribed with certain
assumptions and values:

> These include the paramount importance of individualism and
> selfhood; the assumption of a permanent nuclear household, with a
> prime carer and a lone dependent child as the focus of adult atten-
> tion; the need to encourage choice from a wide range of material
> goods; and various kinds of nature–nurture dualisms. The practices
> advocated are neither neutral nor scientifically established (even if
> this were possible) . . . [Yet] World Bank advisers have uncritically
> accepted the assumptions of DAP, which introduces us to a kind of
> 'core' child who is paradoxically both embodied brain and a highly
> individual being, upon whom adults act.
>
> (Penn, 2002: 125)

A further clutch of technologies *monitor and assess children and workers* in preschools. Some measure whether the correct conditions are in place in preschools to secure the predetermined outcomes required of them, what might be termed the technology of quality. 'Quality' has become the great cliché of our age. In most instances of its use, 'quality' is devoid of any substantive meaning, an empty concept supposed to make the reader or observer feel well disposed towards a product. But if we peer behind the vacant public face of quality, we can discern a technical claim: that it is feasible and desirable to find and apply scientifically based, value-free and stable standards for evaluating preschool (or other) services. Such criteria, the claim goes, replace the need for making a 'subjective' evaluation with the application of a technical, 'objective' practice. Once reduced to a set of criteria that constitutes a norm, quality can be assessed using a technical instrument that measures the conformity of a service to the norm. The best known example of such an instrument is the Early Childhood Environmental Rating Scale – ECERS – originating in the United States, but now used in many other countries to offer a universal standard for evaluation (for a full discussion and critique of the 'discourse of quality', see Dahlberg *et al.*, 1999; some of the main arguments are summarised in Chapter 5).

Measuring quality is just one of a variety of technologies deployed to regulate practice in preschools. Preschools are increasingly bounded by other normalising frameworks – either required by government or offered by experts: standards, curricula, accreditation, guidelines on best practice, inspection, audits, the list rolls on. Like quality, these guides to technical practice purport to provide decontextualised 'benchmarks' – generalisable standards – of what is necessary or desirable. What these normalising technologies have in common is an administrative logic, an intention and capacity to govern more effectively by ensuring that correct outcomes are delivered.

Other technologies measure *outcomes*, monitoring whether services deliver what is expected of them, information needed both by managers, the better to govern, and by parents, the better to act as consumers. Outcomes are increasingly quantified, expressed as a normative framework of performance indicators. Quantified performance indicators permit comparisons – within countries or, increasingly, globally, between countries. So far, cross-national comparisons of preschools have been confined to descriptions of systems and structures, though it is probably only a matter of time before the appearance of global performance indicators.

Their use, however, is becoming well established in cross-national comparisons of schools, exemplified by two major surveys: Trends in International Maths and Science Study (TIMSS) and the Programme for International Student Assessment (PISA). The former has tested 14-year-olds in 52 countries in 1995 and/or 1999, while the latter is a three-yearly survey of the performance of 15-year-olds in reading, mathematics and science in 32 countries, first conducted in 2000. Such cross-national comparisons are taken very seriously, not least by national governments, with an increasing tendency for 'performance in international surveys . . . to explain or justify national policy changes' (Le Métais, 2003: 9).

These assessment exercises are focused on very specific skills, arguably just one part of a larger concept of education. The danger they pose is that far larger claims are made for the results from these surveys. For example, a recent report that combines results from PISA and TIMSS argues that they provide:

> the first 'big picture' comparison of the relative effectiveness of education systems across the developed world . . . [It] reflects the relative success or failure of each country in preparing its young people for life and work in the 21st century . . . [T]he big picture shows that some OECD countries are consistently performing better than others when it comes to educating and equipping their young people for life in the 21st century.
>
> (UNICEF, 2002: 5, 18)

As this example shows, measures of very specific skills, a very partial view of education, can readily be equated with large, complex and contestable concepts such as 'education', 'educating' and 'life'. Rather than stimulating or contributing to a broad debate about the meaning of education and processes of learning, these international comparisons may have a quite opposite effect. Debate may become focused, instead, on the narrow and technical: what changes, governments ask, are needed to improve future performance scores and our position in the league table? Greater attention may be paid to formal methods of teaching in compulsory schooling. Emphasis may be placed on other services (such as preschools) supporting schools to improve educational performance as defined by the global testing regime. In this way, technical measures of outcome may come to reduce a profoundly complex and political subject into a question of standardised and technical practice.

Developing the argument

A foregrounding of technical practice connected to a highly instrumental rationality is nothing new. It is the product of a particular mindset or paradigm that has been highly influential for more than two centuries, and which has often seen children as redemptive agents, ideal subjects for technical practice through which we will fix problems without having to address their structural causes. But there are also particular contemporary reasons why a technico-instrumental approach to institutions for children and young people has become a dominant discourse today – why we hear so much talk about audits, goals, inspection, programmes, outcomes, quality and so forth, yet treat such talk as natural and incontestable. Yet at the same time, the foundations on which this approach is based are showing some signs of wear and tear – suggesting possibilities for transgression, for slipping between the cracks appearing in a seemingly monolithic structure. We shall develop these analyses in Chapter 2.

We then turn to the possibility that intrigues and inspires us – preschools as sites for ethical and political practice. Ethics hardly figures in current discourses about the preschool – or indeed other institutions for children and young people. It has not featured in any of the recent batch of cross-national studies of early childhood education and care, and it occupies a very marginal place in national policies. Curricula may refer to certain moral codes or underpinning values. One of the 'early learning goals' set out in the Curriculum Guidance for the Foundation Stage (i.e. for children aged 3 to 6 years) in England is that children should 'understand what is right, what is wrong and why' (English Qualifications and Curriculum Authority, 2000: 38). This document also includes a list of 'principles for early years education'. Most of these are technical (e.g. 'well-planned, purposeful activity and appropriate intervention by practitioners will engage children in the learning process' [*ibid*.: 11]), but some express values (e.g. 'no child should be excluded or disadvantaged because of ethnicity, culture', etc.).

In Sweden, the preschool curriculum (and indeed the curriculum for schools) has a section on 'fundamental values', including democracy, the inviolability of human life, individual freedom and integrity, equality and solidarity. It also refers to ethics:

> The foundation on which these values rest expresses the ethical attitude which shall characterise all preschool activity. Care and consideration towards other persons, as well as justice and equality,

in addition to the rights of each individual shall be emphasised and made explicit in all preschool activity.

(Swedish Ministry of Education and Science, 1998: 6)

While ethics may not appear much in current policy discourses, having at best a 'walk on' part, this does not mean it is absent from the preschool. In our view, the preschool is never outside ethics, even if technological practice masks the ethics' presence. But what ethics? When we speak of preschools (or other provisions) as sites for ethical and political practice, the issue is not simply one of quantity, of how much ethics and politics there should be. We are not talking just about 'more ethics' or 'more politics'. Nor are we speaking of ethics and politics as subjects for the curriculum, for example the need to have more time allotted to learning the difference between right and wrong or the workings of democracy, or the need for more codes of ethics to regulate behaviour. For us, the critical questions are 'What ethics?', 'What politics?', 'What sort of practices?' and 'What would it mean to understand preschools as, first and foremost, loci of ethical practice and minor politics?'

In Chapter 3 we will suggest that a particular approach or concept of ethics currently underpins discourse about preschools, although usually implicitly, its presence having to be deduced from a number of clues. This is a universalistic ethics, which treats ethics as a standard, norm or code – fixed, impartial, incontestable and generally applicable. The example above from the English 'early learning goals' provides a rather extreme example, implying that early education can inculcate children with such a code which, once successfully transmitted, will enable children to tell the difference between right and wrong. Perhaps a more widespread clue to the presence of universalistic ethics is the recurring discourse of 'quality', with its search for generalisable codes that will enable us to know with certainty what is good. But we see it too in the discourse of rights, another attempt to provide a code of correct behaviour and relationships founded on stable and universal criteria, a discourse to which we return below and in a later chapter.

Our intention is twofold: to *vitalise* the place of ethics, making it explicit and central to the life of the preschool – something that is openly and knowingly practised; and to *diversify* the ethical possibilities open to preschools. So we go on to propose other ethical approaches that we find particularly sympathetic, ethics which foreground responsibility and the relationship to the Other. Rather than ethics being a matter of prescribing, transmitting and applying a code of rules, we are interested in ethical practices which foreground active personal responsibility for making ethical choices – but not as an autonomous subject seeking objective truth, rather as an ethical actor in relationship with others and located in a particular context. We are also interested in ethics as relational in another sense: ethics conceived in terms of an ethical relationship between persons, in particular how we do or might relate with the Other in a way that is respectful of alterity and does not grasp the Other to make the Other into the Same.

These interests will lead us to explore a number of ethical approaches – such as Bauman's discussion of 'postmodern ethics', the 'ethics of care' proposed by Joan Tronto, Selma Sevenhuijsen and other feminist scholars, and, of particular importance for us, the 'ethics of an encounter' from the work of Emmanuel Levinas. These ethical perspectives have much in common including a 'sensitivity to the "violence" of our stand-ard modern modes of thinking' (White, 1991: 99), concerns with radical difference, and the importance of regenerating 'an ethic of respons-ibility which has been undermined by the prevalence of a modern legislative coding of rules of conduct' (Smart, 1999: 98–99).

What is the relation between ethics and ethical practice? All preschools (indeed, all schools and other provisions for children) are spaces for ethical practice in the sense that people strive to put ethical approaches into their daily practice – although with varying degrees of awareness of the ethical nature of their endeavours. But different ethics require different practices. A universalistic approach requires the application of prescribed codes, a form of technical practice: the aim is closure through the application of universal rules. The other approaches we discuss require listening, reflection, interpretation, confrontation, discussion, judgements open to question: there is no escaping the provisionality of this practice, nor its messiness. The one holds out the security of certain foundations, the other the uncertainty and responsibility of needing to make a choice.

In Chapters 4 and 5, we look at the relation between ethics and practice more specifically. We consider the implications of the ethical approaches we favour, in particular the ethics of an encounter, for evaluation, the place of care and pedagogical practice in the preschool.[2] What, we ask, would it mean to give ethics a higher profile in the pedagogic work of preschools and schools? In particular, what would it mean to reconfigure pedagogy as a locus of an ethics of an encounter? The answers are, we think, very provocative. For example, working with the ethics of an encounter requires the preschool pedagogue (or indeed the preschool researcher or policy maker) 'to think an other whom I cannot grasp [which] is an important shift and it challenges the whole scene of pedagogy' (Dahlberg, 2003: 273). Our enquiries into pedagogy as the locus of an ethics of an encounter lead us to the concept of 'a pedagogy of listening', and the importance of certain concepts, images and methods: thought, listening, radical dialogue, the intelligent child, co-construction and invention, connections and experimentation, the preschool as laboratory, project work and pedagogical documentation. These are very much at odds with concepts, images and methods that occupy the educational mainstream today and constitute the educational project of modernity: objective knowledge, transmission, monologue, the incomplete child, reproduction and recognition, the preschool as factory, curriculum, classification systems.

If ethics has little recognition in current early childhood discourses, politics has an even lower profile. Mainstream or programmatic politics – with its particular institutions (government, ministries, parliaments) and processes (general elections, parliamentary votes, budgets, the making and implementation of policy) – is of course the arena within which policy decisions about early childhood education and care services are made, for example about the extent and nature of government involvement. Should the state support 'childcare' for very young children or encourage parents (mothers) to care for these children through systems of parental leave? To what extent should the state provide, fund and regulate services? How should it do so? Do preschools fall within the welfare or education systems?

This arena is of the utmost importance: it can create very different policies, provisions and practices at different times and in different places. What is often missing though is recognition or discussion of other political arenas, including the one that interests us: preschools themselves as potential spaces for political practice, preschools as a stage for political actors rather than simply political objects. We will explore this possibility in Chapter 6, arguing that preschools (and other institutions for children) have great potential as spaces for political practice in today's world, not least because they are regular meeting places for many children and adults. One concept we find particularly interesting in relation to the political role of preschools is 'minor politics'. What might this mean? With inspiration from Deleuze and Guattari, Rose refers to this as 'minor engagements . . . [which] are cautious, modest, pragmatic, experimental, stuttering, tentative . . . [and] concerned with the here and now, not with some fantasized future, with small concerns, petty details, the everyday and not the transcendental' (Rose, 1999: 280). Yet the small concerns, the petty details (at least 'small' and 'petty' as viewed from the perspective of traditional 'programmatic politics'), the everyday lives of children, families and preschools open up a wide arena for politics – understood as recognising the contestability (the not-to-be-taken-for-grantedness) of many issues and decisions.

'Minor politics' might therefore be understood as both a localisation of politics (in terms of where politics is conducted) and at the same time a broadening of politics (in terms of subject matter). 'Minor politics' brings back into the political arena subjects that politicians or practitioners or researchers may define as technical – and therefore uncontestable – for example, practice in preschools. Minor politics also has the potential to become more than the sum of its parts through the ability, as Rose puts it, to 'connect up with a whole series of other circuits and cause them to fluctuate, waver and reconfigure in wholly unexpected ways' (*ibid.*). In this way it may be capable, on occasion, of confronting the programmatic or major politics of local, regional and national government, influencing public policies that affect the lives of children, parents and preschools.

We do not suggest that minor politics is, or could ever be, a substitute for major politics. Many of the big issues of our day – the damaged environment, capitalist irresponsibility, the violence of inequality – require action at the level of the nation state and in international political structures. Both politics – minor and major – have an important part to play in future democratic practice.

'Minor politics' might be seen as one way in which the nation state and democracy are being pushed in new directions, towards wider participation in more negotiations about more issues. Given the wide range of issues that preschools as sites for democratic practice and minor politics can address, one way of characterising this complex political role is as resistance to power. We explore this role in relation to three examples of preschools as sites for confronting: dominant discourses, those 'regimes of truth' which govern what we can think and do; processes of subjectification, by which we are created as a particular type of subject; and certain dimensions or forms of injustice in particular domination and oppression.

We use examples throughout the book. Some come from the municipal preschool centres in Reggio Emilia in northern Italy, which from our perspective provide a vivid example of foregrounding ethics and politics without discarding technical practice (for a fuller discussion of the pedagogical theories and practices created in the 33 municipal preschools in Reggio for children from birth to 6 years, see Dahlberg *et al.*, 1999; Giudici *et al.*, 2001). But we also introduce examples from other places, and indeed not only from preschools themselves but from other fields too, such as research. Chapter 7 consists of a number of such examples, illustrating what we consider to be the practice of minor politics. We do not claim that the examples we cite, here or elsewhere in the book, see themselves in the same light as we do. But we think they illustrate the possibility of thinking and practising differently, of getting beyond technical practice and creating a space for ethics and politics.

These examples show that change is possible, perhaps not universal and perhaps in specific conditions, but change nevertheless. In our last chapter we consider possibilities and conditions for change, covering such matters as Utopian thought and action, networks and other alliances, creating conditions for experimentation and the question of time.

Dominant discourses, governmentality and the subject: three important analytic concepts

We need to introduce here three concepts that play an important part in our thinking about what preschools are and what they might be. In all three cases we owe a debt of gratitude to the French thinker Michel Foucault (1926–1984) and his extensive and influential investigations into the nature and workings of power. We shall consider his work and its implications for 'minor politics' in more detail in Chapter 6. But for the moment we will start by considering disciplinary power, the application of a range of 'techniques of power' that work principally on the body, which is approached primarily as an object to be analysed and separated into its constituent parts. The aim of this disciplinary technology is to forge 'a docile [body] that may be subjected, used, transformed and improved' (Foucault, 1977: 136).

These techniques, which have developed from the seventeenth century, have become so established and pervasive – in the field of early childhood, as elsewhere – that we often take them for granted, rather than as the relatively recent technologies of governing that they are. They include surveillance, exclusion (the defining of the abnormal), classification (differentiating groups or individuals from one another), distribution (arranging, isolating, separating, ranking), individualisation (giving individual character to oneself or another), totalisation (the specification of totalities, giving collective character to a group) and regulation (controlling by rule) (Gore, 1998).

But of particular importance is normalisation, defining the normal, with its associated concepts of normality and the norm, and the role of the expert who can define what is normal and desirable. Rose describes how normalisation, and the capacity to identify, measure, instil and regulate through the idea of the norm, emerged as 'a key technique of government' during the nineteenth and early twentieth centuries. Institutions such as schools, prisons and workhouses became places of normalisation, in the sense of determining what was normal, identifying the abnormal and setting normality as an outcome or purpose.

> Normality was natural, but those who were to be civilised would have to achieve normality through working on themselves, controlling their impulses in their everyday conduct and habits, inculcating norms of conduct into their children, under the guidance of others. Many would aspire to this role as experts of conduct: religious authorities and philanthropists would soon be accompanied by all manner of reformers, child-savers, campaigners for social purity; later they would be joined, but never supplemented, by those who claimed to ground their norms, and their codes of conduct, in objectivity: the proliferating scientific experts of the moral order. In the process, free individuals became governable . . . as normal subjects.
>
> (Rose, 1999: 76)

Disciplinary techniques do not act in isolation, but connect up to contribute to the formation of dominant discourses or regimes of truth. Such discourses function through the concepts, conventions, classifications, categories and norms that we use to analyse, construct and describe reality, and which determine what is seen as true or false, normal or abnormal, right or wrong. They provide the mechanism for rendering reality amenable to certain kinds of actions (Miller and Rose, 1993). By the same token, they also exclude alternative ways of understanding and interpreting the world. In short, dominant discourses make assumptions and values invisible, turn subjective perspectives and understandings into apparently objective truths, and determine that some things are self-evident and realistic while others are dubious and impractical. We find ourselves talking and doing in certain ways as if they were natural and obvious, rather than the product of particular power relations, particular mindsets, particular ways of seeing – the Emperor's New Clothes being a classic example of how a dominant discourse operates to govern what can be said and what is treated as the truth in a particular time and place.

The growing attention given to preschools today is shaped by a dominant discourse. It is an Anglo-American discourse spoken in English – though it is increasingly to be heard across the world and translated into other languages. It governs our ideas, thoughts and actions through language: in this discourse concepts such as 'early intervention', 'investment in the future', 'child development', 'outcomes', 'quality', 'cost-benefit', 'best practice', 'readiness for school' become natural ways of speaking, as if they were the only ways to think about early childhood services. It offers itself as truth, but it is the product (as is any discourse) of particular power relations that privilege certain perspectives over others. It is located in a liberal political and economic context, inscribed with Enlightenment assumptions about objectivity, mastery and universality. It constructs particular understandings of childhood, learning, evaluation and so on; generates particular and technical problems and questions; and relies on certain tools and methods. And it is dominated by certain disciplinary perspectives, in particular psychology and economics, and the knowledges that they produce.

Knowledge is strongly implicated in dominant discourses. Knowledge and power 'operate in history in a mutually generative fashion' (Dreyfus and Rabinow, 1982: 134). Knowledge, or what is defined as legitimate knowledge, is a product of the power relations that form the dominant discourse. But knowledge in turn acts as an instrument of power. It produces power, because it informs our perception of reality: 'knowledge can never be of an absolute or final nature but is instead a selecting out, among the many readings and possibilities present in a concrete instance, of those characteristics and aspects that will promote the goals of the individual or group doing the selecting' (Ransom, 1997: 19).

Such dominant discursive regimes or regimes of truth serve a disciplinary or regulatory function: 'discourses that carry public authority shape identities and regulate bodies, desires, selves and populations' (Seidman, 1998: 235). They also shape or mould individuals – both in their subjectivity and conduct – without resort to violence. Through the concepts, classifications, norms and categories that we use to represent reality, they provide means by which we govern others, for they are about 'who can speak, when, where and with what authority . . . [so that] certain possibilities for thought are constructed' (Ball, 1994: 21–22).

But we also govern *ourselves* through these regimes. For they order or organise our everyday experience of the world, influencing our ideas, thoughts and actions. They exercise power over our thought by governing what we see as the 'truth', what we accept as rational and how we construct the world – and hence our acting and doing. Or rather, since we are ourselves inscribed in dominant discourses, we govern ourselves through dominant discourses, acting upon ourselves rather than being directly acted upon: 'we do not speak a discourse, it speaks us. We are the subjectivities, the voices, the knowledge, the power relations that a discourse constructs and allows' (*ibid.*: 22).

So rather than an external coercive force dictating to us, discipline often operates through the self governing the self, 'something like an inner compulsion indistinguishable from our will, immanent to and inseparable from our subjectivity itself' (Hardt and Negri, 2001: 329) – the concept of governmentality. We first introduced the term earlier in the chapter, in a quotation from Lynn Fendler in which she described governmentality as 'a current pattern of power in which the self disciplines the self'. Governmentality therefore refers to the way in which people and populations come to be governed or managed not through external coercion, but by more subtle and more effective practices. These practices work directly *on* us, steering us towards desired behaviour. But they also work *through* us, acting on our innermost selves, reaching to the innermost qualities of being human: our spirit, motivations, wishes, desires, beliefs, dispositions, aspirations and attitudes. So though we are directly governed, the most important effect is that we govern ourselves – conduct our own conduct – in ways that conform to the dominant regime.

We will come back to governmentality later in the book in the context of 'minor politics', which may provide a means for being governed less in this way. But for the moment, we should give some examples using preschools. Mostly preschools are not governed using a big stick, with the threat of punishment if practices stray from what is expected. Practices, generally, are shaped in very different ways. Regulatory frameworks – such as standards, curricula or guidelines – provide external norms, which may be reinforced through processes of inspection. But practitioners also create their own internal norms, just as important, indeed more so, in determining their conduct. Various sources – including disciplinary knowledge, professional traditions and government policy – inscribe a certain way of reasoning, which has very practical consequences: systems of categorisation and norms, for example, are brought to bear on children through observation and assessment procedures, and systems of ideas construct an understanding of who children are and who they should become. The earlier quotation from Fendler refers to *developmentality* to describe 'the self-governing effects of developmental discourse in curriculum debates'.

Via dominant discourses and the practice of governmentality, human beings are continually constructing themselves, forming themselves as subjects – what have been referred to as processes of 'subjectification' or 'identification'. Like governmentality, the subject will be a recurring theme of our book. Subjectivity is not essential, not some pre-given substance. It is shaped by social forces and produced in the functioning of major social institutions, including family, (pre)school and workplace (*ibid.*: 195). But we are not just acted upon, not only made; we also continually make ourselves, and in this process of constituting ourselves we are strongly influenced by dominating discourses and practices of power.

Subjectification, the shaping of a certain kind of subject who will govern herself or himself, replacing the need for coercive force, has become the most common and effective means of government in modern times. The ideal of modernity, especially from the time of the Enlightenment, was, as Readings argues at the beginning of this chapter, the autonomous subject. This subject was rational, knowing, stable, unified, self-governing, and freed of obligation – also, by implication, adult, male and white.

This, too, was the ideal subject of liberal government, which emerged in the nineteenth century. Subjectification became the answer to an apparent contradiction confronting liberalism: it sought to exclude government from certain private areas, such as markets and families, yet recognised that good government depended on the well-being and good-functioning of these self-same areas. The answer to this apparent contradiction was to foster the subject who could be relied on to govern himself (and his family) and so exercise responsible judgements and do what was right and necessary.

This gives liberalism a Janus-face with autonomy on one side, control on the other. Because liberalism depends on the exercise of responsible autonomy by subjects, 'it seeks to form subjects and their capacities' (Dean, 1999: 205). Rose speaks of 'a kind of despotism of the self at the heart of liberalism' (Rose, 1999: 43), and goes on to argue that liberal political rationalities 'are committed to the twin projects of respecting the autonomy of certain private zones, and shaping their conduct in ways conducive to particular conceptions of collective and individual well-being' (*ibid.*: 48–49). The subject, in short, must be formed to be able to exercise freedom and responsibility.

(As the word 'autonomy' has been introduced and recurs, we should at this point clarify our understanding and use of the word. Within a liberal discourse, 'autonomy and independence tend to be conflated, and autonomy, in the sense of autonomous judgement, is linked to an ideal of independence as self-sufficiency' [Sevenhuijsen, 1998: 63]. Like Sevenhuijsen we would problematise 'autonomy' when used to imply this ideal of independence from others, with self-sufficiency as a desirable goal. However, like many other words that recur in this book, 'autonomy' is 'Janus-faced'. It can mean the individual acting alone in a state of self-sufficiency. But it can also be used to mean the individual taking responsibility, for example for making ethical choices [Bauman, 1999], even while recognising the importance of relationships and interdependency in forming such choices. So, like Sevenhuijsen, we consider 'connection and dependence [to be] part of human life and moral subjectivity' and that 'the quality of autonomous judgements can be regarded as enhanced . . . [when] the illusion of a solipsistic subject is replaced by an idea of "being in the world with each other"' [1998: 63]. In this book, we use 'autonomy' in its liberal meaning that equates to independence, unless explicitly stated otherwise.)

But more recently, towards the end of the last century, with the emergence of advanced liberalism and neoliberalism as increasingly dominating forms of political and economic regime (discussed in more detail in Chapter 2), this ideal subject has assumed additional qualities. She or he must be re-formed after the interlude of the social state when she or he became too dependent on shared responsibility, pooled risk and social security. This neoliberal subject remains independent, assuming responsibility for himself or herself (and his or her 'dependants') – but over an ever-increasing range of domains (Dean, 1999). This subject is a risk manager, who can survive in an uncertain and individualised world by learning how to calculate, which renders reality amenable to action and therefore some degree of order and control. Heightened awareness of risk and individual responsibility, and the insertion of contractual relations into ever more areas, requires the adoption of a suspicious disposition and a calculative rationality: the responsible subject must be on the constant look-out for the signs that she or he and her or his family are at risk or getting a bad deal, and once spotted must take 'appropriate' preventive or remedial measures.

The liberal subject is an active consumer, facing a vast array of material goods and services. She or he is also constantly seeking self-realisation – through the creation of personal life-style, the discovery of who she or he really is, the achievement of personal potential. Rather than attaining a stable end state, a condition of completion, she or he is a fluid, flexible being, ready to respond and adapt to conditions of constant change. Fendler (2001) refers to 'current social circumstances [calling] for "flexible" and "fluid" ways of being . . . [pertaining] to a shift away from the rigidly defined social roles characteristic of modernity', and to the 'education of flexible souls' (119, 137). (The term 'soul', which recurs throughout the book, refers to 'aspects of humanity that were previously sacrosanct [such as desire, fear and pleasure] but that have recently been constructed as objects of psychological and regulatory apparatuses . . . [It] deliberately alludes to what have been the innermost qualities of being human [and has been used] to emphasize the depth to which modern technologies of discipline have extended' [Fendler, 2001: 123].) This competent subject is engaged from birth in a continual process of self-improvement and adaptation to the world as it presents itself, through the application of knowledge and techniques. The subject is an entrepreneur of the self 'conducting his own and his family life as a kind of enterprise seeking to enhance and capitalise an existence through calculated acts' (Rose, 1999: 164). This involves asserting individual rights, locating and processing information, solving problems and entering into contractual arrangements requiring repeated calculation of cost and benefit to ensure finding the best value.

Despite a surface diversity of appearances and self-identities, this autonomous subject is normative, the benchmark for all to follow. The exercise of free choice – the practice of freedom – is essential for this subject: 'modern individuals are not merely free to choose, they are obliged to be free, to understand and enact life in terms of choice' (Rose, 1999: 87). The only choice that is not available is choice itself.

We said at the start of this section that these concepts are important to our approach. For if you choose to work with these concepts, and the theories which give rise to them, then it becomes impossible to view preschools as neutral technologies. It becomes impossible to view the purpose of all concerned with preschools – whether educators or researchers, parents or politicians – as seeking the best means to achieve self-evident goals for a self-evident child. It becomes impossible to believe any of us can stand outside power relations, offering disinterested and stable knowledge.

Instead, preschools are inscribed in particular discourses, they are places for the exercise of discipline and governmentality, they participate in shaping subjectivities. We cannot escape from this and our own involvement in the power relations out of which dominant discourses emerge. But we can make the preschool an object of critical thinking, we can deconstruct and reconstruct discourses, we can ask 'What is going on here?' We have to make decisions about purposes and practices, but these must always be provisional and contestable. We are therefore confronted by choices which are not in the first place technical (what is the best means to our ends), but ethical and political – and these are choices for which we must take responsibility.

Some assumptions

The need for border crossing

Our thinking is provoked by a wide range of ideas, including: dominant discourse, governmentality, and the subject, which we have just introduced; the ethics of an encounter and minor politics; and the significance of the linguistic turn and its implications for knowledge, of which more in the next chapter. We are also particularly interested in the thought and writings of certain people: Bill Readings, Michel Foucault, Jacques Derrida, Emmanuel Levinas, Nikolas Rose, Loris Malaguzzi, Chantal Mouffe and so on. What these ideas and writers have in common is their diversity, for example in their disciplinary backgrounds: few in fact have taken a particular (or any) direct interest in early childhood and preschools.

For us border crossing – literally in terms of exploring writers and traditions from different places, metaphorically in terms of moving into disciplines not normally connected with early childhood – is important. It has been important too in the history of the Reggio preschools; for example, it enabled Loris Malaguzzi (1920–1994), the first head of the municipal preschools there, to open up 'new possibilities, a new space, outside the ahistorical laws and imperatives of contemporary science and philosophy' (Dahlberg, 2000: 178). We need the provocation of different perspectives, viewing a particular field from across borders.

But border crossing can take other forms, including moving beyond early childhood into other fields of work with children. We have already said, but want to reiterate, that our argument, and the possibilities that we discuss, are not confined to preschools. We focus on this form of provision for children, but the arguments encompass *all* public provisions for *all* ages of children and young people, including the school and the university: hence the occasional bracketed addition of 'and schools' to remind the reader that preschools are only part of a larger story. For instance, a book to which we make frequent reference – *The University in Ruins* by Bill Readings (1960–1994), a Canadian working in the field of comparative literature – is about higher education institutions. Yet the ideas, especially about pedagogical relations, resonate for preschools and schools.

In many countries, there is an increasingly close relationship between preschools, schools and 'school-age childcare' (OECD, 2001). This process has gone furthest in Sweden where all of these provisions are now within the education system, schools and free-time services (school-age childcare) have often merged to form 'whole day schools', and the three former occupational groups (preschool teacher, school teacher and free-time pedagogue) have been brought together within a single training framework, on the completion of which they have a common qualification and are known as teachers. In England and Scotland there is a movement to extend the range of services provided on school sites, including early childhood education and care and school-age childcare, with the development of what are called, respectively, extended schools and integrated community schools. In such conditions, to focus on only one type of provision in isolation and to ignore the rest both denies possibilities to many children and risks undermining attempts to re-form.

In particular, the school is a powerful institution that often harbours imperial tendencies towards preschools and other neighbouring territory. We can see this in the language of 'school readiness' – which implies that preschools should shape children to fit the demands of compulsory school, without questioning those demands and that institution – and of 'readiness to learn' – which implies either that children do not learn before school or that they do not do so in the prescribed, school way. We can also see it in the priority attached to the 3 Rs in preschool policies in some countries.

This language is prominent in the education policies of the most powerful country in the world. The 'mission' of the Head Start programme in the United States, intended primarily for 3- and 4-year-olds from low-income families, is 'to promote school readiness'. In an initiative announced in 2002 – *Good Start, Grow Smart* – the Bush administration has attached further importance to this role. From 2003, Head Start centres were to assess 'standards of learning in early literacy, language and numeracy skills', while a national programme was to be introduced for all Head Start teachers to train them 'in the best pre-reading and language teaching techniques for young children'. A further initiative is aimed more broadly at all preschool services, with the administration calling on all states 'to take steps that will help prepare children before they enter school to be ready to learn . . . for example, States should help coordinate the public schools with the early childhood programs that serve the children they later educate' (the White House, 2002).

In its recent review of ECEC, the OECD notes that 'there are concerns in some countries that as ECEC becomes more integrated with compulsory schooling . . . downward pressure on early childhood education and care could lead to a school-like approach to the organisation of early childhood provision' (OECD, 2001: 79). The review recommends 'a strong and equal partnership . . . [providing] the opportunity to bring together the diverse perspectives of both early childhood education and care and schools' (*ibid.*: 128–129). But a 'strong and equal partnership' is difficult to envisage unless the school itself is re-formed: otherwise the relationship will become more unequal, with the school 'schoolifying' preschools and other provisions for children, young and old alike, spreading its traditions, constructions, methods and rationality down the age range. To try and change the preschool without changing the school seems like an uphill, perhaps impossible, struggle against superior odds. (For a discussion of the changing relationship between preschools, schools and school-age childcare services in England, Scotland and Sweden, countries which have integrated administrative responsibility for all of these services within the education system, see Cohen *et al.*, 2004; for an analysis of Swedish reforms, see also Lenz Taguchi and Munkhammar, 2003.)

So in talking about sites for ethical and political practice and, later on in this chapter, more broadly about 'children's spaces' full of possibilities, we are offering a 'vision of a possible meeting place' (Dahlberg and Lenz Taguchi, 1994) for *all* public provisions for children and young people which provides the possibility of a 'strong and equal partnership'. With these concepts of space or place we hope to encompass not only preschools but also out-of-school childcare (or, the term used in Sweden, 'free-time services'), schools, clubs, playgrounds and much else besides. In so doing, we want to offer one alternative to what seems to us to be an other, pervasive concept of such provision – as enclosures or factories for the production of predetermined outcomes, instrumental, technical and regulatory.

Avoiding dualistic thinking

We recognise the perennial risk of falling into oppositional dualisms, the 'either/or' of modernity. In particular, we have already appeared to pose a total opposition between preschools as sites of technology and as sites of ethical and political practice. We do not want to dismiss technical practice: it is necessary and important to have methods, tools and procedures for evaluation and to put pedagogical ideas into practice.

Furthermore, to imagine preschools without some degree of instrumentality, expressed in some predetermined outcomes allotted them by the government or the community that funds them or the parents who decide to send their children to them, is probably naïve and, in our view, also mistaken.

The issue facing us, therefore, is not whether or not to be instrumental. It is the relationship between technology and instrumentality on the one hand and ethics and politics on the other. What socially agreed knowledge and values should be defined as predetermined outcomes? And how much space should be left, in Readings's words quoted at the start of this chapter, 'to listen to Thought, [to] think beside each other and beside ourselves, [and] to explore an open network of obligations that keeps the question of meaning open as a locus of debate'? The question of the balance between specified goals and experimentation is itself a matter for the most careful deliberations: it is highly contestable, indeed a prime subject for ethical and political practice. It also challenges our imagination, for we in so-called developed countries are so steeped in instrumentality and outcomes that it is very hard to think an other idea of the preschool, or indeed of other services for children provided through public policy, an other idea in which other rationalities and purposes are also important. Can we imagine the preschool as (to take just some examples) a space of possibilities, or as a network of obligations, or as a work of art, or as part of a local cultural project concerned with a good childhood and the relationship between children and the larger community?

At risk of exclusion

One of the consequences of dualistic thinking is that it leads to exclusion, since it sets up oppositional categories – one that is wanted against one that is not, one that is desirable and the other that is not, one that is right and the other that is wrong. We want to avoid falling into this position, which automatically excludes: because we are critical of something, does not necessarily mean that we banish it from our presence. So despite our critical comments about scientific method and knowledge, and about disciplines such as developmental psychology, we recognise their contribution. We want to avoid the extremes of both scientism and obscurantism – infatuation with and rejection of science.

We need, as Critchley (2001) reminds us, to 'return to the classical distinction, first coined by Max Weber, between explanation and clarification, between causal or causal-sounding hypotheses and demands for elucidation, interpretation or whatever . . . Natural phenomena require causal explanation, while social phenomena require clarification by giving reasons or offering possible motives' (121). Or, viewed another way, science can tell us certain things about the world, but cannot supply wisdom.

Similarly, we do not want to set up a dualism which divides the world into a few patches of light, surrounded by darkness. We are not suggesting that, apart from a handful of exemplary places such as Reggio Emilia, all preschools are the same, passively conforming to a technico-instrumental approach in their pedagogical work, unwitting lackeys to the demands of the state and international capital! In practice, there is much experimentation, much transgression, much seeking to think and do differently – by individual practitioners or groups of practitioners, sometimes openly, on other occasions concealing their transgression behind a public face of conformity.

One of our aims in writing this book is to give support and encouragement to such local projects, established or emerging islands of dissensus, and to contribute to the forming of global networks of preschools that want to contest dominant discourses. Books such as this, just like existing islands of preschool dissensus, are part of a resistance movement to these discourses, which by their nature try to strait-jacket what we can think, say and do by laying claim to tell the truth. At times, such resistance may seem hopeless. There are enormously strong structural forces, which we discuss in the next chapter, pressing a strongly technico-instrumental approach to preschools. Relations of power, buttressed by knowledge claims, are pervasive and normalising. The tide of uniformity is rising, the experts are fanning out across the world offering technical assistance that guarantees appropriate practice, desirable outcomes and reliable measurement of performance (of children and preschools) against universal norms.

But we are not without hope. Structure is powerful, but agency is always possible and at many levels, from the individual, through the group, to local government and the nation state. Green (2003) discusses the continuing influence of nation states over education reminding us that education systems are not all 'converging on a single model', and that though 'new global policy rhetorics – like lifelong learning – are certainly emerging . . . in practice they are interpreted and applied in quite different ways' (87). We can see this in practice if we compare Britain and Sweden and the very different policies they have adopted in relation to preschools and schools (Cohen *et al.*, 2004). While at the micro-level, Foucault, the great analyst of power, reminded us that relations of power are 'changeable, reversible and unstable' and that in them 'there is necessarily the possibility of resistance' (Foucault, 1987: 12). Narratives can be made to stutter and transgressions are possible since 'as soon as one can no longer think things as one formerly thought them, transformation becomes both very urgent, very difficult and quite possible' (Foucault, 1988: 155).

Positioning ourselves

In relation to preschools

Our approach throughout the book is to recognise multiple perspectives and identities, the importance of individual choice and responsibility, and to welcome the ensuing diversity and plurality. This does not mean, however, that we adopt a position in which every perspective is of equal value and merit, a relativism in which anything goes. We make choices, which we recognise as ethical and political, and we take responsibility for those choices: they cannot be determined for us by some objective assessment of evidence or by the weight of expert opinion.

One important choice and position that we take is to contest certain understandings of education (in Chapters 4 and 5). Another is to contest a certain understanding of preschools (and other institutions for children), which we have already referred to as 'producers of predetermined outcomes', but which we might also term institutions as 'children's services'. The concept of 'children's services' is deeply instrumental. The metaphor is the factory, for the concept understands institutions as places for applying technologies to children to produce predetermined, normative outcomes, for the efficient processing of children by workers-as-technicians.

We choose an other concept of institutions for children. The concept of 'children's spaces' has a very different rationality to that of 'children's services' – aesthetic and ethical rather than instrumental. The metaphor is the forum or meeting-place, for the concept understands institutions for children as environments where the coming together of children and adults, the being and thinking beside each other, offers many possibilities – cultural and social, but also economic, political, ethical, aesthetic, physical. Some of these are predetermined, but many others are not, some initiated by adults, but many others by children. The concept of 'children's space' does not just imply a *physical* space, a setting for groups of children. It also carries the meaning of being a *social* space, 'a domain of social practices and relationships' (Knowles,

1999: 241); a *cultural* space, where values, rights and cultures are created; and a *discursive* space for differing perspectives and forms of expression, where there is room for dialogue, confrontation (in the sense of exchanging differing experience and views), deliberation and critical thinking, where children and others can speak and be heard. In this sense, the concept of 'children's space' implies possibilities for children and adults to contest understandings, values, practices and knowledges.

Another and increasingly widespread understanding of preschools that we oppose is as an enterprise or business providing private commodities ('childcare', 'education', 'preparation for school', etc.) within a competitive private market, trading these commodities with individual 'consumer' parents. This understanding has established itself firmly in the English-language world (for the example of England, see Cohen *et al.*, 2004; Osgood, 2004), though not as yet so strongly in most countries of Continental Europe. It is part of a larger process, by which a neo-liberal belief in market rationality is extended to all areas of life, making everything economic and subject to the logic of commodification, consumerism, calculation and contract.

In our view, preschools should be understood as a public good, of great social, cultural and political importance. They should be viewed as part of that wider network of public provisions that makes society meaningful and creates possibilities for solidarity and democracy. Rather than competing with each other within a market, preschools should work together collaboratively. Rather than enterprises producing tradable commodities, we argue that not only *can* preschools be seen as sites of ethical and political practice, but that they *should* be seen in this way.

Our view of preschools is radically at odds with a market rationality, and this determines our views about policy. Like schools, preschools should be publicly funded and children should be entitled to go to them either from birth or, as in Sweden, from 12 months of age (after a period of well-paid parental leave shared between mothers and fathers): going to a preschool should not be conditional on, for example, the employment of a parent or on a child being categorised as 'in need'. They should be provided by organisations whose first commitment is to the public good, unconditional universal access and democratic practice. These organisations may take many forms – including local authorities, co-operatives and other non-profit organisations – but they are unlikely to be for-profit businesses. The staff working in preschools should be well trained, at least to the same level as those in schools, and should have the same pay and conditions of employment.

If this sounds more like Sweden than Britain (and most other countries), this is because we think that the Nordic welfare regime has proved uniquely capable of providing universally available preschools with a professional workforce. We doubt whether liberal regimes such as Britain, with their commitment to private market solutions, can achieve as much. Sweden is far from perfect. But it has provided good structural conditions that create space for producing pedagogical work that is permeated by strong ethical and political practices.

In relation to rights

An important discourse today about children, and provisions made for children, is about rights. Where does this discourse of the rights of the child fit into our thinking on ethics and politics? We are sceptical supporters of rights, sceptical because we see the concept as neither neutral nor unproblematic. The concept of rights is constituted by particular legal and liberal discourses (it is no coincidence that the prominence given to rights coincides with the political dominance of advanced liberalism and increasing recourse to the law as a means of mediating relationships), and premised on particular values and a particular understanding of the subject as a rational, autonomous individual. There is some tension between the concept of rights and, for example, the ethics of care or the ethics of an encounter, ethical approaches we discuss in Chapter 3. Rights entail a contractual and finite exchange between calculating and independent individuals; care and encounter foreground inter-dependence, infinite responsibility and the impossibility of being free of obligation. Rights are one example of universal codes set up to govern actions; care and encounter pay more attention to the need to make ethical choices in relation to particular contexts and conditions.

This does not mean that we wish to discard rights. Rather, we want to put them in perspective, treating them more as a tool than an icon. Rights have a tactical value within the political arena, increasing the agency of those with less power and providing a modicum of protection against oppression. They can give visibility and legitimacy to issues, making them more readily contestable. We would go along with Burman (2001) when she argues that 'we should recognise the tactical character of our engagement with the discourse of individualism via rights approaches and work alongside this towards formulating more genuinely interpersonal and intersubjective approaches to development and education' (14–15). In short, they are useful, not to be dismissed at a time when children (and others) have begun to acquire an established position in the rights discourse.

The problem comes when they are discussed in a decontextualised way, as if they are free of value, when too much is expected of them or when 'human rights doctrine [becomes] so unthinkingly imperialist in its claims' (Ignatieff, 2000: 323). For 'human rights can command universal assent only as a decidedly "thin" theory of what is right, a definition of the minimum conditions for any kind of life at all' (*ibid.*: 322).

Rights as codes of conduct rooted in liberal individualism have their uses, but they provide no substitute for more relational, contextualised and responsible ethical and political practices. Indeed, rights often end up the subject of such practices, as people seek to interpret their meaning and application in a particular place and time. Without such practices, rights simply become another technical practice that preschools, for example, may be required to observe, another code of conduct containing a prescriptive set of dos and don'ts.

In relation to the academy

What is our responsibility as members of the academy? Universities are increasingly becoming 'transnational bureaucratic corporations' (Readings, 1996), operating in national and international markets, offering their traditional roles of teaching and research to potential consumers. This means tailoring their offers to actual or perceived demand. One consequence is that academics in universities are increasingly made into technicians (another example of subjectification), whose task it is to produce outcomes as efficiently as possible. In the field of research, for example, agendas, questions and funding are increasingly supplied by 'customers', the task of researchers being to produce a particular type of supposedly value-free knowledge – 'policy relevant' information – ever more efficiently. They also get drawn into the design, development and application of technical practices for preschools and other institutions, offering a guarantee of objective and expert knowledge.

There is a place for instrumentality in universities, as in preschools, for some predetermination and delivery of outcomes. But universities should also be communities for provoking dissensus and crisis, for critical thinking, an activity vividly described by Rose, as

> partly a matter of introducing a critical attitude towards those things that are given to our present experience as if they were timeless, natural, unquestionable: to stand against the maxims of one's time,

against the spirit of one's age, against the current of received wisdom. It is a matter of introducing a kind of awkwardness into the fabric of one's experience, of interrupting the fluency of the narratives that encode that experience and making them stutter.

(Rose, 1999: 20)

Academics retain a responsibility to be reflective, sceptical and critical, whilst recognising that rather than being Masters of Truth and Justice we can at best offer one perspective from one particular situation within relations of power. We have a responsibility to resist the forces seeking to reduce us to mere purveyors of information and expertise, the production of which can be costed and offered for sale in the market place. We have a responsibility to resist closure and to hold open the question of meaning. The question 'posed to the university is thus not how to turn the institution into a haven for Thought but how to think in an institution whose development tends to make Thought more and more difficult, less and less necessary' (Readings, 1996: 175).

What is interesting for us about this discussion on universities and the role of the academic is that it could equally well be applied to the preschool and the school, and to the pedagogues working in these institutions. We are once again drawn to see the commonalities not only between preschools and schools, but between both institutions for children and universities – and therefore possibilities for solidarity and mutual learning.

Endnotes

1 'Preschool' is the literal English translation of the Swedish term *förskola*, and refers to centres for children below compulsory school age. In the case of Sweden, these centres take a wide age-range of children from 12 months or so – when parental leave ends – to 6 years when school starts. But in other countries, centres may be more age-segregated, for example taking children under 3 or from 3 to 6 years. We have chosen to use 'preschool' because the term encompasses a wide range of different types of centre-based provision for children prior to admission to primary school which come with a variety of names: nurseries, crèches, kindergartens, nursery schools, etc. It suggests to us the idea of a space prior to compulsory schooling, which is in relation to school but can shape its own identity.

We recognise that many young children in many countries are in family day care, a service which is not centre based. There is a fruitless discussion which tries to answer the question 'Are centres better/worse for young children than family day care?' – fruitless because the answer depends on various assumptions and understandings about childhood, upbringing, learning and so on, about which there is no consensus – nor need there be. We favour centre-based provision as a site for childhood, and that is therefore what we choose to explore in this book; others better qualified than we may choose to write about ethics, politics and family day care.

2 In this book we use the terms 'pedagogy' and 'pedagogical' to define the practice and purpose of the preschool and school, and 'pedagogue' as a generic title for workers in preschools and schools. We use these terms rather than those often used in English-language articles and books, such as 'education', 'childcare', 'education and care', 'childcare worker' or 'teacher'. The concept of pedagogy has a long history in Continental Europe, originating in nineteenth-century Germany. Today pedagogy is an important theory and practice in work with children and young people (and sometimes too with adults) in most European countries (with notable exceptions such as Ireland and the UK). Over time, though, pedagogy has taken somewhat different forms in different countries. The form we refer to, which is rather prominent in Sweden, combines a particular concept of learning (foregrounding relations, dialogue and the construction of meaning rather than the transmission of predetermined knowledge) with a broad idea of care that goes well beyond physical caretaking to a concern for and engagement with all aspects of life (social, physical, aesthetic, ethical, cultural, etc.).

Chapter 2

Technology as first practice

From Educating the Flexible Child *by Lynn Fendler (2001)*:

> The term 'flexible' has recently been used to describe traits, not only in education but also in business and politics. Analyses of developments in these fields and others have shown that current social circumstances call for 'flexible' and 'fluid' ways of being. These terms rightly pertain to a shift away from the rigidly defined social roles characteristic of modernity, such as the assembly-line positions in a Fordist factory or the efficiency models in a Taylorist school. The conception of a fixed role or position has now shifted to a more multifaceted and response-ready capacity, exemplified in a recent television commercial in which the members of a chamber orchestra drop their musical instruments to play basketball when a ball is thrown into their midst. Flexibility is vaunted as the cutting-edge solution to the challenges of productivity in a fast-moving global economy, and the goals and objectives of education reinscribe the values of flexibility through curricular and pedagogical practices.
>
> The shift from fixed role to situation response does indicate a new kind of flexibility relative to modern organisational structures, and on that basis many liberal and critical analyses of education suggest that this flexibility entails some essential sort of freedom, liberation, or release from regulation . . . The use of the term 'flexible' to describe methods – management, pedagogy, diagnosis – and to describe the subjective outcome – educated subject, worker, facilitator – gives the impression that regulations have been lifted, or that more possibilities have been opened. I argue, instead, that flexible and interactive technologies are constituted in historical relation to developmentally defined outcomes. In this historical relation, the education of flexible souls does not necessarily constitute an instance of emancipation, release, or empowerment. Rather, the educated subject is produced as the effect of the confluence of current discursive practices.
>
> (119, 137)

We have argued that preschools are often conceptualised in overly instrumental ways, as means to produce predetermined and calculable ends through deploying human technologies. Technical practice, finding the most efficient methods to achieve predetermined ends, is the main focus of attention, what might be termed 'technology as first practice'. But we have already begun to argue that this understanding of the preschool is not self-evident, that there are other possible understandings that we could choose. The questions for us are what these other understandings might be? And why is one particular understanding treated today as if it was true, as, what Foucault termed, a 'regime of truth'? Before seeking an answer to the first question, in this chapter we consider the second – why is a technico-instrumental construction of the preschool so widely taken for granted?

Later in this chapter, we shall discuss how 'cognitive-instrumental rationality' has been gaining ground, overcoming other forms of rationality, for more than 200 years. We shall also suggest that some of the pillars supporting this rationality are eroding, so that just as it becomes more influential than ever, so too its position is increasingly subverted. But first, we want to note some contemporary conditions which privilege this way of relating to the world above others, making a technico-rational approach appear to be self-evident.

Some contemporary influences

Neoliberal capitalism

New economic conditions require a reconfigured labour force, in particular more women employed overall with particular attention paid to increasing employment among women with young children. The consequent need for 'childcare' drives the growth in preschools. These changes in employment come at the same time (but not coincidentally) as the increasing dominance of a particular form of capitalism, given various names – neoliberal, flexible accumulation, free market, disorganised, Anglo-Saxon.

Capitalism takes different forms, with deep cultural differences between capitalisms, for example with respect to the role of the state or the responsibility of businesses to different groups such as shareholders, workers and suppliers (Hutton, 1995; Gray, 1999). As Joseph Stiglitz, the 2001 Nobel Prize winner for Economics, observes:

> There are striking differences between the Japanese version of the market system and the German, Swedish and American systems

... While the market is at the center of both the Swedish and American versions of capitalism, government takes on quite different roles. In Sweden, the government takes on far greater responsibilities for promoting social welfare; it continues to provide far better public health, far better unemployment insurance, and far better retirement benefits than does the United States. Yet it has been every bit as successful, even in terms of the innovations associated with the 'New Economy'.

(Stiglitz, 2002: 217)

Neoliberal capitalism is driven by an untrammelled search for profits, untrammelled in the sense that responsibility is owed only to one group expressed in its aim of maximising 'shareholder value'. This form of capitalism is characterised by the high value attached to free markets, the commodification of everything, competitiveness, inequality (as the motor driving competitiveness), economic and financial deregulation, and flexibility both personal and organisational. In the mindset of neoliberalism, everything is reduced to economics, 'all things desired or valued – from personal attributes to good government – are commodities' (Radin, 1996: 2), including children (Becker, 1976). All commodities can be expressed in monetary terms, at prices determined through the market, and traded on the market:

From the perspective of the ideal market, values that cannot be reduced to market values are flaws – interferences with rationality and free exchange. Social relations such as trust and caring are invisible. A person may have preferences that include making another person happy, but making another person happy for the other's sake rather than to satisfy the preferences of the person makes no sense. In the ideal market every social interaction is an exchange between individual entities and the notion of a social tie disappears. The ideal of the market teaches that everyone is always motivated by self-interest, that firms seek to maximise profits, that economic value is the only kind of value that matters.

(Held, V., 2002: 25)

From its heartlands in the Anglo-American world, neoliberalism spreads its Utopian vision that the market can and should permeate every aspect of human activity and behaviour, and that the exercise of choice within markets, by the autonomous subject, 'is a fundamental human faculty that overrides all social determination' (Dean, 1999: 57).

Instrumentality is all – 'how much the available means may bring in is the only question one can ask about their available use' (Bauman, 1995: 262). Relationships are calculating and contractual. Everyone and every organisation should be entrepreneurial, all actions and relations should be 'business-like' – everything becomes 'businessified'.

It is not just that neoliberalism has become the dominant form of capitalism; it is also relatively unfettered. Polanyi (1957) argued that capitalist development has been characterised by a 'double movement', with the main principle of economic liberalism, unfettered markets, confronted by 'the principle of social protection aiming at the conservation of man and nature as well as productive organisation' (132). Typically, therefore, periods of capitalist expansion have been followed by counter-movements checking its self-destructive capacity. At the moment, neoliberal capitalism is strongly on the offensive. Social regulation of its excesses has had little impact, partly due to current developments in globalisation that require strong measures to be taken at the international level.

The emergence of this particular form of capitalism as a star player on the global stage is significant for the preschool in a number of ways. It is not just that the 'new capitalism', linked to changes in employment and the labour market, requires 'childcare for working mothers' to ensure a sufficient supply of trained, flexible and increasingly female labour (and we recognise that there are other rationales for making provision that enables parents to work, not least the promotion of gender equality). It also focuses the minds of legislators and business people on the formation of the future workforce, a workforce inscribed with the prevailing values and able to compete successfully in a world of global free markets.

New economic regimes require new subjects to work for them. (Economic regimes also require the production of new subjects who will consume their ever-growing output – but that is another story.) It is not just a question of a sufficient supply of subjects; nor of subjects with trained hands and developed minds. Souls must be governed through processes of subjectification, to constitute the subject who will govern himself or herself and her or his effective participation in the new world order. Institutions are required that can produce these subjects – not just families, schools and workplaces (as was the case under Fordist capitalism) but now a whole network of services for children including preschools, and all connected ever more closely through technologies that ensure continuous co-ordination and control (an issue we return to below).

Popkewitz and Bloch (2001) suggest that the 'new' form of constructivism, prevalent in the field of education today, with its talk of the 'empowered' child that can analyse, reflect and problem solve, seeks to govern the soul by creating a particular subjectivity. This subject is created to fit the neoliberal workforce – as well as advanced liberalism's ideal of citizenship (a theme we also pick up shortly). This subject is an entrepreneurial self, a flexible 'actor', ready to respond to new eventualities and empowered through self-reflections and self-analysis: 'the twenty-first-century child has to be prepared to be a global citizen/ worker, flexible, adaptable, ready for uncertainties in work as well as in the family' (103).

The apparent autonomy of this subject is more apparent than real, since constructivism works within normative frameworks, embodying a subject defined in terms of flexibility, entrepreneurship and development. The constructivist self 'involves images of the universal child that intersect scientifically derived age norms with the normalizations of the dispositions and sensitivities of a problem-solving child or person . . . [T]he notions of development [therefore] intersect with a new normality of the child' (*ibid.*: 103). Put another way, despite a rhetoric of freedom, in effect the self is taught to govern the self – an example of governmentality – through 'the cultural production of individuals who work on themselves through self-improvement, autonomous and "responsible" life conduct and lifelong learning' (*ibid.*).

Echoing this theme, Fendler (2001), a quotation from whom starts this chapter, identifies the shift from one form of economy to another and argues that much current educational practice is intended to meet the demands from the state and the neoliberal economic system for flexible souls and problem solvers. She argues that the construction of this 'educated subject' involves particular technologies, 'the confluence of whole child education, developmentality, and interactive pedagogy' (120). These are practices that 'may appear to be exercises of freedom but, on closer examination, turn out to be repetitions and reiterations of the status quo' (121).

We have already referred in Chapter 1 to developmentality as a technology of normalisation which connects 'developmental psychology, efficiency, and behaviourism in educational curricula' and which becomes a means by which 'the self disciplines the self'. Fendler implies that this is an example of governmentality. Whole child education provides a further means for governing the soul, for the thrust of whole child education is that the child's entire being – desire, attitudes, wishes – is caught up in the educative process. Educating the whole child means not only the cognitive, affective and behavioural aspects, but the child's innermost desires . . . No aspect of the child must be left uneducated: education touches the spirit, soul, motivation, wishes, desires, dispositions, and attitudes of the child to be educated.

(Fendler, 2001: 121)

While such flexible and interactive technologies are often spoken of as freeing the child, in practice they serve to produce developmentally defined outcomes constituting a flexible self where flexible 'has come to mean response-ready and response-able; and the definition of "freedom" has come to mean the capacity and responsibility for self-discipline' (*ibid.*: 137). Rather than emancipatory, they are extremely instrumental and regulatory.

Kjørholt (2001) has also explored the relationship between practices in the preschool and subjectification. Analysing practices that became widespread in Nordic preschools in the 1990s, such as giving children increasing rights to make their own decisions, she relates discourses about 'the competent child' and children's rights to the creation of a particular subject – autonomous, individualistic, self-determining, rights-bearing, a consumer who expresses personal preferences, in many ways the ideal subject of Anglo-American liberalism. Thus, to take a very specific example, 'common meals', children and adults eating together, were seen as very important. But they are now seen as a 'threat to self-realisation' and increasingly dropped in favour of individual children choosing when and where they will eat.

Preschools are not confined to the production of the flexible subject for a neoliberal world. They are also intended to be instruments for reducing or preventing the unwanted consequences produced in the course of creating the neoliberal Utopia. For while neoliberalism seems to generate dynamic if erratic economic growth, it also seems to produce a commensurate growth of social problems.

Neoliberalism seeks to spread its values and practices into every part of life, and sees this as a beneficent act. But some writers view such spillover as more of a curse than a blessing. Sennett (1998) identifies 'new capitalism' with short-termism (rather than 'flexibility', the term of choice for advocates of neoliberal policies). He argues that the corrosion of long-term commitment in the workplace – and the trust, loyalty and mutuality that such commitment fosters – is dysfunctional for personal and family life:

> It is the time dimension of the new capitalism, rather than hi-tech data transmission, global stock markets or free trade that most affects people's emotional lives outside the workplace. Transposed to the family realm, 'no long term' means keep moving, don't commit yourself and don't sacrifice . . . This conflict between family and work poses some questions about adult experience itself. How can long-term purposes be pursued in a short-term society? How can durable social relations be sustained? How can a human being develop a narrative of identity and life history in a society composed of episodes and fragments?
>
> (Sennett, 1998: 27)

Similarly, Bauman traces a connection between the economic values of 'new' or 'neoliberal' capitalism, in particular flexibility, and adverse social consequences, including 'a new inter-societal and intra-societal polarization' and 'making precarious the situation of those affected and keeping it precarious' (Bauman, 1999: 27–28). Like Sennett, Bauman sees this precariousness of employment as having wider, serious social consequences: for

> in the world in which the future is at best dim and misty but more likely full of risks and dangers, setting distant goals, surrendering private interest in order to increase group power and sacrificing the present in the name of future bliss does not seem an attractive, nor for that matter sensible, proposition . . . [B]onds and partnerships tend to be viewed and treated as things to be consumed, not produced.
>
> (Bauman, 2000: 163)

While Gray (1999) observes that

> it is odd that there are still those who find the association of free markets with social disorder anomalous. Even if it could itself be rendered stable the free market is bound to be destructive of other institutions through which social cohesion is achieved. No society can opt for the free market and hope to avoid these consequences . . . By privileging individual choice over any common good it tends to

make relationships revocable and provisional . . . [A]ll relationships become consumer goods.

(36–37)

In this context, preschools (and other 'children's services') assume a role of social regulation, intended to bring a technical fix to bear on the wider societal consequences of the economic deregulation demanded by neoliberalism. Within the Minority World, this role is most apparent in two countries that have opened themselves wide to neoliberalism – the United States and the United Kingdom. Both countries have had very high levels of child poverty. Comparison in the mid-1990s between 23 OECD member states showed that the USA had the second highest level, the UK the fourth (UNICEF, 2000). Using a broader measure of poverty – the Human Poverty Index (HPI2) – across 17 OECD member states, the USA scores highest, the UK third highest (United Nations Development Programme [UNDP], 2002).

In both countries, major government programmes of early inter-vention (Head Start in the USA, Sure Start in the UK), targeted at poor families or areas, are seen as means to reduce poverty and its attendant ills. The rationale for public investment in such programmes is the expectation of a demonstrable and calculable return, a quasi-contract in which preschools receive funding in return for delivering certain outputs (with a growing industry of technical researchers employed to measure these outputs). The implicit assumption is that poverty and related social ills derive from individual failures – of children and/or parents – which interventions through preschools can rectify. These programmes avoid the need to question the 'new capitalism' under which material inequality has thrived.

(Cross-national comparison would, however, suggest the need for such questioning, given that countries with similar income levels pro-duce different amounts of poverty and inequality. Sweden's per capita GDP [applying Purchasing Price Parity to eliminate differences in price level] is much lower than the USA's and comparable to the UK's: $25,600 compared to $36,500 and $25,400 [figures for 2001, from OECD, 2002]. Yet comparisons of child poverty for the mid-1990s show the USA had the second highest level of 23 OECD member states, the UK the fourth highest, while Sweden had the lowest level: children in the USA were 9 times as likely to be in poverty as children in Sweden [UNICEF, 2000]. On the broader measure of poverty – the Human Poverty Index – the USA had the highest level of 17 OECD member states, the UK the third and Sweden the lowest (UNDP, 2002). This suggests that the Swedish welfare state, with its strongly redistributive regime of high tax levels and universal and generous benefits and services, has been rather successful both in preventing poverty in the first place and in providing accessible and affordable preschools to all families who want them.)

In the Majority World, the same rationale for early childhood programmes is on offer: that early intervention will provide an effective and relatively inexpensive technology to reduce poverty and its damaging consequences. Committed to neoliberal economics, the World Bank also believes in the possibility that increased technological expertise can solve global problems, with early intervention now added to the armoury of technologies:

> If professionals can only find the right parenting programme, the right level of stimulation and toys for children and the right kind of feeding programme to use when children are especially young and malleable, and their brains as yet unformed, many of the ill effects of poverty can be offset . . . [The approach] is both technological and redemptionist – the world is a difficult place to reform but young children are innocent and unformed and we can really make a difference if we can get in soon enough with the right kind of stimulating programme for the children and convert their parents to a right or better way of bringing them up.
>
> (Penn, 2002: 126, 129)

This technical approach is, as Penn goes on to suggest, diversionary. It focuses attention on parents and children, whilst distracting attention from the power relations that create poverty and inequality in the first place. Technology depoliticises profoundly important social and economic issues, while technical programmes are based on a logic of exchange, a financially calculable trade-off between inputs and outputs.

Neoliberalism enhances instrumental rationality and technical practices in another way. It commodifies preschools (and other services) as producers of private goods traded on the market. This represents, Dean argues, a transformation of the social: 'the social is not inscribed in a centralised and coordinated state, but as a set of constructed markets in services and expertise, made operable through heterogeneous technologies of agency and rendered calculable by technologies of performance' (Dean, 1999: 193). Especially in the English-language world, preschools (or rather those preschools conceptualised as 'childcare services for working parents') are viewed by government as producers selling services (i.e. 'care') to consumers (i.e. working parents) in a private market, and indeed many preschools operate as private businesses selling their services to whomever can afford them. This reaches its most extreme form in the United Kingdom where 86 per cent of nurseries are commercial undertakings run for profit (Laing & Buissson, 2003). A recent government 'childcare review' slips easily into the language of preschools and other services as commodities traded by businesses: 'The primary mechanism for delivering new places is through pump-priming funds to encourage childcare business start-ups . . . More needs to be done to address areas of market failure . . . Branding is confusing parents and providers' (Cabinet Office Strategy Unit, 2002). Even more bluntly, a consultancy firm that specialises in 'health and community care' states that 'the Children's Nursery sector is one of the fastest growing health and care markets in the UK . . . all market trends point to a continued rise [in demand]', so that its events are 'a must for all potential market entrants, established nursery chains, banks, venture capitalists, equity houses and other investors seeking to enter this growth sector' (Laing & Buisson, 2002).

The UK is at one extreme of the spectrum. Other countries – where other forms of capitalism and other values still retain some currency – still locate preschools (including nursery education) within public or non-profit private sectors, and treat them as part of public infrastructure. In Sweden, for example, over 80 per cent of preschools are provided by local authorities, and the remainder, though independent, are publicly funded; while, as already noted, the world-famous preschools of Reggio are a cultural and political project of the local commune.

But everywhere there are pressures to privatise these and other provisions for children including schools, businessifying and exposing them to market disciplines, including the application of managerial technologies with increasing emphasis on calculable and predefined outcomes. In their study of school reforms in Australia, New Zealand, the UK and the USA, but also Sweden, Whitty *et al.* (1998) note, despite some national variance, common trends summed up as a 'strong state and free economy' – the strong state steering education, but at a distance, and the free economy leading to a 'marketised civil society in which services are increasingly offered to individual consumers by competing providers' (35). Through these processes, instrumentality further saturates provisions for children. The instrumental language, assumptions and ideology of management predominate, and business values (competitiveness, entrepreneurship, individualisation) increasingly permeate every aspect of pedagogical work. Parents are constituted as private consumers: as such, they are expected to demand information on the performance of institutions on a range of predetermined outcomes, in the knowledge that if they make the wrong choice they risk consigning their children to being unsuccessful competitors in the labour market (and therefore in life itself) and as such, failed entrepreneurs.

Advanced liberalism

Economic neoliberalism is partnered politically by advanced liberalism. Indeed, the boundaries between the economic and the social increasingly blur as the former colonises parts of the latter previously out of bounds. The shift from the social state to the advanced liberal state occurs at different rates in different countries, but as it occurs the relation of the social and economic is rethought: 'all aspects of *social* behaviour are now reconceptualised along economic lines – as calculative actions undertaken through the universal faculty of choice' (Rose, 1999: 141). The market becomes a common feature of the economic and the social, providing a universal form for relationships and the provision of services.

The ideal citizen and ideal worker also merge, becoming one and the same: an autonomous subject, in no way dependent, with rights but also matching responsibilities, self-governing and responsible for managing his or her risks through making market choices – whether it be childcare, schools, health, pensions, or maintaining employability through lifelong learning. The individual reckons the price of everything and holds it in the balance as a contracted obligation. The ideal is enterprise and the entrepreneur – the entrepreneur in business, but also becoming an entrepreneur of oneself, conducting one's life and one's family as a kind of enterprise: 'the powers of the state are donated to empowering entrepreneurial subjects of choice in their quest for self-realisation' (*ibid.*: 142).

This self-contained individual citizen is connected with others through two types of contractual relationship: *market relations*, constantly making choices about the purchase of products (which through commodification extend to an ever wider range of goods and services) or engagement in the labour market; and *rights relations* involving exchange between equal and separate individual rights holders. Relations, therefore, are envisaged as taking place between detached, self-contained, rights-holding individuals, secure in a condition of independence. The opposite and undesirable condition is dependency, either on other individuals or, worse, the state.

The role of the state in an advanced liberal regime is not so much to provide benefits and services to its citizens. It is to create a certain kind of subject – a flexible, enterprising subject capable of exercising freedom-as-choice, above all self-sufficient and independent. Independence is 'the central normative idea for human personhood', and normality is constructed as self-sufficiency, the ability to lead an independent economic, social and political life. This has important implications for how services (such as provisions for children) are understood and provided:

> The idea of the self-sufficient individual fits into the current programme of privatisation of public services and the growth of market-oriented forms of regulation. 'Normal' citizens are constructed, then, first and foremost as individual participants in the exchange of labour and provisions. These individuals are supposed to translate care needs into market-oriented behaviour, thus conceiving of themselves as care consumers, participating in a system of care provisions which works according to the principles of supply and demand.
>
> (Sevenhuijsen, 1998: 130)

The state's task is also to enable this autonomous subject's exercise of freedom-as-choice, especially through competent participation in the market place and rights-based contractual relationships. This is done through a variety of means such as the provision of information (e.g. league tables of schools performance, the publication of inspectors' reports about preschools or schools), some regulation of the market (e.g. minimum standards for services), some rectifying of market failures (e.g. subsidies to low income families to enable them to buy 'childcare' on offer in the market) and a framework of law that supports rights and contracts.

The advanced liberal state, like neoliberal economics, espouses a strategy of freedom – but of a certain kind. It is the freedom to make individual choices, to enter the market as an informed consumer calculating best value in relation to cost and preference, to be oneself and do one's own thing. Freedom, as Rose puts it, 'is seen as autonomy, the capacity to realize one's desires in one's secular life, to fulfil one's potential through one's own endeavours, to determine one's own existence through acts of choice' (1999: 84) (see our discussion of the Janus-face of 'autonomy' in Chapter 1). The state thus governs not through coercion, but through citizens governing themselves through the practice of such freedom.

But this is one way of understanding freedom, and it is only this way of understanding and exercising freedom that is compatible with liberal arts of rule. The paradox is that such freedom is, in effect, a way of administering the population, creating citizens who govern themselves as particular types of subject exercising a particular form of freedom: the system cannot cope with a widespread choice to reject this form of freedom. To create such subjectivity requires particular forms of control; and it faces the dilemma of what to do about those individuals, families and groups who cannot or will not become such subjects. Freedom turns out to require a lot of governing:

> In order to act freely, the subject must first be shaped, guided and moulded into one capable of responsibly exercising that freedom through systems of domination. Subjection and subjectification are laid upon one another. Each is a condition of the other . . . On the one hand [advanced liberal practices of rule] contract, consult, negotiate, create partnerships, even empower and activate forms of agency, liberty and the choices of individuals, consumers, professionals, households, neighbourhoods and communities. On the other hand, they set norms, standards, benchmarks, performance indicators, quality controls and best practice standards, to monitor, measure and render calculable the performance of these various agencies. The position of 'freedom' in advanced liberal regimes of government is exceedingly ambivalent.
>
> (Dean, 1999: 165)

Advanced liberal regimes are great proponents of instrumentality and technical practice. To circumvent old centres of professional and bureaucratic governance, deemed incompatible with economic rationality, freedom of choice and best value, services must be marketised and sometimes privatised, in a combination of decentralisation with an 'evaluative state'. The state appears to devolve its responsibilities; but in fact it keeps tight control but indirectly through public management techniques, such as targets, quality assurance regimes, performance indicators and external inspection systems. This state 'governs at a distance' deploying a raft of new 'technologies of performance' to regulate agencies and render them, with their managers and practitioners, more calculative and entrepreneurial (Dean, 1999). Areas previously governed according to professional or bureaucratic norms are now subject to new forms of accountability, which undermine or dispense with expertise and govern professional activity in new ways. In particular there has been an 'audit explosion', a term subsuming a wide range of programmes for accountability and control, with an increasing emphasis on self-control and regulation, a form of governmentality in which organisations deploy techniques for regulating themselves (Power, 1997), preschool accreditation schemes being one obvious example. Advanced liberal government transforms audit

> from a relatively marginal instrument in the battery of control technologies to a central mechanism for governing at a distance . . . [G]overnment by audit transforms that which is to be governed. Rendering something auditable shapes the process that is to be audited: setting objectives, proliferating standardized forms, generating new systems of record-keeping and accounting, governing paper trails . . . Audits of various sorts have come to replace the trust that social government invested in professional wisdom and the decisions and actions of specialists. In a whole variety of practices – educational, medical, economic, organizational – audits hold out the promise – however specious – of new distantiated forms of control between political centres of decision and autonomized loci – schools, hospitals, firms – which now have the responsibility for the government of health, wealth and happiness.
>
> (Rose, 1999: 154)

Like the head office of a transnational corporation, advanced liberal government delegates responsibility to its business centres, individual services or agencies supplying services, while maintaining control through a complex web of specified requirements, in particular predetermined results often denominated in numerical terms. Technologies are judged to work to the extent they can be calculated to achieve the optimum relationship between 'inputs' and 'outcomes': numbers supersede individual judgement. Indeed, as Rose argues, numbers operate as crucial techniques for modern government, making their methods possible and judicable, and reducing complexity to order.

These new technologies contribute to advanced liberal government not only by enhancing power over services, whilst at the same time distancing government from direct responsibility for these same services, but also by contributing to the constitution of the ideal subject, the citizen able to take responsibility by practising freedom. Accreditation schemes, inspection reports, performance indicators and the like enable this citizen to act as an economically rational consumer, exercising market choice through the faculty of calculation. This becomes all the more important since the autonomous subject as consumer has little time left over actually to engage with the services he or she uses and so has little opportunity to gain understanding of their work and to make his or her own evaluation of that work. That responsibility is devolved to expert evaluations and statistical proxies, audits and numbers.

For paid work in an increasingly neoliberal global economy is ever more demanding – as employment itself intensifies to improve competitiveness, as work income becomes ever more important for the individualised management of risks, and as employment increasingly becomes a source of self-identity and self-realisation. The only way for the harassed parent-cum-worker to survive (that is, assuming she or he has decided to take the risk of undertaking parenthood in the first place) is by improved technology, not only at work but also in relation to life in general. We shall return in the last chapter to this critical issue of the relationship between time, employment, parenthood and engagement with institutions for children.

The nation state

We have talked about changes in the state and its government arising from the growing influence of advanced liberalism. In these cases, the state adopts a new role, with new relations to services: it can be described in various ways; for example as a 'facilitating state', a 'decentralising state' or an 'evaluative state'. It seeks to create a new citizen subject, free, autonomous, taking responsibility for managing risk. It also introduces new ways of governing, adopting a wide range of technologies, especially from fields strongly oriented to normalisation and regulation, such as developmental psychology and management. Power may be given away with one hand, but regained with the other. At one level, therefore, the state is more powerful than ever, with unparalleled possibilities for mobilising, co-ordinating and deploying resources towards certain ends.

At the same time, at another level the nation state has become far less powerful. It has lost power in important areas, particularly economic, as globalisation continues its evolution, most recently with the deregulation of capital and the global application of new technologies. Faced by rootless and restless capital, epitomised by transnational corporations, able and willing to move vast quantities of money at short notice, and jobs that can increasingly be located anywhere, nation states are 'no longer the elemental unit of capitalism' (Readings, 1996: 44). They are reduced instead to 'becoming a bureaucratic apparatus of management' (*ibid.*), or as others have termed them 'competition states' (Cerny and Evans, 1999) or 'social investment states' (Dobrowolsky, 2002; Lister, 2003) focused on sustaining the nation's viability in a global economy by taking measures that will attract rootless global capital.

In this role, the state becomes a sort of glorified development agency offering inducements to capital to bring investment and employment to its particular location. An important inducement is a ready supply of suitable labour – flexible, responsive, skilful. In these conditions, where the hollowed-out nation state becomes increasingly managerial and depoliticised, technologies that promise improved delivery of such economic outcomes have a strong appeal to governments. The preschool is one such technology, both ensuring today's labour force through 'childcare for working parents' and preparing tomorrow's through investment in 'social and human capital'.

International organisations play an important part in this changing role of the nation state. They become means of ensuring the better functioning of the market of competing nation states, to better meet the needs of global capital. Not only do these organisations create global systems of rules, for example regulating trade. But they also offer cross-national comparisons of performance assessed against universal criteria (e.g. the TIMSS and PISA studies referred to in Chapter 1) and create opportunities to exchange information on technologies that will enhance performance (e.g. the recent OECD [2001] review on early childhood education and care). It is in this context that we can understand the growing attention paid by these organisations to preschools and preschool technologies. We can also see that they become means for the formation of a global dominant discourse about preschools, as they strive to identify and disseminate 'best practice'.

As we have already noted, there remain considerable national differences in education. But the combination of a global and highly competitive neoliberal capitalism, the expanding interests of international organisations and the hopes invested by nation states in preschools adds up to a formidable force for normalisation and the spread of what we have called the Anglo-American dominant discourse.

Power and control

We have suggested that the freedom of advanced liberalism brings with it an array of new technologies of governance. This takes us to an important theme of this book, which we have already touched on: that an age of unparalleled individualism, choice and freedom is also an age of unparalleled government, discipline and control. The exercise of power, and its effects, is as big an issue as ever, perhaps more so as power relations assume ever more complex and indistinct forms.

In the previous chapter we introduced the Foucauldian concept of disciplinary power, and some of its associated 'techniques of power'. Disciplinary power has evolved and strengthened over time. But it may, too, be overtaken by events, or metamorphosing into a different form with greater effectiveness. The French philosopher Gilles Deleuze (1925–1995), Foucault's compatriot and contemporary, suggested that today 'societies of control are in the process of replacing disciplinary societies'. Disciplinary societies were based around 'closed' institutions which acted as 'normalising machines', with the individual passing from one institution to the other each with its own laws and disciplinary methods: the family, the school, the barracks, the factory, sometimes the hospital, prison or some other selective enclosure: 'enclosures are molds, distinct castings . . . in the disciplinary societies one was always starting again (from school to the barracks, from the barracks to the factory)'. By contrast 'controls are a modulation, like a self-deforming cast that will continuously change from one moment to the other . . . in the societies of control one is never finished with anything' (Deleuze, 1992: 5).

Deleuze connects his analysis to changes in capitalism and machines. Disciplinary societies went with a capitalism of concentration and machines involving energy, what some would call Fordist capitalism. Control societies are associated with a capitalism of higher order production, essentially dispersive, the factory replaced by the global corporation. The machines are computers that provide a technology for connecting everything up, spatially and temporally. Control in control societies is infinite, continuous and dispersed. Thus continuous training – lifelong learning, emphasising continuity from preschool to old age – replaces the school; and continuous assessment – including developmental assessment – replaces the examination. The new citizen is required 'to engage in a ceaseless work of training and retraining, skilling and reskilling, enhancement of credentials and preparation for a life of incessant job seeking: life is to become a continuous economic capitalization of the self' (Rose, 1999: 161). Surveillance is designed into the flows of everyday existence, enabling the continuous monitoring of conduct (e.g. monitoring by closed circuit television, the detailed records of expenditure provided by credit cards and company loyalty cards, the continuous supervision of call centre staff).

Hardt and Negri (2001) argue that the shift from a disciplinary para-digm to a control paradigm of government is 'a most important qualit-ative leap' (318). However, they argue that this shift does not mean the end of discipline. Governmentality runs like a thread from discipline into control: 'the exercise of discipline – that is, the self-disciplining of subjects . . . – is extended even more generally in the society of control' (330). The corollary of the collapse of the enclosed institutions is that mechanisms for disciplining 'have become less limited and bounded spatially in the social field'. Central to the society of control, they con-tend, is the production not only of the individual's subjectivity, but of a new form of subjectivity:

> The passage toward the society of control involves a production of subjectivity that is not fixed in identity but hybrid and modulating . . . Certainly in disciplinary society each individual had many identities, but to a certain extent the different identities were defined by different places and different times of life: one was a mother or father at home, worker in the factory, student at school, inmate in prison, and mental patient in the asylum. In the society of control, it is precisely these places, these discrete sites of applicability, that tend to lose their definition and delimitations. A hybrid subjectivity produced in the society of control may not carry the identity of a prison inmate or a mental patient or a factory worker, but may still be constituted simultaneously by all of their logics.
>
> (Hardt and Negri, 2001: 331)

What this seems to offer, according to Hardt and Negri, is some protec-tion to the capitalist system from the possibility of organised opposition arising from the transformation of the multitude 'into an autonomous mass of intelligent productivity, into an absolute democratic power' (344). It is central to their argument that if this transformation occurred, then 'capitalist domination of production, exchange and communica-tion would be overthrown' (*ibid.*).

How does this discussion of power relations connect to the instru-mental rationality and technical practice of the preschool? From the nineteenth century onwards, Rose argues, the school was a particu-larly important institution for normalisation: 'the normal child was to be produced through this regime of supervision and judgement in rela-tion to norms of scholarly and moral behaviour' (*ibid.*: 77). Today, the school retains this purpose, but is now complemented by the preschool, although regimes of supervision and judgement change over time, to incorporate new technologies and new definitions of normality.

The preschool, like the school, is an institution where disciplinary power is deployed through a range of knowledges and technologies that form part of a dominant discourse. We have already discussed some of these, such as child development, 'developmentally appropriate curricula' and other applications of child development, constructivist pedagogy, whole child education and quality. Knowledges and technologies expand and increase over time, to create a more effective exercise of discipline. Moreover, these technologies increasingly adopt a global form, for example through the spread of particular programmes of practice and methods of evaluation: the growth of cross-national evaluation tools (e.g. ECERS) and evaluation exercises, whether of policy or children's performance, is a current example of this process of introducing global norms against which countries, institutions and individuals judge their adequacy.

The notion of a shift from discipline to control should further alert us to new forms of technology which connect institutions and practices so that they operate in a continuous way across large swaths of the life course. One example is the re-positioning of the preschool as the first step in a continuous process of lifelong learning and formation of subjectivity that continues through schooling into higher education and adulthood. This has implications for the potential of the preschool as a space for minor politics, an issue to which we return in Chapter 6.

The ambivalent place of modernity

We have related both the expansion of preschools and their often strong technico-instrumental orientation to particular, linked and current phenomena. None of these phenomena is entirely new, all are recently emergent variants of long-established forms – capitalism, liberalism, the nation state and disciplinary societies. We now want to add another, broader influence, a particular paradigm or mindset for making sense of the world – modernity.

Modernity is a contentious subject. There are disputes about when we should identify its beginnings (in the sixteenth, seventeenth or eighteenth centuries?), and whether or not we should speak today of the continuance of modernity but in a late or reflexive form, or the ending of modernity and entry into a period of postmodernity. There is also a widespread ambivalence towards modernity – can't live with it, can't live without it! This ambivalence arises in part from modernity's encompassing different traditions and values.

Toulmin (1990) argues for two traditions of modernity, the first emerging in the sixteenth century and taking the form of a Renaissance humanism that celebrated singularity and difference, accepted uncertainty and contingency of existence and adopted a sceptical tone. Hardt and Negri (2001) similarly describe modernity as 'constituted by at least two distinct and conflicting traditions' with the first tradition celebrating singularity and difference (76). This tradition flourished between the collapse of premodernity and a 'second beginning' for modernity in the mid-seventeenth century. Others identify features of modernity which have more lasting merit than others. Tolerance, equality and democracy are a political side of the Enlightenment 'which most critics are looking to preserve' (Seidman, 1998: 347). Foucault answered the question 'What is Enlightenment?' in terms of its being an ethos of permanent critique which retains its importance. (The Enlightenment of the eighteenth century has been described by Bauman [1993] as when modernity achieved its maturity as a cultural project.)

But there is another tradition in modernity, which emerged in the mid-seventeenth century. Toulmin describes this as a scientific rather than a humanistic modernity: he views both traditions as, in theory, complementary, but in practice often seen to be in competition. Moreover, he argues, this later tradition involved a loss of values from the earlier tradition: 'the seduction of High Modernity lay in its abstract neatness and theoretical simplicity: both of these features blinded the successors of Descartes to the unavoidable complexities of concrete human experience' (Toulmin, 1990: 200–201). For Hardt and Negri this second tradition has no redeeming features, typifying it as a counter-revolution, a repressive force seeking 'to control the utopian forces of the first (tradition) through the construction and mediation of dualisms' (140). They portray a conflict between desire and order: 'modernity is defined by crisis, a crisis born of the uninterrupted conflict between the immanent, constructive, creative forces and the transcendent power aimed at restoring order' (76).

The emergence of this strain of modernity coincides with the growth of disciplinary power and technology, discussed in Chapter 1, which Foucault relates to the emergence of a new type of political thought or rationality: *raison d'état*. The main principle was the state as an end in itself and the need to increase its power, through increasing the number, docility and usefulness of the population (what Foucault refers to as 'bio-power'). In this political branch of modernity, instrumental rationality was predominant:

> The administrative apparatus of the state posed welfare in terms of people's needs and their happiness. Both of these were, of course, goals to which previous governments had dedicated themselves. But the relations have been reversed. Human needs were no longer conceived of as ends in themselves or as subjects of a philosophical discourse which sought to discover their essential nature. They were now seen instrumentally and empirically, as the means for the increase of the state's power.
>
> (Dreyfus and Rabinow, 1982: 139–140)

Modernity in this second form has valued order and universal forms:

> The birth of modernity was accomplished by means of a relentless assault against local traditions, social pluralism, disorder, ambiguity and uncertainty. It is this will to order, classify, design or control everything that is at the heart of modernity.
>
> (Seidman, 1998: 313)

And while the Enlightenment espoused emancipatory values, it also held oppressive ideas and aspirations. Bauman, for instance, argues that

> the true spirit of the Enlightenment revolves around the quest for control and certitude. The triumph of the Enlightenment has meant the victory of what he calls 'legislative reason'. This type of reason is hostile to genuine forms of individuality and pluralism and intolerant of ambiguity and uncertainty. Legislative reason strives to fashion the world in accordance with general principles, laws, rules or norms. The Enlightenment may, in principle, celebrate individualism and diversity; in practice, it is repressive.
>
> (*ibid.*: 314)

At the heart of this tradition lies the privileging of a particular concept of, and relationship between, reason and knowledge. This reason is objective, instrumental, calculating and totalising: it involves an autonomous agent who perceives an atomised world, from which bits of information can be taken and processed to fit into the world-view that he or she has; and who then acts to fulfil his or her goals on the basis of calculating the most economic application of means to a given end

(Taylor, 1991). This knowledge is unified and universal resting on a solid ground of fact and scientific method, revealing the truth about humanity, history and nature, providing a predictability that enables social engineering which in turn produces progress. Reason as access to truth via knowledge, provides the means of bringing the world under control, making it available for human projects.

In this tradition, reason and scientific knowledge are separated from experience and emotion, values and politics. They claim to provide an objective and universal standpoint, the one and only valid perspective, made possible because reason and science are value-free and able to mirror the external world. Scientific knowledge and instrumental rationality gain prominence at the expense of other types of knowledge and rationality, their hegemony expressed in the singular terms of 'reason' and 'knowledge' and the strangeness to the ear of the plural 'reasons' and 'knowledges'.

This reason and knowledge have imperial ambitions. Not only do they deny and overrule other forms of reason and knowledge. But, linked with the idea of progress, they form part of the Enlightenment ideal and project of a universal civilisation. But what this means is a civilisation in which diversity in its many forms is eradicated and 'Westernisation' triumphs – for the universal civilisation is both unified and expressive of the values and assumptions of Enlightenment. Modernisation thus becomes equated with Westernisation, while Westernisation means the triumph of instrumental reason (Gray, 1995).

The Portuguese social scientist Boaventura de Sousa Santos (1995, 1998) has also proposed different traditions within modernity, contending that one tradition has become increasingly dominant. The 'paradigm of modernity' has been rich and complex, consisting of 'twin pillars' – emancipation and regulation. But what has become increasingly apparent during the twentieth century has been that the pillar of emancipation has collapsed into the pillar of regulation: 'no new emancipatory projects are emerging, let alone the energy to fight for them' (Santos, 1998: 82). Santos proposes three types of rationality: first the cognitive-instrumental rationality of science and technology, which we have already discussed at some length. But also an aesthetic-expressive rationality of arts and literature and a moral-practical rationality of ethics and law. The collapse of emancipation into regulation is marked by the growing hegemony of cognitive-instrumental scientific rationality and knowledge which has increasingly overcome other rationalities over the last 200 years. The result has been a 'hyperscientification of the pillar of emancipation':

It is appropriate to speak of a global (that is, Western) model of scientific rationality, with some internal variation, to be sure, but one which ostensibly discriminates against two non-scientific (hence, potentially disturbing) forms of knowledge: common sense, and the so-called humanities. The new scientific rationality, being a global model, is also a totalitarian model, inasmuch as it denies rationality to all forms of knowledge that do not abide by its epistemological principles and its methodological rules.

(Santos, 1995: 7–8)

Santos goes further. Regulation is constituted by three principles: the state, the market and the community. But here again the components making up the pillar have got out of kilter. Just as the pillar of emancipation has become dominated by scientific rationality – 'hyperscientifica-tion' – so too the pillar of regulation has undergone an unbalanced development marked by a process of 'hypermarketisation', the dominance of the principle of the market.

These analyses all point to the growing domination of a particular tradition in modernity, with major implications for our interest in the practice of ethics and politics. This tradition is driven by a will to know, as a way to order, classify and regulate; it privileges the universal over the local; and it accords hegemony to an instrumental rationality and scientific knowledge. The scientific and technical are pre-eminent in this tradition, while the ethical and political are controlled and sidelined, leading to de-politicisation and de-ethicalisation. What are ethical and political problems are recast as scientific and technical problems, soluble through the correct application of instrumental reason, scientific knowledge and technical expertise (Dreyfus and Rabinow, 1982). Conflict is reduced to debates about implementation – 'What works?' – leaving politics 'reduced to a specialised, sectoral, social practice' with a 'strict regulation of the citizens' participation in such practice' (*ibid.*: 51). In its turn, ethics is reduced to a restricted rights/responsibilities reciprocity and the following of moral codes.

How do these analyses of modernity relate to preschools and other services for children? The regulatory or ordering side of modernity bears a strong instrumental rationality. Bauman (1995) refers to modern inventions such as schools as 'factories of order . . . sites of purposeful activity calculated to result in a product conceived in advance . . . making conduct regular and predictable' (107). Scientific knowledge and technical practice provide the means of production. This has led many to believe that children might, through the application of science and technology in the right conditions to their state of dependence and incompleteness, become agents of progress. King (1997) argues that much work to improve the conditions of children has been premised on abiding beliefs in mankind's capacity to control and master to predetermined ends, an Enlightenment-inspired endeavour: 'once we know how people or society really work, proponents of this approach claim, we shall be able to identify those controls, buttons and levers that will enable people or society to be better governed and ordered' (*ibid.*: 188).

The development of social policy informed by emergent social sciences, especially from the second half of the nineteenth century, was inscribed with an expectation that children could be redemptive agents to bring about a better future:

> Emerging reliance on science and technology in the 19th century coupled with a romantic view of the purity and perfectibility of the child, led to the perception that children are appropriate vehicles for solving problems in society. The notion was that if we can somehow intervene in the lives of children, then poverty, racism, crime, drug abuse and any number of social ills can be erased. Children become instruments of society's need to improve itself, and childhood became a time during which social problems were either solved or determined to be unsolvable.
>
> (Hatch, 1995: 119)

This project of social policy might be achieved through the application of science and technology to the family, and in particular the better supervision and governance of mothers:

> [The family of the labouring classes was] to be shaped, educated and solicited into a relation with the state if it was to fulfil the role of producing healthy, responsible, adjusted social citizens. The political task was to devise mechanisms that would support the family [of the labouring classes] in its 'normal' functioning and enable it to fulfil its social obligations most effectively without destroying its identity and responsibility. The technical details of the internal regime of the working-class family would become the object of new forms of pedagogy, for example through medical inspection of schoolchildren and the invention of 'health visitors', to instil norms of personal hygiene and standards of child care. While the mothers of the wealthier classes had been solicited into alliances with medics in the nineteenth century . . . one sees a new specification of the

role of the working-class mother as one who was to be educated by
educationalists, health visitors and doctors into the skills of responsible government of domestic relations.

(Rose, 1999: 128–129)

But the project might also involve the application of science and technology in institutions for children, notably schools. In a secular culture of
redemption, guided by a rational scientific thought, 'a 19th-century view
of schooling [was] as a means to "rescue" children from their economic,
social, and cultural conditions through planned intervention' (Popkewitz,
1998: 21).

Modernity, therefore, sustains a continuity in thinking about and
working with children which is inscribed with instrumental rationality,
scientific knowledge and technical practice. This 'regulatory' tradition in
modernity has become increasingly strong, not least because the world
appears to be more threatening and competitive and less orderly and
controllable. In these circumstances, it is the incompleteness of the child,
the lack of corruption, the ability to inscribe the *tabula rasa* and to govern
the soul that makes the child such a promising agent of redemption: 'in
a world seen as increasingly shifting, complex and uncertain, children,
precisely because they are seen as especially unfinished, appear as a good
target for controlling the future' (Prout, 2000: 306). And it is young
children, perceived to be the most incomplete of all human beings, who
today seem the most promising redemptive agents: in the words of an
international organisation, 'ECEC holds out some hope of addressing
at a fundamental level some of the economic and social problems which
are of increasing concern to society as a whole' (UNICEF, 2002: 28).

But as Prout (2000) points out, there is a sort of paradox in the
current situation. 'Modernity's project of rational control', in particular
via children and through the 'quintessentially modernist idea of prevention', appears to have become more intensive at a time when that
project seems to have met its limits. We clutch tightly to the hope that
powerful interventions with young children and their parents, deploying
developmental knowledge and a range of technologies, will this time
prove a 'philosopher's stone' that converts problems into successes,
without having to ask difficult political and ethical questions about the
causes of our problems or the meaning of success. In the poignant
words of Burman, it is a paradox that

> despite manifest failure of the project of modernity (with its associated
> lexicon of progress, liberation and leisure through technological

assistance, and 'bigger is better' philosophy), developmental discourse seems to be the place where these hopes still persist. Onto the child we heap the thwarted longings of decayed societies and try to figure out something better. It's a hard burden for children to carry. Surely they should be their own futures; not ours.

(Burman, 2001: 9–10)

Turning away

We can now connect up these forces. Increasingly hegemonic economic and political regimes require the formation of a particular subject, autonomous, active, flexible, response-able, a bearer of rights and responsibilities, self-governing, a practitioner of freedom. New and continuous forms of discipline and control provide ever more effective ways to form and govern this subject. The subject is inscribed with scientific knowledge and instrumental rationality, forms of knowledge and reason connected to a regulatory mode of modernity pledged to dispense with uncertainty and ambivalence. Technical solutions are an intrinsic part of modernity's instrumental culture.

In this context, preschools appear self-evident. First and foremost, their purpose is instrumental and their practice technical. We could, if we so chose, conceptualise them differently: as spaces of possibility and surprise; as sites of ethical and democratic practice; or indeed as 'works of art' or in many other ways. We could, if we wanted, apply 'moral-practical' and 'aesthetic-expressive' rationalities to them. But in general we do not. Instead, we choose to view and judge them as means for engineering certain ends, defined in terms of universal criteria – be it child development, educational standards or economically valued qualities.

But things can change. Neoliberalism finds itself increasingly on the defensive, as growing numbers of people question or oppose its calculating and exploitive ways. The utopia of markets has not been reached, and many who have been shown the vision are doubtful or opposed. Markets have their place, most would agree. But some would go on to argue that they also have their limitations and flaws: they can and should be put in their place and governed carefully. Capitalism may be the only economic order on offer, at least for now, but capitalism can take many forms, with different relations between the social and the economic, the state and the market, and different degrees of regulation. The autonomous subject of advanced liberalism feels increasingly exposed in an uncertain world: less confident in his or her ability to manage independently, increasingly ambivalent about flexibility. New forms of solidarity and inter-dependence have fresh appeal. Above all, it is possible that we are living through a period of paradigmatic transition – from one tradition of modernity to another or from modernity to postmodernity.

Disenchantment with modernity – or at least its dominant tradition – has set in: many aspects have begun to lose credibility. As a result of what is termed the linguistic turn (Lyotard, 1984), it is argued that knowledge is no longer a mirror image of reality to be discovered through the application of science and reason, no more a sure foundation of truth on which we can build, for example, policy and practice with confidence. Rather than a given, knowledge is to be understood as constructed through language, within particular contexts and by people situated in different economic and social positions: knowledge, in short, is perspectival, always subject to interpretation and evaluation, contestable and therefore provisional, and plural. Nor can knowledge any longer be described as value-free, objective, neutral or by any other terms which imply we can know the world by somehow standing outside it. Knowledge too, as we have discussed in the previous chapter, is closely connected to power: particular knowledges serve to legitimise certain power relations, which in turn value certain knowledges over others. Developmental psychology, for example, legitimises a certain technical approach to public policy about preschools, while public policy in turn adopts developmental psychology as a 'regime of truth'. Overall, the possibility of finding foundations for universal claims has receded: the existence of 'theoretically neutral, pretheoretical ground from which the adjudication of competing claims can proceed' (Gray, 1995: 151) has come to seem implausible.

For some, modernity has become discredited by its perceived implication in the Holocaust, the Gulags and other horrors of authoritarian rule, 'legitimate offspring of the modern age – of that optimistic view, that scientific and industrial progress in principle removed all restrictions on the possible application of planning, education and social reform in everyday life, of that belief that social problems can be finally solved' (Bauman, 1991: 29). Modernity has been further implicated in a global process of environmental degradation. A few centuries of progress have left the Earth in a condition where it is possible to fear the mass extinction of species, including humans. This is a product, some claim, of a belief in the possibility and desirability of one species controlling and mastering the natural world, turning nature into an object of human will: 'the conception of the natural world as an object of human exploitation and of humankind as the master of nature is one of the most vital and enduring elements of the modern world-view and the one which Westernization has most lastingly and destructively transmitted to non-Western cultures' (Gray, 1995: 158). Overall, both the idea of universalism and of linear progress, assumptions central to the history of modernity, have been discredited.

Seidman describes the paradigmatic transition, the turn from regulatory modernity to what he terms postmodernity, and what is at stake, in this way:

> At the heart of the postmodern culture is an acceptance of the pluralistic character of social experiences, identities and standards of truth, moral rightness and beauty. In place of the abstract, universal self, a postmodern culture asserts selves that are differentiated and individuated by class, gender, race, sexuality, ethnicity, nationality, physical and psychological ableness, and on and on. In place of a unitary concept of reason and uniform cultural standards, in a postmodern culture we speak of traditions of reason and a plurality of cultural standards that express different traditions and communities. If modernity is organized round a series of neat divisions (family/economy, science/ideology, politics/morality) and hierarchies (e.g. reason, science, individualism, the subject, progress, the West, the identity of humanity), postmodernity underscores a process of differentiation or the blurring of these boundaries, the disruption of hierarchies and the questioning of modern foundations.
>
> (Seidman, 1998: 347)

A major casualty has been the status of science, in particular the position of scientific knowledge. It must be acknowledged that the situation is somewhat confusing and ambivalent. On the one hand, we face astonishing feats of science and great claims for what science does or will achieve. Recent decades have seen phenomenal breakthroughs, which have changed our understandings of our selves, our planet and our universe. Yet at the same time, science is the subject of increasing scepticism, fuelled by a realisation that science has not been a source of unalloyed progress but rather has increased the risks we face; we realise we have paid a high price for many scientific discoveries and applications. Modern science, 'previously the pansolution for all the problems of modern Western societies, gradually became a problem itself' (Santos, 1995: 55).

At the same time as this growing disenchantment with science, the very model of scientific rationality, with its accompanying notion of scientific knowledge, has entered into crisis – paradoxically as a result of the great advance in knowledge that the model made possible. Einstein demonstrated that Newton's absolute time and space do not exist, problematising the previously dominant Newtonian paradigm. Quantum physics demonstrated the impossibility of objective observation and questioned the accuracy of measurement, while mathematical accuracy has also been problematised. In the fields of microphysics, chemistry and biology, new conceptions of matter and nature have emerged: 'in place of eternity we now have history; in place of determinism, unpredictability; in place of mechanism, interpenetration, spontaneity, irreversibility and evolution; in place of order, disorder; in place of necessity, creativity and contingency' (*ibid.*: 19).

These new understandings undermine the dominance of a 'rational-linear paradigm' based on a certain idea of objective scientific knowledge. They have precipitated a profound epistemological reflection on this form of knowledge, though mostly carried out by scientists themselves (e.g. Maturana, Varela, Prigogine). This reflection has put into question concepts such as objectivity, laws and causality: 'rationality must be balanced by an ecological approach that looks at human and natural systems holistically, and rather than just knowing them through their parts [attempts] to understand their interrelationship and connections within larger systems' (Fink, 2001: 230). It suggests that scientific knowledge should be viewed as one perspective in a world of perspectival knowledge, a knowledge both valuable and dangerous because of its propensity to close the door to many other ways of knowing the world.

> Scientific rigor, because it is based on mathematical rigor, quantifies, and because it quantifies, it disqualifies. It is a rigor that, by objectifying the phenomena, objectualizes and degrades them; in characterizing the phenomena, it caricatures them. In sum, scientific rigor is a form of rigor which, in asserting the scientist's personality, destroys the personality of nature. The vaunted successes of technology obscure the limits of our understanding of the world and suppress the question of the human value of a scientific endeavour thus conceived.
>
> (Santos, 1995: 21)

Santos argues that one important aspect of the paradigm transition through which we are living is the emergence of a new form of knowledge, which he terms a 'postmodern emancipatory knowledge'. This knowledge is not inscribed with a cognitive-instrumental rationality, nor tied to technical practice. It is instead a

> local knowledge created and disseminated through argumentative discourse . . . Because it is created by the interpretive communities of which it is also creator, postmodern emancipatory knowledge is rhetorical. Herein lies its closeness to aesthetic-expressive rationality. While modern science aims at the naturalization of knowledge through objective truths, descriptions and regularities, postmodern emancipatory knowledge assumes its discursive artifactuality. For postmodern emancipatory knowledge, truth is rhetorical, a mythic moment of rest in a continuous and endless argumentative struggle among different discourses of truth; it is the ever-provisional result of a negotiation of meaning within a given relevant audience.
>
> (*ibid.*: 38)

What we may be witnessing is a general process of disenchantment – with neoliberalism, advanced liberalism, modernity in its regulatory form, a technico-instrumental rationality and scientific knowledge, to which we might also add established forms of party- and parliamentary-based political practice. Disenchantment, however, is far from total, while the alternatives either are unclear or fail, so far, to have gained popular backing. Faced by a troubled and troubling world, and a growing sense of crisis, some still clutch at the well-tried responses of instrumental rationality: better science, technology and management. Others, however, are looking for alternative possibilities, different ways of thinking and acting. New forms of social relations which combine some measure of both autonomy and solidarity. A turn away from the search for certainty and order, unity and closure, into a recognition of multiple perspectives and ambivalence, provisionality and contestation.

With this turn to diversity and uncertainty, a new space is opened up for political and ethical practice itself, so reversing a process which has seen ethical and political practice replaced by technical practice. This new space, moreover, calls for the reconceptualisation of ethics and the ethical, politics and the political. We turn now to consider these concepts, and how they can be the subjects of practice in preschools.

Chapter 3

What ethics?

From Ethics of the Other *by Beatrice Hanssen (2000)*:

[M]uch of twentieth-century philosophy and liberation politics can be seen as an attempt to undo epistemic and ontological regimes of the self that violate the alterity of the other . . . Of the many variants of what collectively has come to be called the 'philosophy of the other' . . . all have sought to bid farewell to the monologism of Cartesian philosophy of consciousness no less than Kant's anti-instrumental, nonstrategic moral philosophy, whose universalizable categorical imperative – even as it mandated that the other be regarded as an end in itself, not a means – could not safeguard against the imposition of violence onto the other . . .

No matter how diverse these proposals for thinking the other may be, one problem in particular invariably has plagued them. Put in its simplest terms: how to combine a commitment to the universal recognition of others – whether it be a matter of ethical, cultural, or legal recognition – with a respect for the concrete particularism, difference, or asymmetry of others? . . . [A]nd most crucially, in what way to redress the epistemic violence enacted by hegemonic Western discourses that silence or slight the subaltern other? . . .

[The real or purported horrors of] Kant's utopian universal history of peacefully coexisting atomistic moral agents, who all will that the maxims governing their actions become universal law . . . seem slight compared to the more disconcerting realities of a globalized strategic, manipulative, pragmatic utilitarianism, including its perhaps most seductive phantasm, that of corporate multiculturalism. Mapped out in Fukuyama's *End of History*, this program for a globalized liberal world order, propelled by a healthy, competitive free-market capitalism . . . transforms the other into nothing but a potential economic competitor.

(130, 166)

What would it mean to treat preschools as sites of ethical practice? To privilege the ethical over the technical? To answer these questions we must first answer another question – what do we understand by ethics? It is, as Sevenhuijsen points out, almost 'impossible to give a single unambiguous definition of ethics', as this is closely connected to the 'particular philosophical school of thought in which [ethicists'] work is situated' (1998: 37). There are, in other words, different ways of understanding and approaching ethics.

In this chapter, we look at some answers to the question 'What ethics?' We begin by considering an important tradition, what we term universal ethics, which has been very influential since the eighteenth-century Enlightenment. We then consider three other approaches which have emerged more recently, and which share some important concerns, in particular the relationship with the Other and how that relationship can avoid violating the alterity of the Other. We pay particular attention to one of these approaches, 'the ethics of an encounter', for it is this ethics that we find most interesting and compelling when considering what it would mean for preschools to be 'loci of ethical practice'.

In the next two chapters we look into the pedagogical implications of adopting a practice based on the ethics of an encounter. For though discussions of ethics do involve theory, they are not just theoretical. Ethics is a very practical matter. It is the 'systematic and critical reflection on human action . . . [and this] is not limited to the domain of academic theory (which one might be inclined to think on reading many academic texts), but takes place in all kinds of social practice' (*ibid.*). Ethics can be – and, we would argue, should be – the basis for preschool (and school) practice.

Universal ethics

A universalistic ethics is an expression of 'the Enlightenment project of refounding morality and social life on universal and rationally compelling principles . . . [based on] autonomous human reasoning alone' (Gray, 1995: 158, 161). It is often linked to the name of Immanuel Kant (1724–1801), the German philosopher:

> Kant's notion of ethics set the boundaries . . . around morality as an autonomous sphere of human life. These boundaries require that morality be derived from human reason in the form of universal principles that are abstract and formal. They require that the social and political connections to morality not be counted as central

to morality itself. They require that morality be rigidly separated from personal interest. And they require that morality reflect what moral thinkers have called 'the moral point of view': morality consists of a set of principles that are universalizable, impartial, concerned with describing what is right.

(Tronto, 1993: 27)

This ethics offers a categorical distinction between right and wrong applicable to and by everyone irrespective of social or historical context or circumstances: it is 'a totality of rules, norms, principles equally applicable to everyone and acceptable to every rational thinking person' (Sevenhuijsen, 1998: 59). Ethics here is the 'should' question: from a normative and universalist perspective, how should we think and act? The task of ethics is to formulate higher principles or criteria within a society that adopts a contractual model of functioning, in cases of conflicting interests, rights and opinions. The search is for a universal objective point of view, a transcendental 'view from nowhere' that would be the same for all rational people, the essential qualities needed being reason, abstraction and impartiality.

These qualities begin to create a subject. The question of the subject – what sort of subject is assumed or required – a question first raised in Chapter 1, runs through the discussion of ethics. This approach of 'universal ethics' assumes a particular idea of the subject as moral agent:

> In Kantian ethics the moral subject is separate from and stands above empirical reality. In this way he can determine what constitute universal moral obligations. According to Kant's categorical imperative – 'I ought never to act except in such a way that I can also will that my maxim becomes a universal law' – a moral subject shall be oriented towards duties which are recognizable and acceptable to everybody. The moral subject can only be held responsible for autonomous choices, whereby freedom is understood to mean being free of dependence and bodily and historical contingencies, as well as the ability to formulate an autonomous will . . . The moral subject is a detached and separate individual, whose central question is how best he can satisfy universal moral obligations.
>
> (*ibid*.: 55)

This moral agent is, therefore, 'an atomistic unit with a predetermined identity', deliberately striving not to become involved in case this should distract from the business of finding and applying the correct principles and rules. He represents a 'male fiction of an individual who imagines himself free from particular relationships and living conditions' (*ibid.*: 48). This moral agent is very similar to the ideal subject of modernity whom we introduced in Chapter 1: rational, stable, objective, autonomous, able therefore to stand outside the world and know it as it really is, his thought and actions assuming the strict separation between mind and body, passion and reason, self and others.

In the approach of universalistic ethics, obligations and rights are closely connected, two sides of the coin:

> Satisfying one's moral obligations makes one eligible to be the bearer of rights. Rights in turn are seen as the cement of social order, as the most important way people can engage in orderly social relations. Kant links this, following many other philosophers, with the idea of society as a contract, a series of legally determined agreements on the central aspects of human society. Being a moral person is thus, almost by definition, linked to the ability and the authority to exercise rights and fulfil obligations. Moral dilemmas take the form of conflicts between rights claims.
>
> (*ibid.*: 55)

What is described here is an idea of ethical relationships – how subjects should relate to each other and society – in which key elements are calculation (a balancing between rights and responsibilities) and contract (an agreement on duties and expectations). This contractual view of ethical relationships is inscribed in liberalism. Santos (1995) refers to a 'liberal micro-ethics' that has become the dominant conception in the rationality of modernity. The calculation at the heart of this ethics is the principle of 'restricted reciprocity', so that 'rights can only be granted to those from whom we can demand corresponding duties' (51). This is an individualistic and narrowly conceived ethics, operating through 'a linear sequence: one subject, one action, one consequence . . . offering us ethical criteria for minor acts, but [denying] us the ethical criteria for the major acts that result from enormous capacity for action made possible by technology' (50).

A universalistic ethical approach underlies much policy and practice in the early childhood field. There is a search on for universal codes that will govern practice and evaluation, 'a totality of rules, norms, principles equally applicable to everyone and acceptable to every rational thinking person'. These codes take the form of curricula, goals and targets, standards, quality measures, standardised measures of assessment.

Such codes offer norms against which to judge what is right or wrong, good or bad, normal and not normal.

This ethical framework does not require an active ethical practice. Instead, it provides guidance for an active technical practice. As Sevenhuijsen (1998) points out, this whole approach is driven by modernity's 'deep-seated mistrust of the moral capacities of its subjects' which results in legislating on 'moral truth claims by laying them down in legal imperatives' (11). What is right, good and normal is specified, by some supra-individual agency or by experts acting as legislators who prescribe what needs to be done. What is called for from the individual – for example, the preschool practitioner – is conformity to the prescriptions of the code and the terms of the contract through the application of correct technology. Responsibility is exchanged for legislation, the need to choose for rule-following, ambivalence for certainty.

The Polish social theorist Zygmunt Bauman (1925–) is one of those for whom this approach to ethics, so much a part of modernity, has been deeply problematic, indeed dangerous. For, he claims, it seeks to divest the individual of responsibility, by setting forth a 'discourse of objective, transnational and impersonal truth' (1992: xxii). An ethical code, designed by experts, has substituted ethical law for moral choice:

> The modern project postulated the possibility of a human world free not only from sinners, but from sin itself: not just from people making wrong choices, but from the very possibility of wrong choice. One may say that in the last account the modern project postulated a world free from moral ambivalence: and since ambivalence is the natural feature of the moral condition, by the same token it postulated the severance of human choices from their moral dimension . . . The focus of moral concerns has been shifted from the self-scrutiny of the moral actor to the philosophical/political task of working out the prescriptions and proscriptions of an ethical code . . . From the moral actor's point of view, the shift has much to be commended . . . Having reduced the vague, notoriously underdefined responsibility to a finite list of duties and obligations, it spares the actor a lot of anxious groping in the dark, and helps to avoid the gnawing feeling that the account can never be closed.
>
> (Bauman, 1995: 4)

Postmodern ethics

The disenchantment with modernity, and with liberalism in its various forms, is paralleled by a turn in ethical thinking away from what we have termed the universalistic approach. This new direction has led to the exploration of a number of connected themes: responsibility, relationships, situatedness, and otherness are particularly important. In the process, 'the concept of ethics and the ethical has been reconceptualized, reformulated and repositioned' (Garber *et al.*, 2000: viii). One casualty has been the ideal of the autonomous and sovereign subject, another the desirability or feasibility of codes or other general prescriptions and the calculation and 'restricted reciprocity' of rights and responsibilities. Rather than seeking the truth, these new approaches to ethics foreground wisdom, which involves an active practice to decide what is best in a concrete situation. They engage with particularities and emotions rather than seeking the dispassionate application of general and abstract principles. They recognise the uncertainty, messiness and provisionality of decision making. Implicit in this turn to active ethical practice is trust in the ethical capacities of individuals, their ability to make judgments rather than simply apply rules.

We have already introduced a major critic of universalistic ethics – or the approach taken to ethics in modernity. Bauman (1993, 1995) argues that modernity has replaced ethics with order, rules and regulations – what Bauman terms morality (although in his writings he often does not maintain this distinction between 'ethics' and 'morality', using the two terms interchangeably). He views ethics as a chance given to moderns, who have though

> been largely unable to take on the challenge . . . [for it was] easier just to follow the rules. By this process morality or conventionalism is substituted for ethics, or care of the self and others; and in turn moralism or hectoring replaces morality, or else morality gives way to law: we let the magistrates and black letter law books tell us how to live.
>
> (Beilharz, 2000: 123)

Underlying this process was a deep mistrust of individuals, an assumption that they cannot act ethically without codes to follow. Modernity, Bauman argues, is built on suspicion of human spontaneity, drives, impulses and inclinations, which it tries to replace 'with the universalising gaze of unemotional calculating reason' (Sevenhuijsen, 1998: 17).

To Bauman, a Jew himself born and raised in Poland between the two world wars, the Holocaust did not occur because of reasons specific to Germany. Rather, it was a 'central fact of modernity . . . a characteristically modern phenomenon . . . an accident waiting to happen in the field of possibilities we call modernity' (Beilharz, 2000: 88, 90, 91). It erupted from the intersection of social engineering – part of modernity's drive for a fully controlled and ordered world – with instrumental rationality and moral indifference. This indifference – which he sees as the dissolution of feelings of responsibility for the Other – arises from the distancing effects of the modern division of labour: 'all divisions of labour create distance between persons by establishing links which take us away from the face of the other . . . The decision-makers do not actually witness the outcomes of the processes which they bureaucratically initiate' (*ibid*.: 96). Power and responsibility thus become detached, and in the process the ethical becomes the technical, creating a situation in which the murder of millions became for thousands of German officials a managerial matter of how to produce most efficiently a particular outcome (while Bauman considers this process of detachment of power from responsibility in relation to the Nazi death camps, Sennett [1998] refers to it as a feature of organisation in the workplace of 'new capitalism').

Moving into postmodernity offers the possibility to re-personalise ethics and assume the responsibility which comes from facing and making choices, rather than following universal codes or laws. Ethics exist, Bauman argues, but without one foundational code that can provide us with certain and universal answers. We have to recognise, and learn to live with, ambiguity and ambivalence.

> It is possible to give up on the grand narrative idea of a single ethical code, without giving up on the idea of moral responsibility as a regulative ideal . . . Choices between good and evil are still to be made, this time, however, in the full daylight, and with full knowledge that a choice is being made. With the smokescreen of centralized legislation dispersed and the power-of-attorney returned to the signatory, the choice is blatantly left to the moral person's own devices. With choice comes responsibility. And if choice is inevitable, responsibility is unavoidable.
>
> (Bauman, 1995: 5)

The absence of foundations and codes does not doom us, as is often glibly asserted, to relativism: 'the demise of universal absolutes does not mean "everything goes" licence' (*ibid*.: 6). Indeed, quite the opposite. For postmodern ethics turns out to be far more demanding than modern morality. There may not be a foundation or code against which everything may be judged, objectively and with certainty. But that does not mean that all views must be considered equal: 'if there is no absolute truth to which every instance can be compared for its truth value, if truth is instead multiple and contextual, then the call for ethical practice shifts from grand, sweeping statements about truth and justice to engagement with specific, complex problems that do not have generalizable solutions' (St Pierre, 2000: 26).

The answer to the bugbear of relativism lies with us, ordinary people. The absence of certain foundations in postmodern ethics means that we must, as individuals, assume more of the burden, be more active in ethical practice. We have to think for ourselves, not rely on codes produced by experts. We must make choices and take responsibility for those choices. And we can do this because 'humans are essentially moral beings' – which does not mean that we are basically good (humans being neither exclusively good nor exclusively bad) but that the human condition is moral:

> Well before we are told authoritatively what is 'good' and what 'evil' . . . we face the choice between good and evil: we face it already at the very first, inescapable moment of encounter with the Other. This means in its turn that, whether we choose it or not, we confront our situation as a moral problem and our life choices as moral dilemmas. What follows is that we bear moral responsibilities (that is, responsibilities for the choice between good and evil) well before we are given or take up any concrete responsibility through contract, calculation of interest or enlisting in a cause. What follows is that such concrete responsibilities are unlikely to exhaust and replace in full the primal moral responsibility which they strive to translate into a code of well tempered rules.
>
> (Bauman, 1995: 2)

Our situation as ordinary people is both exhilarating and scary, stark and complex. We are our own moral agents. We recognise that we have to make choices between good and bad without seeking shelter in a universal code. We must take responsibility for the choices we make.

This, as Bauman observes, is uncomfortable. Human reality is messy and ambiguous. So ethical decisions are ambivalent and uncertain, they are often provisional and contested. There is no black and white, only varying shades of grey. There are no guarantees: 'confronting the choice between good and evil means finding oneself in a situation of ambivalence . . . Dilemmas have no ready-made solutions; the necessity to choose comes without a foolproof recipe for proper choice; the attempt to do good is undertaken without guarantee of goodness of either the intention or the results' (*ibid.*). The dilemmas increase because of the pace of change in today's world, resulting in 'the fast-changing standards of "normalcy" which once – when solid and persistent – offered the benchmark against which injustice, the violation of the "normal" and "habitual", could be measured' (*ibid.*: 43).

Yet far from being pessimistic, Bauman is hopeful. The postmodern era may bring a pace of change that increases the 'moral agony', it may be a bane – but it also offers 'the chance the moral selves never confronted before' (*ibid.*). People show moral competence – indeed, society is made possible by this competence. But this competence is neither technical nor rational, nor governed by instrumental rationality: Bauman argues that 'moral behaviour is more like intuition than reason: we are not ignorant of what is right and what is wrong, but we cannot always fully justify or explain a particular course of action or inaction' (Beilharz, 2000: 123). He welcomes a re-personalising of morality, and the release of morality from constructed ethical codes: personal responsibility is 'morality's last hold and hope' (Bauman, 1993: 35).

This 'personalisation' of ethics does not mean, however, that we cannot construct agreed positions. But these are built from the bottom up, through negotiation, not imposed by experts. Moreover, any agreement is likely to be 'inconclusive, temporary and short of universal acceptance' (*ibid.*: 34).

Bauman's idea of postmodern ethics, or perhaps we should say an ethics for postmodern conditions, has much in common with what Cherryholmes refers to as 'critical pragmatism', although ethics is only one field to which critical pragmatism can be applied:

> [Critical pragmatism] continually involves making epistemological, ethical and aesthetic choices (not necessarily in serial order or this order) and translating them into discourses-practices. Criticisms and judgements about good and bad, beautiful and ugly, and truth (small t) and falsity are made in the context of our communities and our attempts to build them anew. They are not decided by reference to universal norms that produce 'definitive' and 'object-ive' decisions.
>
> (Cherryholmes, 1988: 178–179)

Cherryholmes contrasts 'critical pragmatism', with its connotations of active and contextualised practice, with 'vulgar pragmatism', which is closer to Bauman's idea of 'modern morality' with its application of universal codes: 'vulgar pragmatism tests ideas and practices by comparing them to traditional and conventional norms with little or no sense of crisis or criticism' (*ibid.*: 178).

Gray (1995) envisions the possibility of a concept of ethics similar to Bauman's, inscribed with what he terms an aesthetic rationality. But, to finish this section on a note of uncertainty, he also questions whether we, in the West, can shake off our modern tradition and its pervasive instrumentality – calculative thought – sufficiently to practise such ethics:

> It may be that the Western cultures are so deeply imbued with rationalism that they cannot tolerate a conception of ethics, for example, in which it is an aspect of the art of life, not to be distinguished categorically from prudence or aesthetics in its character, in which it shares with these practical arts a provisional character and a local variability . . . [But it may be] that the calculative and representational mode of thinking which philosophy has privileged in modern times is now so hegemonic that the cultural space is lacking in which an alternative mode of thinking might occur . . . [The wager] turns on the chance that the power of calculative thought in contemporary Western culture is not irresistible.
>
> (183–184)

This wager encompasses very specific and concrete matters, for example policy, provision and practice for children and our recurring question. Is it possible to resist calculative thought and to practise a less instrumental early childhood education and care?

An ethics of care

There are important connections between Bauman's approach to ethics and that of the mainly feminist scholars who have explored another approach, what has come to be called 'an ethics of care'. Both regard ethics as a creative practice, requiring the making of contextualised ethical decisions, rather than following universal rules or codes. Both see ethics as being about care of and responsibility for the Other, both of which arise from proximity, from being confronted by the Other.

Authors who have written about an ethics of care have found inspiration from a number of twentieth-century thinkers including Martin Heidegger, Simone Weil, Hannah Arendt, Emmanuel Levinas, Michel

Foucault, François Lyotard and Paul Ricoeur, so that in many ways the ethics of care 'intersects with other attempts to think about morality and normativity in new ways' (Sevenhuijsen, 1998: 31). Moreover, in a challenge to notions of linearity, work on an ethics of care also draws on the writings of far earlier thinkers, including classical philosophers such as Aristotle, early Christian thinkers in the tradition of Stoa, and contributors to the eighteenth-century Scottish Enlightenment, such as Hume, Hutcheson and Smith – following whom there is a turn to universal ethics.

Tronto (1993) contrasts the ethical approach of the Scots with the Kantian approach, the former concerned with context and the idea of a 'moral sensibility' with which individuals are endowed and which can be cultivated, the latter focused on delineating general moral rules. But with the major social and economic changes of the eighteenth century, including rapid globalisation (a reminder that globalisation is not an event but a long-term historical process), it became increasingly necessary to have not only global – rather than local – units of measurement, but also global rules for regulating behaviour and relationships. There was a shift from 'contextual morality' to a universalistic morality premised on a universal human reason: 'since the late eighteenth century, Kant's model of what constitutes good moral theory, "the moral point of view" [i.e. from the standpoint of disinterested and disengaged moral actors], has stood almost unchallenged, resting upon the notion that morality requires a universal grounding in rules' (*ibid.*: 51). But in the late twentieth century the fortunes of contextual morality began to experience a revival.

From this historical background, Tronto goes on to describe an ethics of care as 'a practice rather than a set of rules or principles . . . It involves *particular acts of caring* and a *"general habit of mind"* to care that should inform all aspects of moral life' (*ibid.*: 127; emphasis added). She defines caring as 'a species activity that includes everything that we do to maintain, continue and repair our "world" so we can live in it as well as possible' (103), broadening the concept to include our relationship with the environment as well as with other people. She outlines a number of elements, or values, of an ethics of care including: attentiveness (to the needs of others), responsibility, competence and responsiveness.

Developing this theme, Sevenhuijsen (1998) proposes that important values in what she terms the 'feminist ethics of care' include empathy, intuition, compassion, love, relationality and commitment. The central values are responsibility and communication. She contrasts universalistic ethics and an ethics of care in terms of their central questions. In the former case, what am I obliged to do in general terms? In the latter case, how should I deal with dependency and responsibility in a specific situation? The former starts from the assumption of a self-interested, calculating and exchange-oriented human being, while the latter starts from the premises of mutual dependency.

Sevenhuijsen goes on to distinguish the ethics of care from a universalistic ethics, or ethics of rights, in four main respects. The ethics of care is concerned with responsibilities and relationships rather than rules and rights; it is bound to concrete situations, rather than being formal and abstract; and it is a moral activity rather than a set of principles to be followed. Finally, the ethical subject in the ethics of care is different from the ethical subject of universalist ethics:

> the moral agent in the ethics of care stands with both feet in the real world. While the universalist ethicist will see this as a threat to his independence and impartiality, or as an obstacle to creating in his moral imaginary, the care ethicist sees this precisely as a crucial condition for being able to judge well . . . The ethics of care demands reflection on the best course of action in specific circumstances and the best way to express and interpret moral problems. Situatedness in concrete social practices is not seen as a threat to independent judgement. On the contrary it is assumed that this is exactly what will raise the quality of judgement.
>
> (Sevenhuijsen, 1998: 59)

Moreover, the ethics of care brings a different image of what it means to be human:

> In contrast to an atomistic view of human nature, the ethics of care posits the image of a 'relational self', a moral agent who is embedded in concrete relationships with other people . . . Individuals are no longer seen as atomistic units with a pre-determined identity, who meet each other in the public sphere to create social ties . . . The self is not conceived as an entity, but as the protagonist in a biography which can contain all kinds of ambiguities and unexpected turns. This implies a radical break with the idea of a pre-social self in liberal ethics. The feminist ethics of care has more to gain from the idea of a processual self, a self which is continually in the process of being formed.
>
> (*ibid*.: 55–56)

Despite its association with feminist scholarship, the ethical agent in the ethics of care is not gendered. Tronto argues against regarding an ethics of care as essentially feminine, a women's morality. Rather, she argues, it is an ethic that includes values traditionally associated with women: she sees it as part of those 'moral theories that rely on compassion, care, emotions and communication' (Tronto, 1993: 149).

At its heart, therefore, the ethics of care is about how to interpret and fulfil responsibility to others. Ethics does not involve conforming to a code but seeking answers to situated questions, i.e. what is the proper thing to do in this situation. Ethical dilemmas arise not from conflicts of rights but from conflicts of responsibility. It is also an ethics of relationships, giving particular attention to how to relate to the Other in a responsive way.

Responsiveness for Tronto (1993) involves finding a relation to the Other based on responsibility and the recognition of difference: 'responsiveness suggests a different way to understand the needs of others rather than to put ourselves into their position ... [O]ne is engaged from the standpoint of the other, but not by presuming that the other is exactly like the self' (135). Sevenhuijsen (1998) also argues that an ethics of care requires and enables a relation to the Other that assumes difference, connected with an understanding of subjectivity very much at odds with the subject of modernity, who is homogeneous, coherent and complete:

> The central values of the ethics of care, responsibility and communication lead to a commitment to deal with differences, not only between individuals and social groups, but also within the self. This is made possible because a definition of the self as multiple and unstable is no longer seen as a threat but rather as a part of life ... A feminist ethics of care grafted on to postmodernism thus has the capacity to deal with diversity and alterity, with the fact that subjects are different and in this sense both 'strange' and 'knowable' to each other.
>
> (60)

Levinas and the ethics of an encounter

The 'philosophy of the Other' and how to respond to alterity is at the heart of the work on ethics of Emmanuel Levinas (1906–1995), a Lithuanian Jew who came to make his home in France. Largely ignored until the mid-1980s, today Levinas is considered one of the greatest

French philosophers of the twentieth century (Critchley, 2001), who has 'played a major role in formulating the contemporary account of the ethical in France' (Readings, 1996: 223).

Levinas challenges some of the most central tenets of philosophical, political and economic thought – as well as, we will show in the next chapter, much in a contemporary dominant discourse of preschools, a discourse we have described as highly instrumental and which puts technical practice first. He confronts the idea of contractual and calculable relationships, the norm of autonomy, the freedom of the autonomous subject, and the primacy philosophy has given to knowing. Indeed, central to his argument is a questioning of what knowledge is and does.

For Levinas, in Western thought knowledge readily becomes *a will to know* which involves making sense of perceptions through applying to them the knower's prefabricated system of understandings, concepts and categories. There is a high price to pay for this will to know. The autonomous and rational subject, Levinas argues, assimilates and makes the Other into the Same in its will to master and make the world comprehensible through the application of abstract and universal systems of knowledge and truth. I come to the Other with my typical ways of knowing, and make sense of the Other by applying them. If I can know the Other then I banish uncertainty and ambivalence for order and predictability, I make the Other an integral part of my world and by so doing affirm my autonomy and independence.

Levinas examines how the striving towards autonomy and independence is oppressive, even violent. When the autonomous self 'understands' or 'knows' the Other, what occurs is the Other's being made into the Same and dispossessed of the possibility to be an Other. Levinas calls this 'the Logos' – a form of transparent understanding which reduces the unknown to the known. To describe the process of assimilation or negation, Levinas uses the metaphor of grasping: to retain his or her freedom, the knowing subject with claims to mastery 'grasps' the Other by means of concepts, categories and classifications, 'grasping' expressing a sort of violence involved by reducing the particularity of the Other into the totalising system of the knowing subject.

> In knowledge there also appears the notion of an intellectual activity or a reasoning will – a way of doing something which consists precisely of thinking through knowing, of seizing something and making it one's own, of reducing to presence and representing the difference of being, an activity which appropriates and grasps the otherness of the known. A certain grasp: as an entity, being

becomes the characteristic property of thought, as it is grasped by
it and becomes known. Knowledge as perception, concept, comprehension, refers back to an act of grasping.

(Levinas, 1989: 76)

Through grasping, the stranger is made familiar and intimate and the
same, and the unknown is turned into something which 'free thought'
can grasp and have at its disposal (Kemp, 1992). Thought becomes self-
reflection and, in this process, neutralises the objects of its attention;
then everything becomes neutral and objectified quantities, rather than
unique phenomena. Originality and novelty are excluded and alterity
disappears, to be replaced by 'the totalitarianism of the same'. Levinas
is quite specific that 'alterity' is not the same as 'difference': 'Alterity
is not at all the fact there is a difference, that facing me there is someone with a different nose than mine, different colour eyes, another
character . . . [Alterity] is the unencompassable, the transcendent. It is
the beginning of transcendence. You are not transcendent by virtue of a
certain different trait' (Levinas, 1988: 170).

Levinas questions the whole Western philosophical tradition.
Western thought, he argues, has been ruled 'by a desire for totalisation,
an attempt to reduce the universe to an ultimate unity by way of
panoramic overviews and dialectical synthesis' (Peperzak, 1998: 4).
Knowledge and knowing, to which since Aristotle Western thought has
given priority, are particularly implicated in this desire for totalisation,
with its consequence of grasping and making the Other into the Same.

Levinas is not alone in recognising the aggression inherent in universal and normative thinking so characteristic of modernity, with its
autonomous and rational subject. Heidegger, feminism and contemporary postmodernism are all connected by a shared 'sensitivity to the
"violence" of our standard modern modes of thinking' (White, 1991).
Butler, in relation to the modernist project, concludes that 'any appearance of unity presupposes and requires a prior act of violence' (1993:
37). Many, following Heidegger and echoing Levinas, argue the problem precedes modernity, dating back to ancient Greece: Western thought
itself is inscribed by ways of thinking which produce 'the drive to know
[which] is often compromised by elements of domination and control'
(Clark, T., 2002: 1). Foucault (1983) writes of 'how an Other is always
pushed aside, marginalized, forcibly homogenized and devalued as
[Western] cognitive machinery does its work' (19). Jacques Derrida
(1930–2004) refers to the Western philosophical tradition as marked
by a foundational violence that seeks to reduce the Other to the same

status as the addressee, while R. Young, too, observes how 'in Western philosophy, when knowledge or theory comprehends the Other, the alterity of the latter vanishes as it becomes part of the same' (1990: 13).

To rethink ethics, Levinas has had to challenge the sovereign and knowing subject of the Enlightenment, by arguing that one must think 'otherwise than being' – beyond essence and the autonomous and rational self. Contesting the primacy given to knowing in Western thought, Levinas argues that ethics has to precede all thought: the ethical relation has primacy, it is prior to logic and reason, it is 'first philosophy'. Contesting totalities and universal sameness, Levinas bases his ethics – an 'ethics of an encounter' – on absolute alterity and the unknowability of the Other. Opposing the Western tradition of totalisation, Levinas 'maintains the human and divine Other cannot be reduced to a totality of which they would only be elements' (Peperzak, 1998: 4). This is an Other whom I cannot represent and classify into a category; this is an Other whom I cannot totalise and grasp, that is, seek to understand through a framework of thought I impose on the Other.

Rather than grasping the Other, Levinas requires respect for the Other. This calls for respecting the Other as absolute alterity: 'the Other is the stranger that disturbs intimacy and whom it is impossible to reduce to myself, to my thoughts and my possessions'. The Other always goes beyond my understanding of her: 'The Other is infinity, and we can conceptualise infinity but we can never comprehend infinity' (Taylor, 1987: 196).

But the relation to the Other is not just a matter of respecting, of not grasping. It goes further. Levinas's ethic is also premised on absolute and infinite responsibility for the Other. It is responsibility for the Other, rather than autonomy, independence and rights of the self, that constitutes an ethical relation. Indeed, for Levinas, freedom comes not from the exercise of choice and independence but through affirmation of the Other and one's own responsibility.

This is a total negation of the independent free subject and of the instrumental rationality of modernity and liberalism. Resuming the theme of non-calculative thinking, Levinas's ethics of an encounter has none of liberalism's logic of contractual duties and rights nor capitalism's logic of calculated marketised exchange. The emphasis is on obligation to the Other without expectation of a profitable return. Rather than a calculated relationship of restricted reciprocity, there is an unconditional responsibility: 'I have to respond to and for the Other without occupying myself with the Other's responsibility in my regard' (Levinas, 1987: 137). Instead of autonomy, Levinas speaks of 'heteronomy', which means a community that has to be understood in terms of dependency (or inter-dependency) rather than autonomy.

Nor is ethics for Levinas anything to do with prescribing rules for what is right or wrong (what Levinas termed 'morality'). They are conceived instead in terms of a critique of 'the liberty, spontaneity and cognitive *empris* of the ego that seeks to reduce all otherness to itself' (Critchley, 1999: 5); and of an ethical relationship between persons involving a form of 'responsibility towards the other' (Levinas and Kearney, 1986: 28), a question of how to relate and how to affirm the irreducible alterity of the world we are trying to construe. Nor should we confuse the affirmation of irreducible alterity with empathy and tolerance, which are ideas Levinas contests as means of representing the Other in your thought – another case of grasping.

This relationship of responsibility or responsivity to the Other takes place at the level of sensibility, not at the level of consciousness and reflection: we *feel* called, engaged, summonsed. It is an asymmetrical face-to-face relation, a relation governed by proximity: 'the face before me summons me . . . The Other becomes my neighbour precisely through the way the face summons me, calls for me, begs for me and in so doing recalls my responsibility, and calls me into question' (Levinas, 1989: 83). What does Levinas mean by 'the face'? He does not mean

> a phenomenon whose mode of being is appearance, but the demand of 'the one who needs you, who is counting on you'. The face in the ethical sense invoked by Levinas is 'a notion through which man comes to me via a human act different from knowing' . . . An act which is fundamentally and originally ethical: that for Levinas is the relation to the other.
>
> (Smart, 1999: 102)

For Levinas, in the face-to-face relation the Other is absolutely other. This is an Other which I cannot represent and classify into a category – and hence not totalise. The face-to-face encounter ruptures my ego, eludes thematisations and formalisations and dissolves the capacity to possess and master the Other. Instead of grasping, I have to take responsibility for the Other: and this relation is one of welcoming, a welcoming of the other as stranger.

The word 'welcome' is frequently used by Levinas, and Derrida (1999) says that the use of the concept of welcoming opens the way for another word – 'hospitality'. Derrida further proposes that Levinas, like Derrida himself, redefines subjectivity as hospitality. In other words, Levinas replaces the autonomous subject with the idea of the subject as host, knowing with welcoming.

The ensuing relationship between the self and the Other is not, however, necessarily harmonious nor what many might understand as close. It is a dissociating relation that can leave room for the radical otherness and singularity of the Other, a separation that 'respects the irreducible non-identity of the Same and the Other' (Peperzak, 1998: 4). It is a relation characterised by uncertainty, dissensus, dissymmetry, ambiguities, interruptions, even, as Derrida has said in relation to Levinas's ethics, 'impossibilities'. But at the same time this relation which opens up to the Other as stranger is also the chance of human togetherness, which is the condition for love and friendship. So there is a paradox: being-together presupposes infinite separation and dissociation. Or as Derrida so intriguingly expresses it, 'the social bond is a certain experience of unbinding without which no respiration, no spiritual inspiration, would be possible' (Derrida, 1999: 92).

While Levinas's influence has grown greatly over the last 20 years, providing a key philosophical resource for the development of what has been termed a 'politics of ethical difference' (Critchley, 2002) or a 'postmodern ethics', he has also been subject to criticism, not least for being too demanding and impractical (Smart, 1999). Levinas's response was to argue that the ethical responsibility towards the other is Utopian. By this he means something 'which, ultimately, guides all moral action' (Levinas, 1988: 178) and which finds many expressions in daily life:

> Its being utopian does not prevent it from investing our everyday actions of generosity or goodwill towards the other: even the smallest and most commonplace gestures . . . bear witness to the ethical. This concern for the other remains utopian in the sense that it is always 'out of place' in this world, always other than the 'ways of the world'; but there are many examples of it in the world.
>
> (Levinas and Kearney, 1986: 32)

Connections

We can see some common threads running through the work of Levinas, Bauman and care ethicists such as Tronto and Sevenhuijsen. They do not adopt a universalist approach, turning away from the search for codes: if, as Mouffe (2000b) puts it, there is an 'opposition between moral-universalistic and ethical-particularistic approaches' (129), then they are all with the latter. They resist the calculative idea at the heart of liberal 'micro-ethics'. All question the subject of modernity and liberalism. None finds enticing or credible the norm of the independent, autonomous, self-sufficient 'atomistic' subject, practising calculative freedom in all matters and situated in a network of moral codes, rights and contracts.

They view ethics as strongly relational, being about how people relate to each other. They refuse a dualistic opposition between independence and dependence (independence good and normative, dependence bad and abnormal), and welcome inter-dependence, 'the recognition that we are all in more or lesser degrees dependent on the care, attention and respect of others' (Sevenhuijsen and Williams, 2003: 17). In particular, the issue of relating to otherness is a shared preoccupation. This reflects a wider philosophical concern with otherness which gained increasing importance during the last century in reaction to mounting realisation of the consequences of making the Other into the same or simply obliterating the Other in the interests of order. At the heart of this discussion is what type of relationship might both connect but also distinguish myself and the Other, might assume responsibility whilst maintaining a distance by which difference can be sustained.

Three themes are closely woven in this concern with otherness. The first is *responsibility*. Bauman is strongly influenced by Levinas when he contends that responsibility for the Other is the central challenge of postmodern morality: 'to take a moral stance means to assume responsibility for the Other. We are, so to speak, ineluctably – existentially – moral beings: that is we are faced with the challenge of the Other, which is the challenge of responsibility for the Other' (1993: 1).

Other contemporary thinkers foreground responsibility. Santos (1995), for example, refers to 'the postmodern principle of responsibility' in his discussion of a new ethics necessary for a paradigmatic transition from modernity to postmodernity. He connects responsibility with care, and extends responsibility to cover not only other humans but other species and the environment we share:

> Postmodern knowledge cannot build solidarity in the technological age except by developing a new ethics, an ethics not colonized by science and technology, like liberal ethics, but, rather, based on a new principle. In my view this new principle is the principle of responsibility . . . The new principle of responsibility resides in the *Sorge*, the caring that puts us at the centre of all that happens, and renders us responsible for the other, whether human beings and social groups, or objects, animals, nature and so on . . . The new ethics must also put an end to the principle of restricted

reciprocity upon which liberal micro-ethics is founded. According to this principle, rights can only be granted to those from whom we can demand corresponding duties. On the contrary, according to the postmodern principle of responsibility, both nature and the future have rights over us without corresponding duties.

(1995: 50–51)

Important here is the turn from a relationship of mastery and calculating contract to a striving after a non-instrumental relationship founded on an open-ended responsibility and sense of obligation.

A second theme is that responsibility entails *respect for otherness*. Tronto, echoing Bauman and Levinas, concludes that 'questions of otherness are at the heart of contemporary theory' (1993: 58). The element of responsiveness in the ethics of care is particularly important because excessive control of the Other is recognised to be a major risk in relationships of care – care can smother. What is required is a relation to the Other based on responsibility and recognition of difference: 'responsiveness suggests a different way to understand the needs of others rather than to put ourselves into their position . . . [O]ne is engaged from the standpoint of the other, but not by presuming the Other is exactly like the self' (*ibid.*: 135). Introducing an important concept – listening – to which we shall return in Chapter 4, care requires a strong 'injunction to listen' to the Other, understood as a willingness to hold open an intersubjective space, 'in which difference can unfold in all its particularity' and which 'entails a hesitancy to "place" the other quickly and firmly within habitual interpretive molds' (White, 1991: 97–98).

Respect for otherness is also openness to and welcoming of difference. But just as Santos argues that liberal micro-ethics is inimical to responsibility, so Sevenhuijsen (1998) argues that a universalist ethics which takes sameness as its basic principle views difference as problematic: 'differences, whether speculative in nature or accompanied by convincing evidence, are always considered deviant and negative in relation to a universal norm' (45). This critical attitude to difference, and the will to construct totalising systems which reduces everything to one principle or law, runs deep in the Euro-American psyche. R. Young (1990) contends that Western philosophy has a long history of desire for unity and the One, so that 'when knowledge or theory comprehends the Other, the alterity of the Other vanishes as it becomes part of the same' (13). Going even further, Critchley (1999) argues that 'the very act of thinking, which lies at the basis of epistemological, ontological and veridical comprehension, is the reduction of plurality to unity and alterity to sameness . . . *the very task of thinking, is the reduction of otherness'* (29; emphasis added).

These shared concerns about otherness owe much in turn to the influence of the German philosopher Martin Heidegger (1889–1976). Heidegger developed a powerful critique of modernity's instrumental-technological orientation to the world, its calculative way of thinking, which 'lets us experience the world only as a standing reserve of potentially graspable stuff' (White, 1991: 38). This concern with the instrumental and totalising nature of modern thought, and its propensity for domination and control, led Heidegger in his later works to the central problem of how we should respond to otherness: 'he wants to delineate a way of experiencing otherness such that it remains other, a mode of posturing the self that "lets the other be" in its difference . . . Attentive concern for otherness means that the gesture of nearing, bringing into one's presence, into one's world, must always be complemented by a letting go, an allowance of distance' (*ibid.*: 67). The idea of attentiveness meaning distancing is to be found both in the ethics of care literature and in the work of Levinas: it enables the Other to be in its difference, in contrast to nearness which implies the possibility of grasping something and, hence, a potential for better control.

The third theme is a *rejection of calculative and rational thinking* in relations with the Other, and as a basis more generally for ethics. Morality, in the view of Bauman (1993):

> begets an essentially unequal relationship: thus inequality, non-equity, this not-asking-for-reciprocation, this disinterest in mutuality, this indifference to the 'balancing up' of gains or rewards – in short, this organically 'unbalanced' and hence non-reversible character of 'I versus the Other' relationship is what makes the encounter a moral event . . .
>
> [M]orality is endemically and irredeemably *non-rational* – in the sense of not being calculable, hence not being describable as following rules that are in principle universalizable. The moral call is thoroughly personal; it appeals to my responsibility, and the urge to care thus elicited cannot be allayed or placated by the awareness that others do it to me, or that I have already done my share by following to the letter what others used to do.
>
> (48–49, 60)

The ideas of Bauman, ethicists of care and Levinas are therefore non-rational in a particular way: they are radically at odds with an instrumental rationality and a capitalist logic in which the price of everything can be determined.

Having set out some ethical approaches, and discussed the opposition between moral-universalistic and ethical-particularistic approaches, we now turn to consider how these approaches might be practised in preschools (and, by implication, other institutions for children including schools). How might postmodern ethics, an ethics of care or the ethics of an encounter become central concerns and with what effect? What might it mean if preschools were first and foremost loci of ethical practice?

Chapter 4

Preschools as loci of ethical practice

From Pedagogy as a loci of an ethics of an encounter *by Gunilla Dahlberg (2003)*:

[P]utting everything which one encounters into pre-made categories implies that we make the Other into the Same, as everything which does not fit into these categories, which is unfamiliar and not taken-for-granted has to be overcome. Hence, alterity disappears. This betrays the complexity in children's lives and closes down possibilities to view the child in relation to multiplicity and change . . .

To think an other whom I cannot grasp is an important shift and it challenges the whole scene of pedagogy. It poses other questions to us as pedagogues. Questions such as how the encounter with Otherness, with difference, can take place as responsibly as possible – as something which the so-called 'free thought' cannot grasp through categories, classifications and thematizations.

Following Levinas we then need to vitalize and intensify ethics so it can be possible to open ourselves for alterity, by *a welcoming of the stranger.* From this perspective teaching and learning have to start with ethics – with receiving and welcoming – and it is the receiving from the Other beyond the capacity of the I which constructs the discourse of teaching (Derrida, 1999), a teaching that interrupts the philosophical tradition of making ourselves the master over the child. This requires restructuring of subjectivity through challenging the universal subject. To be able to hear the ungraspable call of the child, and to have the capacity to relate to absolute alterity, one needs to interrupt totalizing practices which give the teacher possibilities to possess and comprehend the child. We have to open up for the unexpected and affirm what is to come.

(270, 273; original emphasis)

It is now time to move from outlining some ethical approaches in general terms, to examining how they might form the basis for pedagogical practice. Our intention is to show what the idea of teaching and learning as loci of ethical practice, and of particular ethical practices, might mean in reality. We begin by applying ethics to two familiar topics: evaluation and the relation between education and care. But we shall devote most attention to the ethics of an encounter and its relevance to pedagogical thought and practice in the preschool (and the school).

When we come to the ethics of an encounter, Levinas sets a new agenda. In the preschool, how can the encounter with otherness take place as responsibly as possible? How can the pedagogic relationship avoid grasping the child? How could it build on welcoming and hospitality? Seeking answers to such questions leads into areas of theory and practice that confront and problematise much of the dominant discourse about preschools and preschool education, including learning and knowledge, and the child and the teacher.

Getting beyond quality

Both postmodern ethics and the ethics of care suggest an immediate focus for ethical practice: evaluating pedagogical work in the preschool. Inscribed with universalistic ethics, such evaluation is often today a matter of assessing conformity to a norm or code. No active ethical practice is required, just the ability to apply a set of stable, generalisable and reason-dictated criteria to children or workers or the institution itself and a belief that this can be done objectively. A classic and topical example of this approach to evaluation is the 'concept of quality' (and its *doppelgänger* 'excellence', to be found frequenting universities where it is the subject of fierce critique from Readings [1996]).

We have written about quality at considerable length elsewhere (Dahlberg *et al.*, 1999; Moss *et al.*, 2000). We have argued that though the concept is usually treated as neutral and self-evident, in practice it is permeated with particular modernist values and assumptions:

> The concept of quality is about a search for definitive and universal criteria that will offer certainty and order, and a belief that such transcendental criteria can be found. It asks the question – how far does this product, this service or this activity conform to a universal, objective and predetermined standard? It has no place

for complexity, values, diversity, subjectivity, indeterminacy and multiple perspectives.

(*ibid.*: 108)

In other words, quality can be understood as a means to make judgements about what is good or right, within a framework of universal, normative ethics. Like Cherryholmes's definition of 'vulgar pragmatism', quality tests 'practices by comparing them to traditional and conventional norms with little or no sense of crisis or criticism' (1988: 178). As the subject of universal ethics, the evaluator of quality is assumed to be rational, objective and detached, not needing to ask any questions of the code (in this case the measure of quality), only how far the subject of evaluation conforms to the code.

This introduction to quality also problematises the distinction we have drawn so far between 'technical' and 'ethical' practice. No practice is outside ethics: in this sense technical/ethical is a false distinction. But some practices – like evaluating with quality or excellence – claim to be technical, that is they claim to offer objective and standardised procedures for solving problems (e.g. evaluation) which deny their own ethical dimension. Thus evaluation with quality (or excellence) claims to provide an objective statement of fact based on a technology of measurement rather than a subjective judgement of value.

In our earlier work, too, we offered an other approach to evaluation, which made no attempt to mask its ethical dimension. This took the position that evaluation is essential but unanswerable; it is something we must attempt without, however, expectation of achieving a definitive position. We termed this approach the concept of meaning making.

The concept of quality is about establishing conformity to predetermined standards. It seeks closure, in the sense that it wants certain answers about conformity, often reduced to numbers. The discourse of meaning making, in contrast, is first and foremost about constructing and deepening understanding of the early childhood institution and its projects, especially its pedagogical work – to make meaning of what is going on. It assumes that the meaning of pedagogical work is always open to different interpretations, not least because there is no homogeneous standard of value that can produce a single scale of evaluation (Readings, 1996): in short, meaning is always contestable. Meaning making, therefore, foregrounds provisionality, multiplicity and subjectivity, rather than closure, standardisation and objectivity (a concept which, in the words of the bio-physicist Heinz von Foerster [1991], can be seen as 'a subject's false view that observing can take place without him').

Meaning making also takes place in relationship with others. In place of the 'autonomous, self-regulating subject' making judgements from 'the moral point of view', in meaning making understanding of the early childhood institution and its pedagogical work is co-constructed in relationship with others. From constructing these understandings, people may choose to continue by making judgements about the pedagogical work – a process involving the application of values to understanding, in order to produce a judgement of value. Judgement can seem a rather severe concept, with its connotations of the last word and the lawcourts. But we can treat it in another way, by viewing a judgement as a provisional position taken in a particular context, a statement of value and as such incapable of closure, part of a continuing discussion rather than a finality (Readings, 1996).

People may further choose to seek provisional agreement with others about these provisional understandings and judgements, both about what is going on and its value. However, the discourse does not assume that all three stages must be followed. Indeed, it may be considered sufficient in some cases to concentrate on deepening understanding without going on to judge or to seek agreement.

All stages of meaning making are done in the context of constant democratic debate about a range of critical ethical and political questions, such as: What do we want for our children? Who do we think the child is – what is our image of the child? What is the role of the preschool or school in society? What do we mean by terms such as 'education', 'knowledge', 'care'? In this way, our evaluation of pedagogical work can never be divorced from ethics and politics.

This concept of meaning making has much in common with Bauman's discussion of postmodern ethics, with its recognition of contingency, ambivalence and 'messiness', as well as his notion of 'ethical negotiation and consensus', with its recognition of the likely provisionality of any agreement reached in negotiation. But the concept of meaning making also has much in common with Sevenhuijsen's discussion of 'judging with care', which seeks to achieve judgements 'in a situated way, proceeding from an interpretative, dialogic and communicative moral epistemology' (1998: 64). Acting ethically is based on interaction with and attentiveness to others, not derived from an ethical code. Sevenhuijsen foregrounds heterogeneity and plurality of view rather than consensus, since moral identities are diverse and culturally formed: 'it is exactly by engaging in an active dialogue with different moral perspectives and moral considerations that we can improve the quality of normative judgements' (ibid.: 87).

Viewed in this way, evaluating pedagogical work can be seen as an active practice inscribed with a particular ethical approach or sensibility. It calls for making some form of contextualised judgement, rather than calculating how the work fits a predetermined normative framework. It requires the work to be made visible, for reflection, for interpretation, for discussion and, possibly too, for argument and perhaps eventual (but always provisional) agreement. In this and other ways, the ability to make ethical judgements can be cultivated and improved: it is a quality constantly to be worked upon, not a technique to be mastered. It also suggests the importance of holding meaning open, of being prepared to judge the judge, of treating judgement as always contestable and open to reconsideration: 'we should not cease to judge, but we should recognize the fragility and provisionality of judgement' (Beilharz, 2000: 81).

How can meaning making be put to work in practice? One well-tried tool (or, using Vygotsky's term, mediation), gaining international interest from its origins in Reggio Emilia, is pedagogical documentation, by which practice is made first visible and then the subject of interpretation and evaluation. We shall discuss this process in more detail later on, in Chapter 5.

The place of care in the preschool

An other way of making an ethics of care part of an active ethical practice in the preschool is to consider it to be the 'care' in 'early childhood education and care'. At present, early childhood policy and provision – at least in the English-language world, which lacks the encompassing concept of pedagogy (as discussed in Chapter 1) – has become snared in a care/education dualism. In many countries, two traditions – of 'early education' and 'childcare for working parents' – are being brought closer together, and there is an increasing discourse about the inseparability of 'care' and 'education', at least for children below compulsory school age. The assertion in a recent government document in England that 'there is no sensible distinction between good early education and care' (English Department for Education and Employment, 1998: paras. 1.4) is typical of this discourse. Terms linking 'care' and 'education' are now widely used: for example a recent cross-national study by the OECD (2001) was described as a review of 'early childhood education and care'.

Yet the relationship between the two concepts proves difficult to define and understand, at least in the English-language world. The meaning of 'care' is rarely gone into with any rigour, leaving it loosely defined by association. Thus the term 'childcare' associates care in many people's minds with a secure place for keeping children while their parents are at work, a sort of standing in for the mother, a limited notion which 'reduces care to a "function" of employability and labour market participation' (Sevenhuijsen and Williams, 2003: 16). In another case, care becomes associated with a welfare or therapeutic idea, 'care in the community', taking children 'into care'. In a third case, care is associated with a sort of nostalgic longing for the good old times: care conjures up images of a cosy place like home, a place free of difference, power and conflict, with an ever-present mother.

All these associations seem to us to be problematic. They produce a very narrow idea of what the preschool is or might be. They naïvely ignore the ever-presence of power relations and the possibilities that can arise from difference. They suggest care as the opposite of learning or, at the very least, offer no help in conceptualising a relationship between care and education. Nor do they provide any help with other questions. If it is widely recognised that 'childcare' settings need to be 'educational', in what way do 'educational' settings – most notably the school – need to be 'caring'? If care and education are inseparable for young children, why not older children too? Why, for instance, do we not talk about 'older childhood education and care'?

One way of answering these questions, of constructing a relationship between 'care' and 'education', is (as we have already suggested) to adopt a concept like 'pedagogy', which for us encompasses learning and caring within a broad concern with all aspects of life. Another way is to connect the concept of an ethics of care with a recurring discussion in this book: about how preschools (or schools) might be understood as spaces in civil society where children and adults can engage together in a potentially wide range of possibilities. Then we can view 'education' as one of the many possibilities (though recognising that the meaning of 'education' is always contestable); and conceptualise 'care' as an ethical approach applicable to all possibilities (including education) undertaken within the institution, as well as to all practices and relationships and to all children irrespective of whether or not their parents are employed. Care as an ethic, in this sense, becomes a choice. It is a dimension that can be absent or present, to a greater or lesser extent, not only in preschools or schools but across a wide range of social institutions:

> [The ethic of care can be used] as a sensitising concept to evaluate a range of social practices . . . [M]any social practices have or should have caring dimensions. Care is not confined to an activity for children, sick and elderly persons in the private sphere, but is in

fact practised in many social locations, ranging from the work place, institutions of welfare, health care and social work, to scientific research and the halls of policy making itself.

(Sevenhuijsen and Williams, 2003: 17)

The care ethic, so applied, would foreground attentiveness, responsibility, competence and responsiveness to the Other. Following Tronto's definition, it would involve both practice and thought, 'particular acts of caring and a "general habit of mind" to care that should inform all aspects of moral life'. Viewed in this way, the preschool (or indeed the school) is transformed from a locus of instrumentality and for technical practice into a locus of diverse possibilities and for the practice of an ethics of care in all of these possibilities and in all aspects of its everyday life and relations.

Pedagogy as a locus of an ethics of an encounter

In our view, we are at a historical moment when we need new inspiration about the meaning of education; inspiration that can help us to contest neoliberalism and managerialism, with the great value they attach to instrumentality, calculation and the autonomous subject, and their powerful technologies for governing and subjectification. Inspiration that can confront what we have termed the dominant Anglo-American discourse in early childhood, with its universal and normative thinking and totalising practices that smother difference through giving the teacher possibilities to possess, comprehend and govern the child.

Postmodern ethics and the ethics of care can provide two sources of inspiration. A third and particularly important source, we believe, is Levinas's ethics of an encounter. For this opens up the possibility to think an Other that I cannot grasp – an idea that challenges the whole scene of pedagogy by foregrounding respect for otherness. We begin our exploration of pedagogy inscribed by an ethics of an encounter by reviewing some of the ideas of Bill Readings, since his thinking, before his untimely death in 1994, was so rich and full of potential about the relationship between pedagogy and ethical practice.

Bill Readings and listening to thought

As we have already noted, *The University in Ruins* is in many respects as relevant to preschools and schools as to institutions of higher education, for the book is an enquiry into the meaning of pedagogical work. In this, his final book, Bill Readings has much to say which throws light on how pedagogy might embody an ethics of an encounter. Indeed, Readings specifically recognises that his ideas 'parallel' the work of Levinas. This work, he says, diverges significantly from Anglo-American philosophy and is particularly important for what it shows about the relation to the Other.

Pedagogy, in the view of Readings, involves listening, relationships and obligation. Readings argues for the importance of 'listening to thought' in pedagogical work, defining thought as the voice of an Other, and by so doing to draw out the otherness of thought. This requires, in the words of the French philosopher Maurice Blanchot, an infinite attention to the Other, which 'is to think besides each other and our-selves to explore an open network of obligation that keeps the question of meaning open as a locus of debate' for 'doing justice to thought . . . means trying to hear that which cannot be said, but which tries to make itself heard' (Readings, 1996: 165). Rather than closure – the conclusion, for example, that comes with giving marks or grades – pedagogical work that seeks to be transgressive is engaged in a struggle to hold open – the question of meaning, space for listening to thought.

Pedagogy for Readings is a relationship. But if the Other is to be heard, if meaning is not to be closed off, if the Other is not to be grasped, it means a very particular relationship. To leave room for radical difference and the singularity of the Other, the pedagogical relationship must also leave space between, it must be a dissociating relationship. As we touched on in the previous chapter, there is an apparent paradox: the welcoming and hospitality that Levinas and Derrida speak about, the importance of being together with the Other; and, at the same time, the importance of an infinite separation, a distance to enable the possibility of difference. The child becomes a complete stranger, not a known quantity through classificatory systems and normative practices whose progress and development must be steered to familiar and known ends.

Listening to the Other also requires a relationship of respect and obligation.

> [Respect for the Other] must precede any knowledge about the other. The other speaks and we must owe the other respect. To be hailed as an addressee is to be commanded to listen and the ethical nature of the relation cannot be justified. We have to listen without knowing why, before we can know what we are listening to. To be

spoken to is to be placed under an obligation . . . We are obligated to them without being able to say exactly why. For if we could say why, if the social bond could be made an object of cognition, then we would not really be dealing with an obligation at all, but with a ratio of exchange. If we knew what our obligations were, then we could settle them, compensate them, and be freed from them in return for payment.

(*ibid.*: 162, 188)

The use of obligation here has much in common with the description by Lyotard (1984) of a 'dissensual society', where the social is an effect of a duty towards others, a duty which we cannot wholly understand and predict. The pedagogical relationship arising from the ethics of an encounter envisages 'the absolute future, the welcome extended to an other whom I cannot, in principle, anticipate . . . It is a gift that gives itself without return, whenever the occasion calls for it' (Caputo, 1997: 200). Readings contrasts such an open-ended and incalculable commitment in a pedagogical relationship inscribed with the ethics of an encounter, to the fixed-term and calculable responsibility of capitalist relations:

The capitalist logic of general substitutability (the cash-nexus) presumes that all obligations are finite and expressible in financial terms, capable of being turned into monetary values . . . Of course, once one begins, as I have done, to speak of a non-finite obligation, people think of religion . . . But I am not trying to sound mystical. I am saying something rather simple: that we do not know in advance our obligations to others.

(Readings, 1996: 188)

To make such a pedagogy possible we need to think in terms not only of the centrality of listening to the Other and respect for difference, but also of radical dialogue and negotiation. We need to move away from modernist ideas of autonomous knowledge and education as the transmission of this knowledge to fill empty heads, taking the form of a monologue controlled by the sender. We need to move away from a relationship of sender and receiver, in which the former is privileged. And we need to move away from the modernist goal of education as a site of emancipation, understood as creating the autonomous subject, whereby knowledge frees the subject from obligation to others including the obligation to listen. Instead of such autonomy, pedagogy related to the ethics of an encounter can be seen as a social movement where we examine the question of being together.

Turning from the modernist project to a pedagogy of listening

So many of today's discussions about education and learning are locked into what Readings calls 'the modernist project of autonomy and universal communicability' (*ibid*.: 154). They bear little relation to the times in which we live. They are inscribed with the values, assumptions and ideals of modernity, instrumental rationality and scientific knowledge. But today, the modernist project is questioned and a new paradigm is emerging which foregrounds the construction of meaning, complexity and multiplicity, relations and contexts, subjectivity and perspectivism, provisionality and contestability.

It is true that most of today's discussions are about different approaches to education, with much argument about their respective merits. To take just two examples: there is the 'back to basics' approach, born out of a nostalgia for the 'old school', with its emphasis on the structured transmission of knowledge from the teacher to passive pupils (Whitty *et al.*, 1998); then, in apparent opposition, there is a 'constructivist' approach, in which the child is 'empowered' to be an active problem solver, acquiring knowledge and skills (such as flexibility) through analysis, reflection and classroom interaction.

Yet despite their differences, both of these approaches seem to share a common idea of education and learning as being about children attaining normative development and knowledge and so achieving a set of predetermined outcomes. All value children's development and learning in terms of whether it is right or wrong, whether children achieve the required and defined standards. All share an Enlightenment image of the child as lacking, incomplete, immature, and of education as a process of '[transforming] children, who are by definition dependent on adults, into independent beings' (Readings, 1996: 158). All view the teacher as someone who knows the one right answer to every question, as the privileged voice of authority with a privileged relation to the meaning of knowledge; and the complementary image of children as receptacles for the teacher's explanation and transmission of preconstituted and unquestionable knowledge. All work with fixed categories and classificatory systems to define, assess and normalise children – whether these categories and systems are expressed in terms of development, standards or grades and practised through observations, portfolios, tests or exams. All, in short, make the Other into the Same and remove the possibility of otherness, through the exercise of power and grasping the child. The tactics (or methods) may differ, but the basic assumptions are the same.

Our argument is that the ethics of an encounter and the inspiration of thinkers such as Bill Readings open up for a new and quite different idea of education, learning and pedagogical practice. This idea is inscribed by concepts such as thought, listening and radical dialogue. It calls for images of the child, the teacher and the school that are very different to those within the modernist project. We might call this idea and its practice a 'pedagogy of listening'. We turn now to consider this idea and practice in more detail.

Chapter 5

Towards a pedagogy of listening

From 'The construction of the educational project' *by Carlina Rinaldi (forthcoming a):*

> The teacher is not removed from her role as an adult, but instead revises it in an attempt to become a co-creator, rather than merely a transmitter, of knowledge and culture. As teachers we have to carry out this role in the full awareness of our vulnerability, and this means accepting doubts and mistakes as well as allowing for surprise and creation . . .
>
> If we believe that children possess their own theories, interpretations, and questions, and are protagonists in the knowledge-building processes, then the most important verbs in educational practice are no longer 'to talk', 'to explain' or 'to transmit'. . . but 'to listen'. Listening means being open to others and what they have to say, listening to the hundred (and more) languages, with all our senses . . . Listening legitimizes the other person, because communication is one of the fundamental means of giving form to thought. The communicative act that takes place through listening produces meanings and reciprocal modifications that enrich all the participants in this type of exchange.
>
> The task of the teacher is to create a context in which children's curiosity, theories and research are legitimated and listened to, a context in which children feel comfortable and confident, motivated and respected in their existential and cognitive paths and processes.

In this chapter we explore in more detail the concepts, images and practices of what we have termed a 'pedagogy of listening', an approach to pedagogy that is inscribed with the ethics of an encounter. The term 'pedagogy of listening' is not original. It comes from Reggio Emilia, and we shall make frequent reference in this chapter to the pedagogical ideas and practices of this Italian city, including how they understand 'listening' – which has much in common with Readings's discussion of 'listening to thought'. We end on the subject of thought, when we open up to the ideas of Gilles Deleuze who, we believe, may provide important new directions for pedagogical work, but who shares an ethical perspective that foregrounds the importance of otherness.

Listening and radical dialogue

In what way does 'thought' shift our understanding of learning and education? Thought starts from the child (or the adult) and her or his experience of the world. It assumes that we are all constantly engaged in searching for meaning, which we do by developing ideas or theories – thought – that are provisional and re-worked in relations with others and through processes of testing, reflection and further thought. Carlina Rinaldi, a former pedagogical director of the municipal preschools in Reggio and now pedagogical consultant to Reggio Children, describes the process of thought in these terms in explaining the pedagogical work in Reggio:

> [One of the] first questions we should ask ourselves as teachers and educators is this: 'How can we help children find the meaning of what they do, what they encounter, what they experience? And how can we do this for ourselves? . . .
>
> [The search for meaning is] a difficult task especially for children who nowadays have so many references in their daily lives: their family experience, television, the social places they frequent in addition to family and school. It is a task that involves making connections, giving meaning to these events, to these fragments that are gathered over the course of many and different experiences . . .
>
> For adults and children alike, understanding means being able to develop an interpretive 'theory', a narration that gives meaning to the events and things of the world. These theories are provisional, offering a satisfactory explanation that can be continuously re-worked . . . It has to please us and convince us, to be useful and able to satisfy our intellectual, affective, and aesthetic needs . . . Our theories need to be listened to by others. Expressing our theories to others makes it possible to transform a world which is not intrinsically ours into something shared. Sharing theories is a response to uncertainty.
>
> (Rinaldi, 2001b: 79–80)

Listening to thought is about being able to hear the ideas and theories of the Other, and to treat them seriously and with respect, neither ignoring them nor dismissing them for not providing the right answer. But what is listening? Listening plays a critical role in the pedagogical work of Reggio Emilia. This has led the preschool workers to conceptualise in some detail what they mean when they speak of 'listening' – unlike more technical discourses that are very widespread today which take 'listening' as a given, an unproblematic and taken-for-granted term involving unmediated transmission from mouth to ear, brain to brain, and focus their attention on the most effective methods for transmission. But in Reggio, listening is understood to be a complex and multi-faceted concept. It is an active relationship that is dialogic and interpretive. It involves many forms of communication, invoking Malaguzzi's famous expression, 'the hundred languages of children'. And it is saturated and mediated by values and emotions.

Here is Rinaldi again, defining her understanding of the term 'listening' from the perspective of Reggio Emilia:

Listening as sensitivity to the patterns that connect, to that which connects us to others; abandoning ourselves to the conviction that our understanding and our own being are but small parts of a broader, more integrated knowledge that holds the universe together.

Listening as a metaphor for having the openness and sensitivity to listen and be listened to – listening not just with our ears, but with all our senses . . .

Listening to the hundred, the thousand languages, symbols and codes we use to express ourselves and communicate . . .

Listening as time, the time of listening, a time that is outside chronological time . . . [I]nterior listening, listening to ourselves, as a pause, a suspension, as an element that generates listening to others but, in turn, is generated by the listening that others give us . . .

Listening is emotion, it is generated by and stimulates emotions, including curiosity, desire, doubt, interest . . .

Listening as welcoming and being open to differences, recognising the importance of the other's point of view and interpretation . . .

Listening as an active verb that involves interpretation, giving meaning to the message and value to those who offer it . . .

Listening that does not produce answers but formulates questions; listening that is generated by doubt, by uncertainty, which is not insecurity but, on the contrary, the security that every truth is such only if we are aware of its limits and its possible falsification . . .

Listening is not easy. It requires a deep awareness, and at the same time a suspension of our judgements, and above all our prejudices; it requires openness to change. It demands that we have clearly in mind the value of the unknown and that we are able to overcome the sense of emptiness and precariousness that we experience whenever our certainties are questioned . . .

Listening as the premise for any learning relationship – learning that is determined by the 'learning subject' and takes shape in his or her mind through action and reflection . . .

Listening, therefore, as a 'listening context' where one learns to listen and narrate, where individuals feel legitimated to represent their theories and offer their interpretations of a particular question.

(*ibid.*: 80–81)

Here we see many of the themes we discussed earlier: welcoming the Other; a dialogic relationship; learning as a creative process rather than transmission; living and working with uncertainty; being open to difference; respecting, not grasping the Other. To listen means being open to the Other, recognising the Other as different and trying to listen to the Other from his or her own position and experience and not treating the Other as the same. It means listening to thought – the ideas and theories, questions and answers of children – and struggling to make meaning from what is said, without preconceived ideas of what is correct or valid or appropriate. 'Good' listening distinguishes dialogue between human beings, which expresses and constitutes a relationship to a concrete Other, from monologue, which seeks to transmit a body of knowledge and through so doing make the Other into the Same.

In particular Reggio's concept of a 'pedagogy of listening', and its practice, foregrounds the idea of respecting otherness. Respect for an absolute Other means a respect that must precede grasping: the child speaks and is doing, and we have to take what the child says and does seriously. A 'pedagogy of listening' exemplifies Readings's reference to pedagogy as listening to thought and what cannot easily be heard, rather than the production of the autonomous subject or objective knowledge. It gives life to Blanchot's contention, referred to so approvingly by Readings, that the condition of pedagogical practice is an infinite attention to the other. Yet at the same time as recognising the singularity of each member of the preschool – child or adult – the 'pedagogy of listening' emphasises relationships, 'social bonds', and the importance of being in a community for creating and re-creating theories (many, diverse and provisional) as part of a continuous process of learning that involves theorising, dialogue, reflection and negotiation.

In a 'real' listening to the child, in a welcoming and an encounter, then, something incalculable comes on the scene. What children say surprises us, and helps us to interrupt predetermined meanings and totalising practices, totalising practices such as the concepts and classifications of developmental psychology which give us as teachers or researchers possibilities to possess and 'comprehend' the child. Doing this one realises that what the child has got to say has often been excluded, marginalised, ignored or just been seen as something cute or funny. Listening can make us both surprised and shocked as we find out how rich and intelligent children's thoughts are.

Listening is highly interactive, or intersubjective to use Readings's term. Indeed, a pedagogy of listening has a strong commitment to radical dialogue that does not resolve into a monologue, a monologue where the teacher claims to know and speak or explicate for the other, the child. It is a move away from monologic transmission – as well as from the idea of just paying attention to determining the conditions for the child's reception of the teacher's transmission, which is so common on the school agenda today, e.g. to assess if the child is response-ready and response-able. This is the common 'sender and receiver' model of communication, with the child seen as a container to be filled while for the teacher it makes no difference to whom he or she is talking as the child's thoughts and meaning making are not allowed to interrupt the teacher's.

In radical dialogue, based on listening, as a teacher you have to participate together with the child, entering a space together where both teacher and child are actively listening and trying to construct meaning out of the situation. Readings, in his discussion of the communication between teacher and child (or, in his case, university student) finds inspiration in Bakhtin's dialogism, which is not simply the capacity for reversed or serial monologues, an exchange of roles which allows people to take turns as monologic senders. According to Bakhtin

> the addressee's head is full of language so that the story of communicative transmission cannot adequately describe what happens in linguistic interaction . . . Communication cannot be the transfer of a prefabricated meaning, since the meaning of words does not remain the same from one utterance – or more precisely one idiolect – to the next. What a sender says takes its place amid a crowd of

idiolects in the listener, and their conversation acquires its sense in a discursive act of which neither is the master.

(Readings, 1996: 155–156)

Meaning making and knowledge construction occur in this relational activity, in a continuous process of formulation and reformulation, testing and negotiation. Learning, including the acquisition of 'objective knowledge', requires attention and the best friend of attention is interest (Liedman, 2001: 26). Through listening to thought and radical dialogue, the child's interest is aroused.

The child, the teacher and the school

Education based on the transfer of objective knowledge divides the world into two: the knowing and the ignorant, the mature and the unformed, the capable and the incapable (Rancière, 1991). The child, like women and people of colour, has been marginalised in the project of modernity. This has come to characterise the knowledge process itself in modernity, the process being understood as one of development and progress: a passage from infancy to adulthood, from dependency to emancipation, from lacking to maturity.

But this image of the child changes in a pedagogy of listening. The child is no longer understood as lacking or incomplete but, as they say in Reggio Emilia, intelligent: intelligent, that is, as a person capable of making meaning of the world from his or her own experiences, not as a person who scores more than so many points on an IQ test. Just how revolutionary this image of the child can be is vividly illustrated in a book called *Le Maître ignorant* ('The Ignorant Schoolmaster'), written by the French philosopher Jacques Rancière (1991). The book tells the story of the French teacher Joseph Jacotot who, working in exile, discovered in 1818 a very unconventional method for learning, a method that caused consternation throughout the learned community of Europe. For Jacotot had found out in his own work that knowledge and explication were not actually necessary for teaching; instead, what was important was to start from the idea that all human beings are equally intelligent. With this as a starting-point he developed a philosophy and a method which he called 'intellectual emancipation', a method which allowed, for example, illiterate parents to teach their children how to read.

In relation to Jacotot's works, Rancière asks the question: What would happen if all education took as its starting-point the idea that all human beings are intelligent? What would it mean if one took such equality as a presupposition instead of as a goal, equality and parity as a practice and process instead of a reward situated in a remote future? As it is, rather than constructing equality the explanations of the teacher in the transfer process create inequality through a system of postponements; that is, a bit further on you will become competent but right now you are not. So rather than eliminating inability, transmission of knowledge creates it – for to do this is a way to tell the other that she or he does not know. It again expresses a division of the world into two parts or rather two intelligences: one superior, which understands things through reason; the other inferior. The intelligent teacher decides when the act of learning will begin and, having thrown a veil of ignorance over everything that is to be learned, appoints himself or herself to the task of lifting it. Until the teacher came along, the unintelligent child has been groping blindly, figuring out riddles; but now the child will learn.

Learning, we would argue, is most likely to happen when we start with listening to thought and the image of an intelligent child. From a different perspective, the same idea is expressed by van Glasersfeld (1991), a prominent researcher in the field of conceptual analysis, cybernetics and epistemology. He argues that the most successful learning starts from taking whatever the child produces as a manifestation of something that makes sense to the child in the context of that child's present construction of her or his experiential world. A teacher who wants to challenge the child's concept must begin, therefore, by constructing a viable model of that particular child's ways and means of organising experience.

The image of the child and teacher are connected. A lacking child requires a teacher who is the privileged voice of authority. But an intelligent, meaning making child calls for someone else. To extend intelligence to the child is not about replacing the teacher with the child, which is sometimes implied in extreme reactions to transmission pedagogy. It is not a case of inverting the traditional hierarchy, so that to be educated the child needs only to affirm what she or he already is. It does not mean the teacher should be just a passive listener, a mere sounding-board off which the child bounces thoughts and theories.

The challenge for the teacher is, as Carlina Rinaldi says at the start of this chapter, to 'create a context in which children's curiosity, theories and research are legitimated and listened to', a context in which children feel comfortable and confident, and at the same time, to be able to widen and extend children's horizons by creating complexity in the child's environment and by introducing new theories, concepts, languages and materials, as tools for children's theorising and meaning making. Loris Malaguzzi captured this idea of the teacher's complex role when he once said that Reggio needed 'a teacher who is sometimes the director, sometimes the set designer, sometimes the curtain and the backdrop, and sometimes the prompter . . . who is even the audience – the audience who watches, who sometimes claps, sometimes remains silent, full of emotion, who sometimes judges with scepticism, and other times applauds with enthusiasm' (Rinaldi, 2001b: 89).

Rather than simply implementing predefined tasks (whether they be labelled curriculum, programme or plan), transmitting disciplinary knowledge in the traditional way, teachers in the pedagogy of listening and the ethics of an encounter are 'authors of pedagogical paths and processes' (Rinaldi, forthcoming d). They keep their distance 'from an overriding sense of balance, from that which has already been decided, preconstituted or considered to be certain' (Rinaldi, forthcoming c). The teacher is an intellectually curious person who, like the child, is searching constantly for meaning, co-constructing knowledge as provisional theories and understandings: '[She] rejects a passive approach to knowledge and prefers to construct knowledge together with others rather than simply to "consume" it' (Rinaldi, forthcoming a). Her education should be broad-based and range over many areas, not just psychology and pedagogy: she is 'a cultured teacher, not only because she has a multi-disciplinary background but primarily because she possesses the culture of research, of curiosity, of working in a group' (Rinaldi, 2001b: 88).

Above all, the teacher has to be welcoming to the Other. She recognises the importance of respecting and paying attention to singularity, to the radical heterogeneity of an individual and an event. She starts from an original affirmation, a welcoming of the Other and an openness to the difference of the Other, 'yes' to the Other, a 'yes' which for her is responsibility and engagement in a future to come. This means being able to let go of any absolute truths and totalising systems of knowing, for new knowledge can only be generated when we abandon the presumption that we possess incontrovertible truths (Rinaldi, 1998). She appreciates 'the impossibility of controlling, deciding or determining a limit, the impossibility of situating, by means of criteria, norms or rules' (Derrida, 1999: 35).

This means seeing uncertainty and dissensus as possibilities not dangers, and an openness to being surprised and finding new meanings: 'as teachers, we have to carry out this role [as co-constructors] in the full awareness of our vulnerability, and this means accepting doubts and mistakes as well as allowing for surprise and curiosity, all of which are necessary for true acts of knowledge and creation' (Rinaldi, forthcoming a). Abandoning systems of classification does not mean ignoring enquiry about children and their learning. Rather it means a rigorous study – in Reggio, they would say researching – of the learning strategies of children, both individually and as a group, using pedagogical documentation (which we discuss below) as a means for reflection, analysis and creation of new and provisional knowledge, without being subjected to the governing effects of totalising systems of disciplinary knowledge with their predetermined concepts, norms and categories.

Finally, what does a pedagogy of listening mean for how we understand the preschool? We have already discussed, in Chapter 1, how these and other institutions for children can be understood in different ways, offering two examples: the preschool as 'children's service', a technology to achieve predetermined ends, and the preschool as 'children's space', a place of many possibilities. But in Reggio they have other understandings, or at least understandings that complement and elaborate the idea of 'children's space'. Understanding knowledge as constructed, and valuing the creation of new knowledge, the preschool can be conceptualised as a laboratory or a workshop of learning and knowledge: 'I now like to say [observes Carlina Rinaldi] that the whole school should be a great *atelier* [workshop], where doing, reflecting, action, sensory perception together with the virtual, and the local together with the global, can find their expression in a school that is now transformed into a great laboratory of research and reflection' (Rinaldi, forthcoming b). The preschool, too, can be viewed as a system of relationships and communication involving children, teachers and parents. And through this system of relationships, the preschool can be understood as, first and foremost, a space or context for multiple listening (Rinaldi, 1998: 6). The space, therefore, is constructed not only by what possibilities can and do take place in it, but also by how these possibilities are conducted.

What does this mean in practice?

What happens in a pedagogy of listening? We have discussed what such pedagogy means for the child, the teacher and the preschool. But what does it mean for the way pedagogical work is actually practised? We consider two tools that are very important: project work and pedagogical documentation.

Project work

In Reggio Emilia they prefer to use the term 'project' rather than 'curriculum' – although many visitors try to fit Reggio into a curriculum model, by so doing grasping Reggio and exemplifying the process of making the Other into the Same. But 'curriculum' in its various forms (e.g. 'emergent' or 'integrated', 'expert' or 'framework') and related terms (e.g. 'curriculum planning' or 'lesson planning') are not suited for representing the understandings of learning or knowledge that they have chosen to work with in Reggio. Learning, Rinaldi has observed,

> does not proceed in a linear way, determined and deterministic, by progressive and predictable stages, but rather is constructed through contemporaneous advances, standstills and 'retreats' that take many directions . . . [In the co-construction of knowledge] conflict and disturbance force us to constantly revise our interpretive models and theories on reality . . . [While the theories that children produce] have their own values and meanings, as well as their timing . . . [which] must be understood, respected and supported.
>
> (forthcoming a)

In short, the idea of curriculum is too normative, ordered and confined to live alongside the complexity, unpredictability and respect for difference that define a 'pedagogy of listening'.

Instead, in the municipal preschools in Reggio they prefer to talk of their pedagogical work in terms of projects (*progettazione* in Italian), to express the complexity of their practice:

> [We prefer to use this term] to describe the multiple levels of action, which are definite and indefinite at the same time, carried out in the dialogue between children and adults. The word 'project' evokes the idea of a dynamic process, an itinerary. It is sensitive to the rhythms of communication and incorporates the significance and timing of children's investigation and research . . . The statement of the hypothesis on how the project might proceed is valid only to the extent it is seen precisely as a hypothesis and not as a 'must' . . . *Progettazione* is also a way of thinking, a strategy for creating relations and bringing in the element of chance, by which we mean 'the space of the others', i.e. that undefined space of the self that is completed by the thought of the others within the relational process.
>
> (*ibid.*)

Project work, seen from the above perspective, differs not only from 'curriculum' but also from how project work is usually understood: as work where the teacher gives the children problems to solve already knowing the solutions and has preplanned not only the process but very often its conclusion. In a pedagogy of listening and radical dialogue, the teacher has to dare to open herself or himself to the unexpected and to experiment together with the children – in the here-and-now event (a concept that reappears later). The teacher and children become partners in a process of experimentation and research, in which the children invent a problem before they search for solutions.

In this context, as we have already said, the teacher needs to challenge the children by enlarging the number of hypotheses, theories and concepts, as well as helping them to develop their more technical work. By so doing, the teacher enlarges the choices that can be made rather than narrowing them down to one correct solution. Through this, children make a specific relation to the different themes of the project – for example time, light, machines, birds etc.; and they get a responsible relation to other children by listening, but also by negotiating between each other.

This whole approach contests the question-and-answer pattern so common in pedagogical practices, a pattern which can easily have the effect that the child has got nothing to say as she or he is forced into a predetermined position. It is a pedagogy that, in the words of Readings quoted at the beginning of this book, 'keeps the question of meaning open as a locus of debate' and resists the closure of attaining goals or standards. Or as Deleuze and Parnet (1989) say,

> If you are not allowed to invent your questions from all over the place, from never mind where, if people pour them into you, you haven't much to say. While encountering others, and while each child is bringing in her/his lot, a becoming is sketched out between the different perspectives. Then a block starts moving, a block which no longer belongs to anyone, but is 'between' everyone . . . Like a little boat which children let slip and loose, and is stolen by others.
>
> (9)

Pedagogical documentation

In a previous book (Dahlberg *et al.*, 1999) we described pedagogical documentation as a process of making practice visible, and therefore subject to interpretation and critique. It involves a process – reflecting upon and discussing material in a rigorous, critical and democratic way – and the production and selection of the material (videos, photographs, tape recordings, written notes, etc.) that documents the practices and relationships of children and educators. From her experience in Reggio Emilia, Rinaldi (2001a: 150) writes about documentation as making experience visible and thus 'open to the "possibles" (possible interpretations, multiple dialogues among children and adults)', as part of a process: 'while each fragment is imbued with the subjectivity of the documenter, it is offered to the interpretive subjectivity of others in order to be known or reknown, created or recreated' (Rinaldi, 2001b: 84). Subjectivity and interpretation, doubt and uncertainty, provisionality and reinterpreting are unavoidable – but welcome since they preserve a political approach to pedagogical practice, an approach that is strongly open and democratic:

> The reader [of documentation] can be a colleague, a group of colleagues, a child, children, parents, anyone who has participated or wants to participate in this process. The documentation material is open, accessible, usable and therefore readable. In reality this is not always the case, and above all the process is neither automatic nor easy.
>
> (*ibid.*: 86)

It should be admitted that pedagogical documentation carries risks. In earlier chapters we referred to Lynn Fendler's work, where she shows how new devices of governing, related to the idea of the autonomous, problem-solving, constructivist child, devices such as portfolios and self-evaluations, have entered the educational agenda, and circulate globally. According to her these devices can be seen as new strategies and technologies for governing the child down to her or his very soul. More of the child's personality, emotions, creativity, capacity for empathy and co-operation are opened up for judgements and governing, something which the British sociologist Basil Bernstein (1977) observed in his discussion of what he called visible and invisible pedagogy.

From this perspective documentation can be viewed as a potential act of power and control, just another new device for better governing the child. But does the power to see and make visible through pedagogical documentation inevitably become a means of normalisation and governmentality? Or are there other ways of working with documentation and portfolios which try to avoid this possibility?

From our way of understanding Reggio Emilia, they have been able to use documentation to resist power, by treating this method as a means to create a space where it is possible to attempt to overcome the techniques of normalisation. In their hands, documentation is not what it can easily become, 'child observation' that assesses children's progress (usually in terms of development) against predetermined and normative categories, and that simply reduces the other to the same. Instead, they have shown how documentation, used in a critical way, can make us observant of the contingency of our constructions, and hence, make it possible to destabilise the meaning of that which we take for given and see as natural and true about the child. Indeed, documentation can help in the study of how dominant regimes establish processes of normalisation and surveillance and how these processes go hand in hand with science. That has helped them to refuse to codify children into prefabricated developmental categories, and hence they have been able to transgress the idea of a lacking and needy child.

So as well as a learning process (learning about learning), in Reggio they have been able to use documentation to deconstruct dominant discourses and, as such, to create a possibility for subverting governmentality and subjectification:

> Through documentation we can unmask – identify and visualize – the dominant discourses and regimes which exercise power on and through us, and by which we have constructed the child and ourselves as pedagogues. Pedagogical documentation, therefore, can function as a tool for opening up a critical and reflective practice challenging dominant discourses and constructing counterdiscourses . . . Through documentation we can more easily see, and ask questions about, which image of the child and which discourses we have embodied and produced, and what voice, rights and position the child has got in early childhood institutions . . . The point of departure here is that the greater our awareness of our pedagogical practices, the greater our possibility to change through constructing a new space, where an alternative discourse or counter-discourse can be established producing new practices. It is, above all, a question of getting insight into the possibility of seeing, talking and acting in a different way, and hence cross boundaries, in particular to transgress the grandiose project of modernity and its determination to map all human life in the search for Truth, Beauty and Goodness.
>
> (Dahlberg *et al.*, 1999: 152–153)

Working in this reflective and critical way, Reggio suggests several ways in which pedagogical documentation can contribute to pedagogical practice. It can provide the means for evaluation as meaning making (as discussed in Chapter 4), enabling practice to be understood in great depth (and if necessary then judged). It enables pedagogical work to become a contestable subject of minor politics, as we discuss in Chapter 7. And it becomes a means for researching pedagogical practice and children's learning, and creating something new. In this last usage, for fostering learning, documentation is an integral part of learning, woven into the process of theorising, verifying and revising, rather than being a means of assessing whether or not children have attained a predetermined stage or goal: for it is not, as Rinaldi says, 'sufficient to make an abstract prediction that establishes what is significant – the elements of value necessary for learning to be achieved – before the documentation is carried out. It is necessary to interact with the action, with that which is revealed, defined, and perceived as truly significant, as the experience unfolds' (Rinaldi, 2001b: 85).

Documentation and resisting normalisation: a Swedish perspective

Interest in pedagogical documentation has spread out from Reggio to many countries in recent years. Preschools across the globe can be found working with this tool. But it has also become a subject for research. A research group at the Stockholm Institute of Education – on the ethics and aesthetics of learning – has been particularly interested in what we have suggested is a critical question: how can a practice of documentation, which carries the possibility of being repressive, be understood and practised as emancipatory for the child and teacher? This question is posed in the context of children (and teachers) today being observed, judged and assessed more than ever. This interest has led to a number of studies involving the use of pedagogical documentation.

One of these Swedish studies – the Stockholm project – was presented in our former book (Dahlberg *et al.*, 1999: Chapter 6). We will here present three more, each of which involves researchers closely engaged with teachers in preschools, listening to thought. The first is by Hillevi Lenz Taguchi. In her study entitled 'Emancipation and resistance: Documentation and cooperative learning processes in the preschool' (Lenz Taguchi, 2000), she has reflected on our critical question by examining the possibility of children and teachers 'having power' over processes of learning and pedagogical practice. She found that this was impossible with the traditional way of understanding power and power production in pedagogical practice, with its assumptions that there are right and unquestionable ways to do things and predetermined goals. But it becomes possible if pedagogical documentation is used as a practice of continuous resistance against such dominating discourses with their taken-for-granted meanings.

This takes place in what Lenz Taguchi calls 'deconstructive talks', between the researcher and the teachers or between the teachers themselves during their daily work together. Using pedagogical documentation teachers questioned their readings (or interpretations) of children's learning and tried instead to make multiple readings – including from the point of view of children's understandings and meaning making. By resisting taken-for-granted ways of understanding and opening up for multiple ways of understanding children's meaning making, it was possible for the teachers to support children's learning in new and unexpected ways. Children, too, were routinely asked to interpret their own work, when revisiting documentation in a group of children, so also opening up learning processes to children's participation and the learning group.

These practices – what Lenz Taguchi calls 'resistance practices' – disrupted teachers' notions of learning, both in general and in relation to specific children and particular content. They were seen as emancipatory: teachers understood themselves as knowledge-constructing subjects, desiring and taking pleasure in making multiple readings of practice and without having to do things 'right'. From a feminist poststructural perspective, resistance practices such as deconstructive talks make possible another form of power production – not only more emancipatory, but also more ethical and responsible.

This work again draws our attention to the difference between pedagogical documentation and child observation. For despite all its emancipatory ambitions, observational work conducted through the lens of developmental psychology, with its stages and its search for the true nature of the child, involves processes of normalisation not practices of resistance. It is many years now since Walkerdine drew our attention to this: how developmental psychology, with its concepts and classifications, constructed what a child is and should be in the project of modernity, observing that developmental psychology 'starts living its own life through processes of normalization, and hence also constructs pedagogues and children and their respective expectations and social practices' (Walkerdine, 1984: 163).

Through documentation within deconstructive talks, resistance is mounted to these processes. This means questioning the power of modernist thinking inscribed in developmental discourse, with the importance it attaches to categorisation, universality, truth, objectivity, rationality, unity and certainty, including a belief in there being one right answer for every question. And it means opening up other thinking, which foregrounds singularity, multiplicity, local knowledge, meaning making, social constructions, emotion, ambivalence and complexity. Drawing on her research, Lenz Taguchi proposes a type of postmodern ethics, which she terms 'an ethics of resistance', where each pedagogical act is examined as having many possible – but often contradictory – meanings and consequences. Through deconstructive talks and pedagogical documentation, the intention is to be able to see the complexity in the pedagogical situation and to become a 'multiplicity thinker' instead of a 'simplicity thinker'.

The second example extends our thinking about the Other beyond human beings, to everything that historically has been marginalised and excluded. This exclusion process has been challenged in Reggio Emilia when they speak of the hundred languages – many of which have not received recognition in traditional education, such as visual language, sound, light, touch, taste, smell (Ceppi and Zini, 1998). From our perspective this is not just a question of recognition, of welcoming these marginalised languages; it is also a question of how these languages are viewed and worked with, in relation to our constructions of the child, since this has important consequences for practice in the preschool (and school).

Working with pedagogical documentation, Ulla Lind has studied visual art discourses in Swedish preschools and schools. In her study entitled 'Postmodern reconceptualisation of aesthetics for education' (Lind, 2003), she shows how teachers rationalise how they govern children through appeals to conditions other than their own thinking and action – this child is tired, that one is not very well, he is a bad boy, she always behaves like that. Lind also relates her analysis to a modernist, educational discourse, which proposes that children become emancipated through art, so linking art to values such as love, truth and devotion. This discourse of modernist romanticism, which surrounds children's creative work, produces processes of normalisation through which teacher and child deny the value of art that is disturbing or complicated as the negation of beauty and purity.

In the final example, research conducted by Elisabeth Nordin-Hultman, in Swedish and English preschools, has explored the relationship between normalisation processes and the preschool environment.

In her study – 'Pedagogical Environments and Children's Construction of Subjectivity' (Nordin-Hultman, 2004) – she finds a strong tendency to individualise children's behaviour: 'processes and problems are individualized, while the educational context more often is taken for granted and left without reflection' (*ibid.*: 202). Children are perceived and described within the normative ideas of how a child ought to act, and activities, materials, the whole preschool context are inscribed with the same ideas.

In her study, Nordin-Hultman attempts to open up other possibilities by moving attention away from children's characteristics to the pedagogical environment, which she views as an important condition for children's behaviour. This means regarding the preschool and school as social spaces for activity and focusing on possibilities for creating environments that will stimulate activities that will be meaningful and interesting to children. From the perspective of the ethics of an encounter and a pedagogy of listening, what children say and do cannot be judged in relation to a predetermined course or programme; rather attention is focused on what happens in the child's encounter with her or his environment, in paying close attention to the unique events of the here and now. Nordin-Hultman argues that it is in these events – unpredictable encounters with their environment, when children become involved in what is interesting and meaningful for them – that 'good' practice takes place, a new becoming.

Gilles Deleuze: opening up to 'new' thought

We want to end this chapter with an opening, an opening to the work of the French philosopher Gilles Deleuze and its relationship to our discussions in this chapter. In particular, he connects together many of the themes in our discussion of ethics by his attempt to work with a 'philosophy of difference'. Deleuze argues that difference 'has never been allowed to exist in and for itself, but has always been mediated, passed through the Same, the Similar and the Negative' (Borgnon, forthcoming: 12). His project was to find a concept of difference that 'escapes western rationalism and essentialism' and that 'acknowledges and welcomes change and fluidity instead of fixed positions . . . and can be seen as an attempt to explode western logical thinking' (*ibid.*: 12, 10).

Deleuze has come into our thinking quite recently and seems to suggest many new directions (Dahlberg, 2003) – but directions we as yet have not followed far. In the spirit of resisting closure and keeping open the question of meaning we want to share with the reader some of the new possibilities or becomings that we have, as yet, only glimpsed in our encounter with Deleuze.

The vitality of thought

We have already met Deleuze in Chapter 2, when we discussed his proposition that we are in transition from societies of discipline to societies of control. But here we want to dwell on his potential for pedagogical thinking and practice, in relation to the ethics of an encounter: in particular, his distinction between knowledge and thought, his ideas about events and the vitality of thought, and the importance he attaches to the encounter with otherness or difference in the generation of thought and the event. In his thinking, knowledge is a dull concept, almost deadly, leading nowhere; it is about recognition of existing facts and the solution of known problems. Thought, by contrast, is life. Thought opens up – to change, innovation, invention of new possibilities. Thought is critical and creative – of new concepts, problems and learning. Thought respects singularity. Thought is that space outside the actual, which is filled with virtualities, movements, forces, that need release. It is what a body is capable of doing, without there being any necessity and without being captured by what it habitually does, a sea of (possible) desires and machines waiting their chance, their moment of actualisation (Grosz, 1999).

Deleuze transgresses the Cartesian understanding of thought as a natural human capacity. Thought is neither innate nor stirred by the reassuring familiarity of encounters with the known. It is, we might say, an involuntary activity that takes place when the mind is provoked by an encounter with the unknown and the unfamiliar – in short, with otherness. As such, it calls for an openness to the unpredictable and new, a willingness to experiment and make new connections. Deleuze puts it this way: 'Thought is what confronts us from the outside, unexpectedly. Something in the world forces us to think. This something is an object not of recognition but of fundamental *encounter*' (Deleuze, 1994: 139; emphasis added).

Thought as an event

Nordin-Hultman, in her study of the pedagogical environment which we outlined above, works with the concept of the event. She refers to Foucault's discussion of why the event has not been the subject of much attention, which he attributes to a tradition of knowledge that has been preoccupied with the abstract, the general and underlying causes. To 'eventualise' existence implies a new interest – in encounters, possibilities, obstacles, the play of forces, and breaking with that which one takes to be natural and necessary.

Deleuze continues with Foucault's idea of the event. The creation of thought through provocation and exposure to what is unfamiliar leads Deleuze to attach importance to how such events can be brought about: 'if you believe in the world you precipitate events, however inconspicuous, that elude control, you engender new space-times, however small their surface or volume' (Deleuze and Parnet, 1987). He talks about constructing assemblages, border crossing, transformations and encounters: all of which involve making connections, which multiply the potential for precipitating events – 'not another moment within time, but something that allows time to take off in another direction' (Colebrook, 2002: 57) – through creating life-giving confrontations and provocations, while undermining techniques of normalisation and totalising systems of classification and representation. To connect is to work with possibilities, with unpredictable becomings, to elude control; to make ever more connections is to produce an intensification of life.

To direct attention to events is to pay attention to process, doing, the here and now. It is an expression of a strong element of pragmatism in Deleuzian thought, but a form of pragmatism not related to instrumentality, not driven by a concern with predictive expertise and calculated outcomes. Rather what is important is to find ways to open up to the unpredictable and the new, to put experimentation before ontology. Borgnon (forthcoming) argues that, from a Deleuzian perspective, we could view the pedagogical relationship as events rather than fixed definitions.

> We could look at it as an encounter of desires. There is a possibility to see them as 'events of encounters of desires'. Instead of thinking of [what happens between teachers and children] as a new way for teachers to tame the children's desires, it can be looked on as an encounter of desires . . . The desires of the children meet with the desires of the teachers . . . [For Deleuze] desire is not lack, desire is force and positive force, desire is the force that creates new compositions.
>
> (11)

This relates to what Lind says in her study of visual art: 'as far as I can see, [it is] the principles of "becoming" behind practicing art work that are the interesting educational questions rather than to induce children to "make art"' (Lind, 2003: 2–3). The importance of becomings foregrounds processes since 'processes are becomings, and aren't to be judged by some final result but by the way they proceed and their power to continue' (Deleuze, 1995: 146). Lind argues that directing interest towards the processes, that is towards how aesthetic learning processes are produced and function and what social effects they have, implies a shift from a discourse about art to a discourse about learning – towards a pragmatic pedagogical practice.

An interest in processes does not, though, mean devaluing results. But usually today it is the result that is seen and assessed as the most important part of art education in preschool and school. Indeed, we can see that more generally in education attention focuses on 'outcomes', with process downplayed and devalued, the end being more important than the becoming. But if we look only for the outcome, and even more so only for a predetermined outcome, we can easily miss the dynamic and intensity of the process and dialogue, and we can all too easily lose the other.

Deleuze's concept of the event expresses a kind of trust and belief: trust that something unexpected, surprising, provoking may happen through making connections; belief in new encounters and forces and thoughts that are not contained and classified in existing programmes and methods. This belief calls for ethical and political responsibility, a heartfelt *yes, yes, yes* to the unknown, whether the unknown is another type of thinking or another human being. This is a form of affirmative ethics that challenges Cartesian certainty, starts in the art of listening and communicates a message of welcome and hospitality (Dahlberg, 2004).

Rhizomatic thought – or 'the tangle of spaghetti'

Respecting the alterity of the Other in the ethics of an encounter has implications for thought and knowledge, understanding knowledge as the construction of new understandings. For if we make the Other into the Same, if everything is always predetermined, if learning and life are about conformity to norms, if surprise and uncertainty are programmed out – then knowledge is endlessly recycled in a process of transmitting prefabricated meaning and life stultifies in endless repetition. But if we learn how to listen to the Other, in a respectful way, we may find ourselves provoked by this encounter to think, to produce new ideas and theories, to abandon our preconceptions.

This brings into being a new image of thought. In mainstream thinking, acquiring objective knowledge (or proceeding through developmental stages) is a linear progression where the metaphor is the tree: the hierarchical and centralised idea of the tree of knowledge, which is so prominent in education. But knowledge produced in the ethics of an encounter can be better understood by the metaphor of the rhizome. The rhizome is a concept that Deleuze and Guattari (1999; see also Deleuze and Parnet, 1989) have used in problematising the classical image of thought, which is related to recognition and linearity, and which Deleuze suggests is a profound betrayal of what it means to think.

In a rhizome there is no hierarchy of root, trunk and branch, nor is it like a staircase where you have to take the first step before you move onto the next. For Deleuze and Guattari, thought is the consequence of the provocation of an encounter, with the rhizome of thought shooting in all directions, without beginning or end, but always being in between. It is a multiplicity functioning by means of connections and heterogeneity, through exposure to difference, and constructed not given. Thought then is a matter of experimentation and problematisation – lines of flight, an exploration of a becoming, being shaken up as we encounter something that does not fit with our habitual ways of seeing and understanding.

In education and child development, linearity and progression are valued qualities. But when, as in the rhizome, there is a multiplicity of interconnected thoughts going off in all directions, linearity and progression are no longer applicable or useful. The Deleuzian desire for multiplicity confronts the binaries of Western thought – reason/ intuition, cognition/emotion, body/soul, logic/fantasy – which have created a world of separation and categorisation and excluded so much experience outside of education, such as sound, light, movement, smell, excluded experiences that, as we have argued, Reggio Emilia has sought to include when they work with 'the hundred languages of children'. And it is the author of this famous saying, Loris Malaguzzi, who made another connection with Deleuzian ideas when he used the metaphor of knowledge as a 'tangle of spaghetti', a culinary image with much in common with the image of the rhizome!

The same paradigmatic shift in thinking, inspired by Deleuze and Guattari, can be extended to other aspects of being besides knowledge; for example to identity. This is vividly illustrated by Shahram Khosravi, an Iranian who has lived many years in Sweden. Writing of a recent visit back to Iran, he describes a growing feeling of homelessness, as he finds himself to be no longer 'at home' in Iran, and seeks some comfort in trying to rethink the meaning of identity in a world of increased border crossing:

> What helps make this burden of homelessness easier is the hope of a new era of nomadity, of a globalisation of people without roots, of a deterritorialisation of culture – that is that all of us, slowly but surely, are becoming modern nomads. More and more of us seem to start living in some form of exile, in forms of life which in existing ways of thinking are seen as deviant, threatening, unnatural. A way to break away from this way of thinking is to try to finish viewing the human being and her identity in botanical terms of a tree, with roots and trunk. Perhaps 'roots' no longer exist, perhaps they have never existed. Instead of roots there exists what the French philosopher Deleuze calls a 'rhizome', different to the idea of a root, with no beginning or end, always being in the middle . . .
>
> If the botanical image of cultural identity is associated with territory, continuity and unit, a rhizomatic cultural identity is characterised by globalisation, discontinuity and multiplicity. My grandfather was a nomad and his life was a continuous wandering on the way to fresh pastures. A couple of generations later, I am the nomad. It is a story of history which I appreciate.
>
> (Khosravi, 1998: 28–29)

The concept and image of the rhizome are both challenging and transformative. They make the familiar – the linearity of development, the progression of knowledge, the essential nature of the subject – strange, or at least no longer self-evident and inevitable. They offer the possibility of resisting normalising practices and of envisaging new ways of relating to the world and to otherness.

Visualising as a force

If one follows the thinking of Deleuze, then to visualise children's theories, hypotheses and work as happens in documentation not only implies a way to follow and visualise children's individual and collective learning processes. It also implies an opening of a space where we can not only overcome the techniques of normalisation but gain new vitality and power through connecting up new forces, constructing new combinations and new assemblages. Visualising through documentation can be seen as a force, as an affirmation, as action and as energy and effectivity, a form of becoming. Following Deleuze, as well as Foucault, one can see power as productive and as vitality and intensity. Visualising then can be seen as a form of construction – as an emotional engagement and participation rooted in the body of experience. Deleuze (1988) says that 'visibilities are neither the acts of a seeing subject nor the data of a visual meaning . . . visibilities are not defined by sight but are complexes of actions and passions, actions and reactions, multi-sensorial complexes' (58–59). Seen from this perspective pedagogical documentation becomes a form of visualisation, which brings forces and energies into a project work, forces and energies that can open us up to new possibilities, to the possibility of transformations – to difference.

Becomings, potentials, vitality, forces, energies, desires, events: these and other terms used by Deleuze express his philosophy of difference, with its central idea, the importance of connections, experimentation and invention for creating new and surprising experience. In this philosophy 'we would be looking for fluidity in our pedagogical work or research analyses [and] to see the learning child as a new learning child every day, to see our observations and analyses as floating and creating new compositions instead of looking to hide differences and adapt to already known patterns and definitions' (Borgnon, forthcoming: 13). We can view the work in Reggio – with its rich combinations of listening, project work and documentation – in this light: it can be understood as a certain kind of inventionalism in the everyday practice. An inventionalism that tries to respect the particularities of each situation and event. This inventionalism challenges representations and puts new thoughts and concepts into work, but only provisionally and tentatively.

But at the same time as they question, the pedagogues in Reggio also affirm what is to come. They are trying hard to listen to the child from the child's own position and experience and not to make the child into the same. They are trying through experimenting to introduce new possibilities and new lines of thought, new potentialities, into their pedagogical practice. So the pedagogy of listening becomes an example of what we described earlier as 'a heartfelt *yes, yes, yes* to the unknown, whether the unknown is another type of thinking or another human being'.

This is not a technical practice of labelling, identification, recognition and judgement. It is about making preschools a locus for ethical practice, ethical spaces of open-ended, experimental, non-programmable reflection and self-questioning. From our perspective, the ethics they practise are the ethics of an encounter, but also, the ethics of resistance of Lenz Taguchi and the affirmative ethics of Deleuze: ethics which foreground complexity and multiplicity and relations of welcome and hospitality that open up to new thought and difference.

Making our choice

In these last two chapters we have explored the implications of particular ethical approaches for the work of preschools. We have paid particular attention to the ethics of an encounter, with the value it places on otherness. We have argued that it finds expression in ideas of listening to thought and the practice of a pedagogy of listening. Making the preschool a locus for ethical practice of this particular kind, with its desire to avoid making the Other into the same through grasping, has focused our attention on how normalising thinking and processes can be resisted and disrupted and how, on the contrary, we can create conditions where encounters with differences can provoke thought and an intensification of life.

We have also made a choice, a choice of the approaches that inspire our thinking about the preschool: what it is and could be, and also what it should not be. Some readers may not share our choice, and that we accept. What we cannot accept, however, is for the importance of ethics to be downplayed or ignored by privileging 'What works?' over 'Why?' In this respect we agree with Rinaldi when she argues that the municipal preschools in Reggio are not technical solutions but fundamental ethical choices: 'we don't forget that behind every solution and every organization, this means behind every school, there is a choice of values and ethics' (Rinaldi, 2001c: 2).

Chapter 6

Major and minor politics

From Powers of Freedom *by Nikolas Rose (1999)*:

In a present when old forms of political mobilization – the party, the programme, the electoral mandate – are losing their attraction, and when a host of new forms of politics are taking shape ... an analysis of the forms of contestation might help us understand the ways in which something new is created, a difference is introduced into history in the form of politics. In particular, it might help us amplify some of those mobile lines of force which have, historically, taken shape on the margins of politics. This is not to say that creativity is never found in traditional political forms. But it is to suggest that something might be learnt from those insurgent, minority or sub-altern forces that have often refused to codify themselves, that have resisted the temptations of party and programme ...

If one were trying to characterize the creativity of what one might term, after Deleuze and Guattari, *a 'minor' or 'minority' politics* ... one would examine the ways in which creativity arises out of the situation of human beings engaged in particular relations of force and meaning, and what is made of the possibilities of that location. These minor engagements do not have the arrogance of programmatic politics – perhaps even refuse their designation as politics at all. They are cautious, modest, pragmatic, experimental, stuttering, tentative. They are concerned with the here and now, not with some fantasized future, with small concerns, petty details, the everyday and not the transcendental. They frequently arise in 'cramped spaces' – within a set of relations that are intolerable, where movement is impossible, where change is blocked and voice is strangulated. And, in relation to these little territories of the everyday, they seek to engender a small reworking of their own spaces of action. The feminist politics that was conducted under the slogan of 'the personal is political' is the most obvious example from our recent past of the ways in which such a molecular and minor engagement with cramped space can connect up with a whole series of other circuits and cause them to fluctuate, waver and reconfigure in wholly unexpected ways.

(279–280; emphasis added)

Our discussion changes course at this point, turning from ethics to politics. What we want to explore in this chapter is the idea that preschools (and, by implication, schools and other institutions for children) could contribute to a process of *re*-politicisation, contributing to the opening up to politics of large areas of life through making them subject to contestation. So as well as 'loci of ethical practice', preschools might also be 'loci of democratic practice': these are both possibilities, both choices that can be made. In the next chapter, we offer some examples of 'minor politics' taking place in and around preschools. But in this chapter, we explore the concept in more detail, including its main features – what it might look like. We suggest two areas in which preschools might have a clear political role: bringing critical thinking to bear on practice and confronting injustice, or at least certain forms of injustice since the concept is broad including a variety of possible dimensions.

Before looking at politics and the preschool, we want to consider the relationship between ethics and politics. In passing from one to the other, how great is the turn? Do ethics and politics keep in sight or at least in contact? Or does politics takes us in an opposite direction to ethics? Is it possible for preschools to be first and foremost sites for ethical *and* political practice?

Ethics and politics

The distinction and relationship between ethics and politics is far from clear-cut; and always the question is 'What ethics?' Tronto (1993) proposes a distinction between morality – 'what one thinks important to do and in what way, how to conduct relations' – and politics – 'usually conceived in Western thought as the realm in which resources are allocated, public order maintained and disputes about how these activities should occur are resolved' (6). But despite this drawn distinction, morality and politics are in fact 'deeply intertwined'. What is needed is a concept that can bring out that inter-connectedness, and for Tronto the concept of care can serve this purpose: 'A concept that can describe both a moral and a political version of the good life can help us escape from the dilemmas of seeing morality and politics as separate spheres. I argue that care can serve as both a moral value and a basis for the political achievement of a good society' (*ibid.*: 9).

For Tronto, therefore, an ethics of care, such as we discussed in Chapter 3, needs a matching political theory of care: 'only if we understand care as a political idea will we be able to change its status and the status of those who do caring work in our culture' (*ibid.*: 157). Care should be understood 'not as a utopian device that will end all conflict, but as a value that should be more central in our constellation of political concerns' (*ibid.*: 172): in short, care as an ethic in politics. An ethics of care challenges many tenets of liberal politics, not least its assumptions about the ideal subject, with the foregrounding of autonomy. It provides a basis for living together in a just, pluralistic, democratic society: qualities such as attentiveness, responsiveness and responsibility 'can inform our practices as citizens'. An ethics of care raises the political importance attached to certain activities in relation to others: for example questioning the predominance in many contemporary societies of the 'work ethic' and the devaluing of care work and those who undertake it.

Levinas distinguishes ethics from politics, but again acknowledges their connectedness. As the focus moves from dyadic relationships, the face-to-face, to relations with third parties, so the ethical relationship is recognised to become increasingly political. Like Tronto, he argues that ethics should guide politics. The political order needs to be based on the ethical otherwise 'it will not be possible to effectively evaluate and challenge problematic manifestations of social and political life, such as, for example, fascism and totalitarianism' (Smart, 1999: 104). For Levinas it is necessary to be continually vigilant for the 'political order of the state may have to be challenged in the name of our ethical responsibility to the other' (Levinas and Kearney, 1986: 30). Levinas, therefore, develops a conception of an ethically informed politics, politics as 'mediated ethically' (Critchley, 2002), ethics as a form of vigilance to place some constraints on politics.

Rose, like others who write of a recent 'turn to ethics', notes a proliferating language of ethics in politics and beyond (as in, for example, 'ethical foreign policy' or 'ethical investments'), which he refers to as a new 'ethico-politics'. He welcomes 'the infusion of ethical discourse into politics' as a counter to 'all those attempts to translate ethical judgements into apparently more "objective", "scientific" rational or uncontestable terms . . . which seek to close off ethical discourse by appealing to the authority of a true discourse and, hence, inescapably, to the authority of those who are experts of this truth' (Rose, 1999: 192). Ethico-politics have the potential, therefore, to escape 'the will to truth' and open up 'the evaluation of forms of life and self-conduct to the difficult and interminable business of debate and contestation' (*ibid.*).

As with Tronto and Levinas, what concerns Rose is what approach to ethics informs politics. Politics can be inscribed by an idea of ethics that emphasises 'diverse ethical criteria', close perhaps to the ideas of postmodern ethics and contextualised ethics discussed in Chapter 3. Or, alternatively, it can be inscribed instead by an idea of ethics as universal codes, to be applied without debate or thought – an ethico-politics operating, in Rose's terms, 'at the pole of morality'. The result is not attractive, a 'moralizing ethico-politics' that uses the language of ethics to secure more effective social discipline and to reduce the scope for democratic practice:

> [S]uch a moralizing ethico-politics tends to incite a 'will to govern' which imposes no limits upon itself . . . Rather than endeavouring to make forms of life open to explicit political debate, it attempts to technically manage the way in which the individual should con-duct him- or herself and his or her relations to others in order to produce politically desired ends. *Ethico-politics operates at the pole of morality to the extent that it seeks to inculcate a fixed and uncontestable code of conduct*, merely shifting the loci of authority, decision and control in order to govern better.
>
> (*ibid.*: 192, 193; emphasis added)

Mouffe (2000a) also sees risks in the relationship between ethics and politics. Like Rose, she fears the consequences of a collapse of politics into a universalistic, rational morality. She speaks of the 'end of politics', as what should be politics is changed into law and morality, enabling conflict and difference to be replaced by a search for a con-sensus. But if Rose is concerned about the consequences for politics of a universalistic ethics, Mouffe fears that the sort of non-universalistic ethical approaches that we discussed in Chapter 3 might have similarly adverse consequences, contributing to a sort of sanitised and therefore ineffective politics, where conflict – 'the dimension of antagonism, which I take to be ineradicable in politics' (*ibid.*: 86) – is erased:

> The kind of pluralism they [ethical approaches] celebrate implies the possibility of a plurality without antagonism . . . As if once we had been able to take responsibility for the other and to engage

with its difference, violence and exclusion could disappear. This is to imagine that there could be a point where ethics and politics could perfectly coincide, and this is precisely what I am denying because it means erasing the violence that is inherent in sociability, violence that no contract or dialogue can eliminate.

(Mouffe, 2000b: 134–135)

(We return at the end of the chapter to consider Mouffe's concept of a politics of 'agonistic pluralism'.)

Another way of distinguishing the ethical and the political, without disconnecting them, is (following Derrida) to locate ethics in the sphere of undecidability, while politics represents the sphere of the decision. In this sense, ethics and politics are paired, the former never fully determinable leaving politics as action based on calculation. The ethical constitutes the (unending) search for determining what is right (however defined); while the political involves the search, through negotiation and compromise, for what is acceptable given others' views about what is right, as well as what is in their interests. Judgements and choices have to be made and all such decisions are political by nature and are always a matter of determining the least bad (Critchley, 2002). But for this reason, politics too is an unending process, involving provisional decisions constantly open to re-appraisal:

> We can never be completely satisfied that we have made a good choice since a decision in favour of some alternative is always at the detriment of another one . . . Politicization never ceases because undecidability continues to inhabit the decision. Every consensus appears a stabilization of something essentially unstable and chaotic. Chaos and instability are irreducible, but this is at once a risk and a chance, since continued stability would mean the end of politics and ethics.
>
> (Mouffe, 2000b: 136)

In all the examples briefly outlined here, ethics and politics are in relationship: ethics can and should permeate politics. Yet the two spheres are, or should be, in tension. Ethics may need to challenge politics; ethics may neuter politics by displacing conflict and violence; ethics is the sphere of undecidability, politics the sphere of decision. There is, too, the ever-present question of 'What ethics?' Politics may become the vehicle of universalistic moral thinking, the search for general moral codes (as in some politicians' hankerings to go 'back to basics'), in which case difference may be smothered by the application of such a code and ethics becomes an accomplice of a 'will to govern'. Or politics may adopt a more pluralist and contingent approach to ethics, which may have the same effect, for different reasons – but might contribute to an 'antagonistic' democracy of conflicting values, interests and interpretations.

The state of politics

Our discussion of politics and the preschool takes place against a background of apparent depoliticisation. One symptom is the hollowing out of political process, or at least of one type of process. 'Traditional' politics, with its institutions (parties, assemblies, occasional elections) and its practitioners (politicians, party machines, spin-doctors and other technicians), are held in ever lower public esteem. Fewer and fewer people participate, whether as party activists, party members or ordinary voters. Complaints are increasingly heard that there is little difference between parties or politicians, that democratic government is reduced to deciding who can best manage the economy and public services, that politicians are too much in thrall to the interests of big business.

Crouch (2001) terms this sense of political malaise 'post democracy', what he describes as an almost inevitable falling off from moments of more vibrant democracy which tend to occur in the early years of achieving democracy or after great crises, such as wars.

> Elections certainly exist and can change governments, [but] public electoral debate is a tightly controlled spectacle, managed by rival teams of professionals expert in the techniques of persuasion and considering a small range of issues selected by those teams. The mass of citizens plays a passive, quiescent, even apathetic part, responding only to the signals given them. Behind this spectacle of the electoral game politics is really shaped in private by interaction between elected governments and elites which overwhelmingly represent business interests.
>
> (*ibid.*: 2)

In this process, Crouch argues, a blurring occurs of the distinctions between public and business interests and ethics. Far from clarifying the boundary between government and business, 'neo-liberalism has linked them in manifold new ways – but all within the former territory reserved to government' (*ibid.*: 61).

Another sign of depoliticisation is the process we have already referred to: the removal of politics from political issues. Political issues are transformed into neutral issues of expertise and management, summed up in the familiar technical question 'What works?' Competing values and views, contested concepts and discourses, conflicts of interest and understanding are reduced to alternative sets of options and costs, assessed against their contribution to organisational performance (Clarke, 1998). This depoliticising of public policy formation, removing it from the field of contestability into the field of consensual rationality, involves defining policy as the province of experts (I. Young, 1990). Experts, in turn, apply 'technologies of government', in particular numbers which 'appear to depoliticise whole areas of political judgement, the apparent objectivity of numbers and those who manipulate them [helping] reconfigure the respective boundaries of the political and the technical' (Rose, 1999: 199).

This extension of expert power into the field of politics is accelerated by the changing position of the nation state in an increasingly globalised economy that we referred to in Chapter 2. Yeatman (1994) sees politics smothered by the growth of the 'performative state', which replaces substantive political content with criteria of efficiency, economy and effectiveness. The identity of the state's populace shifts from social citizens of the welfare state to that 'of actual or potential contributors to the performativity of the competition state' (111), whose task is to become a successful player in the global market place.

Readings (1996), too, associates depoliticisation with the weakening of the nation state, in the face of globalised, deregulated capital:

> Rather than being under national political control, the economy is more and more the concern of transnational entities who transfer capital in search of profit without regard to national boundaries. The erstwhile all-powerful state is reduced to becoming a bureaucratic apparatus of management . . . Under globalisation the state does not disappear; it simply becomes more and more managerial . . . This hollowing out of the state is a process that appears to the erstwhile national population as 'depoliticization': the loss of belief in an alternative political truth that will authoritatively legitimate oppositional critique.
>
> (46–47)

Part of the process of modern globalisation, a particular feature of the post-Second World War world, has been the establishment of increasing numbers of international bodies – the World Trade Organisation (WTO), the World Bank, the OECD, etc. They also contribute to the process of depoliticisation: like national governments, they seek the legitimisation of expertise as a basis on which to offer global prescriptions. But there is a further element. Such international bodies need to find common denominators: cross-national similarities, conclusions that apply everywhere, justifications that claim universal validity. To foreground differences – about values, beliefs, policy, practice – and contestation would undermine their global role, limit their influence on affairs, complicate rather than simplify. Both an Enlightenment belief in universal foundations and solutions, and their own *raison d'être*, make international organisations prone to privilege the technical over the political, the general over the particular.

So, as we have already seen, the World Bank's growing involvement in early childhood seeks a common approach sanctioned by appeals to scientific knowledge, in particular child development. The recent OECD review of early childhood education and care concludes by identifying eight elements of successful policy, which are 'intended to be broad and inclusive so that they can be considered in the light of unique and diverse country contexts, circumstances, values and beliefs' (OECD, 2001: 125). While, as discussed in Chapter 1, in another exercise OECD has developed measures of student performance in three specific areas, intended to permit cross-national comparisons of performance and their relationship to national schooling structures. What these, and similar, exercises have in common is to search, first and foremost, for similarities – of technologies, of policies, of items that can be measured and measurements – as a basis for universal prescriptions which can then be traded globally. In doing so, they downplay differences and the possibility of choices, and remove – but also mask – the political. (For an interesting example of how politics does in fact enter into the work of an international organisation which has claimed a universal, objective prescription for the economic policies of nation states, see Stiglitz [2002] on the International Monetary Fund [IMF].)

Major politics still matters: the case of the preschool

At national level

Yet the process needs qualification. Our reference to an 'apparent depoliticisation' suggests things may be more complex. In many fields, the nation state still has considerable power – and one of these fields is education including the preschool. There may be global forces demanding the expansion of preschools, and international organisations offering blueprints for doing so. But how that is done and how these institutions are viewed remain subjects for determination by the nation state, and by what Rose calls 'a traditional or majoritarian' politics – if the will exists to treat them as political rather than technical subjects.

To be more precise, traditional politics in the shape of the nation state determines a range of policies which shape preschools and their pedagogical practice – types of provision, providers, workforce, content, regulation, funding and so on. Behind these mechanics of government, these blueprints of delivery, lie ideas of how society is and should be, the bundles of theories, traditions, values, understandings and rationalities which shape and justify action. What is still at stake, the major consequences of traditional politics, can be seen in the very different preschools of Sweden and Britain (for a fuller comparison, see Cohen *et al.*, 2004).

The Swedish preschool is viewed as a public good, part of the social infrastructure, and as a legal entitlement to all children over 12 months. Swedish children under 12 months are almost all at home with parents taking well-paid statutory parental leave (in 1999, there were 53 children under 12 months in preschools and family day care, compared with 368,000 between 1 and 5 years of age) (Swedish National Agency for Education, 2000). A recent report emphasises how preschools are now widely accepted as a necessary part of the social fabric and, as such, are regarded as a right:

> What was once viewed as either a privilege of the few for a few hours a day or an institution for needy children and single mothers has after 70 years of political vision and policymaking become an unquestionable right for children and families. As such, families expect a holistic pedagogy of health care, loving care and education throughout the preschool age.
>
> (Lenz Taguchi and Munkhammar, 2003: 31)

Apart from some salaried family day carers, provision for children under 6 years takes the form of 'age integrated' centres, mostly provided by the public sector, i.e. local authorities: in 1999, 15 per cent of children attending preschools were enrolled in an independent preschool, almost half of which were run as parent co-operatives (Swedish National Agency for Education, 2000). Preschools bring together care and education, within the integrative concept of pedagogy: the task of the preschool is to 'provide children with good pedagogical activities, where care, nurturing and learning together form a coherent whole' (Swedish Ministry of Education and Science, 1998). These words come from the Swedish preschool curriculum, a short framework setting out the values, tasks and broad goals for the preschool: implementation rests largely with the local authorities and the preschools themselves. There are no national standards or other normative rules, at least at the time of writing, although the National Agency for Education provides some national overview of preschool services.

The state funds most of the costs of preschools, leaving parents to make an income-related contribution that accounted (in 1999) on average for 16 per cent of total preschool cost (Swedish National Agency for Education, 2000). Overall, Sweden spends about 2 per cent of GDP on preschool services (OECD, 2001). More than half the workforce are preschool teachers. Prior to 2001, they received a 3-year training at higher education level. Since 2001, this has been increased to $3^1/2$ years, as the training of preschool teachers, school teachers and school-age childcare workers (free-time pedagogues) has been integrated within a single framework, combining 18 months of shared training with 24 months of more specialist courses. Graduates of this new training system, whether they propose to work in preschools or schools, will be called teachers.

Since the late 1990s, Britain (or at least England and Scotland), like Sweden, has placed responsibility for all preschool services (as well as school-age childcare) within national education departments. However, a major split persists between 'early years education' (defined as for 3- and 4-year-olds) and 'childcare services'. Without a concept like pedagogy, which starts from the assumption that care and education are inextricably intertwined, it has proven difficult to conceptualise and practise an integrated approach to early childhood services. Early years education and childcare continue to be based on very different concepts and principles.

The former is an entitlement (or at least part-time attendance for 3- and 4-year-olds is an entitlement), fully funded by government, free to parents, mostly taking place in schools with teachers as the main form of staff. However, a 'quasi-market' has been introduced by enabling a wide range of services (not only schools, but nurseries, playgroups and family day carers) to provide publicly funded 'early years education' for 3- and 4-year-olds as long as they meet certain conditions. 'Childcare services' operate in an actual market. They are treated by government as a private good or commodity, mostly provided privately as businesses, to be purchased by parents at the going market rate (though government also exhorts individual employers to provide 'childcare assistance' for their employees). Most 'childcare' provision is in nurseries or family day care, quite separate from schooling.

In addition to funding early years education, government's role is threefold: first, to regulate the market through a centralised system of standards and inspection; second, to rectify instances of market failure, through subsidies paid to lower income parents (as a tax credit) and through stimulating services in poor areas where demand is too weak to create a functioning market; third, to initiate and fund an increasing array of programmes, aimed in particular at disadvantaged areas, and intended to eradicate poverty through early intervention with children and their parents.

Levels of provision, despite recent rapid increases, are much lower in Britain than Sweden. So too is public investment in services. Even after recent increases in public expenditure, Britain still spends only about 0.4 per cent of GDP on 'early years education', 'childcare' (including school-age services) and a major programme of early intervention services targeted on disadvantaged areas. Levels of training and pay in the 'childcare workforce' are low, far below those of teachers in 'early years education'. As well as being bounded by a centralised regulatory system, staff working with 3- to 6-year-olds have to work with a detailed curriculum (the Foundation Stage) and there is a detailed national system for assessing 5-year-olds in their first year of compulsory schooling (Cohen *et al.*, 2004).

Behind these very differing preschool policies in Sweden and Britain are very different politics. The Swedish preschool can be understood as the product of what has been termed the Nordic welfare state, whose characteristics include a high degree of universalism expressed in a wide range of general entitlements, extensive provision of services and generous benefits, and financing through taxation without high user fees (Esping-Andersen, 1999). Now transferred from the welfare to the education system, the preschool has become even more of a universal service: the entitlement to a service for children from 12 months upwards is now open to all children, whereas before it was restricted to children with special needs or with parents who were employed or studying. A period of free attendance is also offered to 4- and 5-year-olds, inserting this educational principle into a system that had previously required that parents always contribute to costs.

Britain, by contrast, adheres more to what has been termed the liberal welfare state, which emphasises private responsibility for welfare provision exercised through the purchase of private services in the market (in the case of preschools, by parents as consumers), with a targeted role for the state focused on children and adults 'in need'. The liberal welfare state places more reliance on the individual paying fees for services and less on financing through taxation. Comparing Sweden with another liberal welfare state, the USA, Esping-Andersen (1999) has shown how welfare expenditure is very similar: what differs is the balance between what the state spends and what families spend. Swedes pay higher taxes, but Americans pay far more in private costs; for example six times as much for childcare services. 'What varies [he comments] is who shoulders the burden, not the total weight of the burden itself' (176). A similar difference in parental fees is apparent when comparing England with Sweden (Cohen *et al.*, 2004).

Sweden's strong system of statutory leave entitlements (parental leave, paternity leave, leave to care for sick children), with generous payments and considerable flexibility operating in favour of employees, displays a willingness to regulate the labour market in the interests of children and parents. Britain's weak system, with low payments and no flexibility, displays an overriding commitment to labour market deregulation. Thus, Swedish parents are entitled to take leave on a full-time or part-time basis and to work reduced hours until their child is 8 years old. But British parents have only the right to ask their employer if they can work part-time!

There is also a striking difference in the relationship between national and local government. In Sweden, a strong role for the state in provision of benefits and services has, in recent years, been matched by a strong measure of decentralisation of responsibility for services both to local communities and institutions (including preschools and schools). For example, responsibility for the interpretation of the preschool curriculum is delegated to local authorities and preschools, and there is no centralised system for regulating services. One consequence is that a rather uniform system of provision (most children going to preschools provided by local authorities) has considerable scope for variation in practice: the OECD review team which visited Sweden in 2000 commented that the Swedish 'preschool education is outstanding . . . in its systemic approach while respecting programmatic integrity and diversity' (OECD, 1999: 41). This potentially opens up space for the 'minor politics' we will discuss next.

England, by contrast, despite a strong emphasis on private provision and markets, operates a strongly centralised system, including a detailed curriculum for 3- to 6-year-olds and a national system of standards and inspection. The result is what Whitty *et al.* (1998) refer to as a 'quasi-market and an evaluative state' or 'deregulation and sharpening rules'. The state remains strong despite appearing to devolve, using new managerial tools focused on ensuring predetermined outcomes; the key relationship becomes that between central government and individual institutions (weakening the role of local government). The end result is that a rhetoric of diversity and choice is actually combined with increasing standardisation and reducing space for minor politics.

As a final observation on national differences between Sweden and Britain, it is apparent that Sweden has shown a far greater capacity than Britain to create a dynamic system that is capable of change based on processes of democratic reflection. Over 40 years, the Swedish preschool system has changed from being based on 'part-time' kindergartens and full-time 'childcare for working parents', via preschools combining care and education but located in welfare, to preschools today, which still combine care and education, but are located within education and foreground an educational (or, to use the Swedish term, pedagogical) purpose. The preschool workforce – originally kindergarten teachers and people who worked in nurseries – has been re-formed, first as a profession of preschool teacher and now as part of a general profession of teacher, and in the process their training, status and conditions have been markedly improved. The relationship between preschool and school has become a major issue, with an awareness that this requires new thinking about both institutions to find a 'common meeting place' (Dahlberg and Lenz Taguchi, 1994: 21). At the same time there has been a rich, active and continuing democratic debate about the meaning of education and increasing diversity of practice supported by strong processes of decentralisation. Over this period, we could say that the Swedish preschool system has been not only completely re-structured but also re-thought and re-located within a re-formed education system.

None of this can be said of the British system. Its structures – both the services themselves and the workforce – and policy discourse remain fundamentally unchanged, split between 'childcare' and education. The relationship between the preschool and school systems has become more distant, dissonant and problematic. The possibility, common in Sweden today, that a preschool worker could be the principal of a school, is inconceivable in Britain. Decentralisation has been associated with increasing regulation. Debate about the meaning of education has been overshadowed by a government agenda of increasing places and improving standards.

Whereas 40 years ago, Swedish and British preschool policies had much in common, today they are far apart. This has something to do with different conditions: Sweden entered into a rapid increase in women's employment before Britain. But it also has much to do with national politics. Governing values have diverged: Esping-Andersen (1999) notes a more general similarity between the Swedish and British welfare states in the 1960s, but a separation with a strong British turn to liberal politics in the 1970s (which was epitomised by the Thatcher regime, but has been a continuous theme of governments of different parties). There are also differences in the traditions and conduct of politics. A more democratic practice is apparent in Sweden, nationally and locally, which draws on a history of public thought and discussion, most obviously a rich tradition of commissions on many aspects of preschools, schools and education. By contrast Britain not only has a more centralised and regulatory mode of politics, but has developed a concept of 'modernisation' which treats the past as either irrelevant or an encumbrance. An active relationship with the past in Sweden has contributed to major change, while a disinterest in the past in Britain has reflected and reinforced strong continuities.

These contrasts show the continuing importance of national and 'traditional' politics. Governments in Sweden and Britain have adopted very different approaches to preschools, which are inscribed with quite different values and understandings, for example about the boundaries between public and private (the preschool as public or private good, as entitlement or commodity), about the relationship between care and education, about the responsibility of national government, local government and individual institution, or about the construction and value of work with children. All these are intensely political issues, but also political issues that need to be decided at the national level.

At more local levels

The importance of major or traditional politics does not end at the national level. Regional or local governments may choose to make preschools a subject of major politics, especially where substantial responsibilities are decentralised to them – or where a weak or disinterested central government leaves space for an active local politics. Perhaps the best example of this process of an active 'traditional' local politics is to be found among many communes (local authorities) in northern and central Italy. The first sign of politics at play was the decision of these communes in the 1960s to provide preschools, not because of central government policy but as an expression of local priorities: many other local authorities in Italy did not make this political choice (Catarsi, 2004; Malaguzzi, 2004).

But these active communes have gone further, to develop distinctive pedagogical practices, which can be seen as a highly political process of making choices – about understandings of the child, of knowledge and of learning. The example of Reggio Emilia is well known, but this local authority is not alone in developing a strong local preschool politics. What many of these experiences share is an image of the child (as competent, strong, full of potential, an image summed up by Loris Malaguzzi as the 'rich child'), of preschools as public spaces of great cultural significance, and of learning as a process of realising possibilities and creating new knowledge rather than producing predetermined outcomes. This is how the head of preschool services in a small commune in central Italy expresses this understanding of learning in conversation with one of the authors (PM):

> Educators have to negotiate with children, develop their capacity to listen rather than transmit programmes. We see the context [of the preschool] as a meeting point, of children and adults, which offers more possibilities than we could think about at the beginning . . . We desire to discover the constructive potentials in the children, to give children the freedom to find out and transform the world. What is important is possibilities, not targets . . . Our education is 'targeted' to develop children's consciousness that not one single world exists. Pedagogy is the cultivation of many worlds, the opposite of *Candide*. We must not do our utmost to justify the existing world, [but support] the creative potential of individuals towards the dimension of diversity.

We do not claim that preschools in such Italian communities are completely without predetermined goals; the issue, as we have already said, is how much space is left in pedagogical work for the unexpected as well as what 'outcomes' are willed and how that political decision is made. Thus the city councillor quoted below was clear about one of the outcomes that Reggio had wanted from its preschools:

> In an interview my colleagues and I conducted with Bonacci [the Mayor of Reggio Emilia during the 1960s and 1970s], it became obvious how important it was for many people in Reggio to break with authoritarian tradition and build a society based on democratic

> values . . . [W]e asked what prompted the people of Reggio Emilia
> to design an early childhood education system founded on the
> perspective of the child. He replied that the fascist experience
> had taught them that people who conformed and obeyed were
> dangerous and that in building a new society it was imperative to
> safeguard and communicate that lesson and nurture and maintain
> a vision of children who can think and act for themselves.
>
> (Dahlberg, 2000: 177)

We can say that in such places in Italy, the discourse of instrumental
rationality is being confronted and contested, that here is a radically
different idea of what it means to be human and to learn. The response
of visitors may be bemusement, unable to grasp a different way of
thinking and practising ('But where are the outcome measures?' 'Has
it been evaluated?'). Or it may be totalisation, making the Other into
the same ('Isn't that rather like we do?' 'Isn't this a good example
of the emergent curriculum?'). Or it may be excitement at finding local
communities making a political choice to explore theory and practice
within a different paradigm, their preschools challenging 'the dominant discourse of our time, specifically in the field of early childhood
pedagogy – a most unique undertaking for a pedagogical practice!'
(*ibid.*: 178).

We shall explore this issue – challenging the dominant discourses of
our time in the field of early childhood pedagogy – in more detail later
in this chapter and in the next, as an example of how preschools, as
individual institutions, can make pedagogical practice a field for minor
politics. Our attention, for the moment, is at the next level up, of
how the local community, as a political entity, can make pedagogical
practice, and childhood more widely, a vibrant and important part of
traditional 'mainstream' politics. The Italian examples we have alluded
to raise the question of whether these communities themselves would
see their work in political terms. We cannot offer a firm answer,
not having enquired systematically of all communes with important
preschool experiences. But there are indications which lead us to think
that many would see their work in overtly political terms.

In Reggio, for example, they describe their experience as only one
possibility of many and say, as we saw in Chapter 5, that their way of
working is a choice of ethics and values. But it is also, in their view, a
political choice. This has arisen because a number of critical questions
have been recognised as political issues, starting with what they describe
as the most fundamental questions of all for their work: What is the

identity of the preschool? How do we understand knowledge? Who is the child? (Rinaldi, 2001c). The great importance attached to this last question, sometimes put as 'What is our image of the child?', reflects an awareness of the many answers that are possible and how the answer chosen is very productive, for better or worse:

> Many different images could be possible: highlighting what the child *is* and *has*, *can be* and *can do*, or on the contrary emphasising what the child is *not* and does *not have*, what he or she *cannot be* or *do*. The image of the child is above all a cultural (and therefore social and political) convention that makes it possible to recognise (or not) certain qualities and potentials in children . . . What we believe about children thus becomes a determining factor in defining their social and ethical identity, their rights and the educational contexts offered them.
>
> (Rinaldi, 1998: 116–117; original emphasis)

The director of preschools in another Italian commune described their experience to one of us as 'a local cultural project of childhood'. This phrase also captures the idea of a political community engaging over many years in thought, reflection and debate about the relationship between children, adults and the community, about understandings of the child and of learning, knowledge and other concepts, and about how these relate to the temporal context, the times we are living in and the changes we witness. The concept of a local cultural project also hints at the creativity that has marked 'traditional' local politics in the engagement of these Italian communes with early childhood. The concept is one that questions the necessity and rationality of programmes and models that claim universal applicability based on technical expertise and true knowledge.

Minor politics

But there is more than this type of 'major' politics. Two images have inspired this book. The first we have already discussed: Readings's vision of teaching and learning as loci of ethical practices. The second, which we consider now, is the idea of 'minor politics', a concept created by Deleuze and his colleague Guattari. Before examining what this concept might mean and how it might be practised in preschools, we want to make it clear that politics does not involve an opposition between minor politics and 'a traditional or majoritarian' politics, in the sense that a choice has to be made between them. A democratic society needs both. Each should provoke the other into creativity and each is best suited to a particular type of political action. Major politics may create conditions for minor politics, minor politics may, as Rose puts it in the quotation that begins this chapter, 'connect up with a whole series of other circuits' and with such force as to disturb and direct major politics.

Minor politics can take a variety of forms – indeed, it might be applied to all political activities outside the field of majority or traditional politics that 'have resisted the temptations of party and programme'. If we consider Rose's reflections on the character of 'minor' politics, from the quotation at the start of this chapter, from the perspective of the preschool, several features catch the eye. Minor politics 'are concerned with the here and now . . . the everyday'; they frequently arise in 'cramped spaces'; they seek to 'engender a small reworking of their own spaces of action'; they involve 'the ways in which creativity arises out of the situation of human beings engaged in particular relations of force and meaning, and what is made of the possibilities of that location'.

These features suggest clearly to us that one location for 'minor politics' – where 'human beings [are] engaged in particular relations of force and meaning' – is public provision for children. Preschools may, therefore, become sites for such 'minor politics', though not necessarily so. In this context, 'minor politics' involves a collective process of critical thinking. The idea of critical thinking, and its importance to re-politicisation, is vividly expressed, again, by Rose. It is

> a matter of introducing a critical attitude towards those things that are given to our present experience as if they were timeless, natural, unquestionable: to stand against the maxims of one's time, against the spirit of one's age, against the current of received wisdom. It is a matter of introducing a kind of awkwardness into the fabric of one's experience, of interrupting the fluency of the narratives that encode that experience and making them stutter.
>
> (Rose, 1999: 20)

Minor politics as critical thinking is about creating opportunities for seeing matters differently and making loud voices stutter, it is about questioning and contesting 'what is given to us as necessary to think and do' (*ibid.*: 277). It should make the familiar seem strange, make visible invisible assumptions and values, remove the 'taken-for-granted' of practices, and 'make explicit the thought that . . . is largely tacit in the way in which we govern and are governed' (Dean, 1999: 36). It should question truth claims based on expertise, technology and management that seek to impose consensus and to close down the contestability of subjects, often expressed in such terms as 'quality', 'excellence', 'best practice', 'benchmarks'. It opens up space 'in which it is possible to think about how it might be possible to do things in a different fashion' (*ibid.*). It is a politics 'whose ethos is a reluctance to govern too much, that minimises codification and maximises debate, that seeks to increase the opportunities for each individual to construct and transform his or her own forms of life' (Rose, 1999: 193).

Viewed from a different perspective, but not very different, 'minor politics' can be seen as part of an expansion of the political terrain, by making more issues political. Yeatman (1994) talks about a *postmodern* politics, which opens up for the contestation of core assumptions and values in *modern* democratic politics. She cites three important examples, large in scale but to which, it seems to us, minor politics in the pre-school could make an important contribution.

Following the linguistic turn, *a politics of epistemology* contests modernity's idea of knowledge: 'this critique is based in a rejection of mirror theories of knowledge, where knowledge, if it is to be true or accurate knowledge, mirrors an order of being outside itself' (*ibid.*: 28). It questions the idea of objective knowledge on which truth claims can be built. Knowledge is always perspectival and always enmeshed with power. Picking up on our earlier discussions, Foucault argued that power produces knowledge, what is taken to be true or false, while knowledge sustains power, lending it authority and justification as well as the means to discipline and control. He claimed

> that discourses that aim to reveal the truth of the abnormal personality or human sexuality or the criminal help to create and control the very objects they claim to know. Scientific knowledge functions as a major social power: through the state, the family, hospital, and therapeutic institutions, the scientific disciplines shape the dominant cultural ideas about who we are, what is permissible and unacceptable, what can be said, by whom, when, and in what form.
>
> (Seidman, 1998: 236)

A politics of epistemology questions the possibility of a neutral, non-positioned, non-perspectivalist knowledge, a possibility accepted as fact by modern scientific or objective knowledge. It does not, though, question the possibility of *contestable* knowledge claims nor the need for them to be subject to rigorous procedures. But no one claim can trump all others in the practice of minor politics – experts, for example, cannot claim a privileged position. Knowledge claims, being 'irresolvably multiple', cannot be used to close debate; they are a stimulus to, rather than a conclusion of, discussion. In minor politics knowledge claims are always open to question and their value is in part a matter of their ability to generate further ideas and argumentation.

Minor politics is not only a place to contest knowledge. It can also provide an opportunity for the construction of new knowledges, what Santos refers to as 'emancipatory' knowledge in contrast to regulatory knowledge represented by the truth claims of scientific knowledge. As we saw in Chapter 2, Santos defines this knowledge as local and created through argumentation. He further states that these two characteristics – localness and argumentativeness – belong together: argumentative discourse can only take place inside interpretive communities (Santos, 1995).

Yeatman's second example – *a politics of representation* – is closely connected. It concerns whose perspectives have legitimacy, whose views merit hearing:

> Central to this politics is the twofold strategic question: whose representations prevail? Who has authority to represent reality? To put the question differently: who must be silenced in order that these representations prevail? Whose voice is deprived of authority so that they may prevail?
>
> (Yeatman, 1994: 30)

Yeatman foregrounds the importance to a politics of representation of opening up public spaces where issues can be made visible through 'turning the techni(econo)cratic representation of state policy into openly contested political issues', so converting 'performative decisions into rhetorical praxis' (*ibid.*: 111). 'Minor politics' conducted in the preschool can be seen as opening such public space.

Finally *a politics of difference* refuses to any group a privileged position of objectivity – a 'god's eye view' – on any contested subject. No individuals or groups can stand outside power relations or have special access to true knowledge, none has views which merit being represented over those of others: 'all then that is possible is for differently positioned groups or individuals to come together to offer their different perspectives on how they should decide and manage their shared life conditions' (*ibid*.: 88). A minor politics in the preschool from this viewpoint involves no parties being able to claim special treatment or authority.

Resisting dominant discourses, governmentality and subjectification . . .

'Minor politics' – understood as expanding the political terrain by introducing critical thought and contestation into areas normally treated as technical or rendered invisible – becomes a means of: being governed less by dominant discourses and through governmentality; resisting processes of subjectification; and confronting injustice. We shall consider each of these possibilities in turn.

The concept of dominant discourses brings us back to the work of Foucault and his study of power and power relations, which we introduced in Chapter 1. To recap, discourses are the exercise of power. They are practices, including ways of naming things and talking about them, that govern how we think and act. *Dominant discursive regimes* exercise particular influence. They organise our everyday experience of the world, exercising power over our thought by directing or governing what we see as the 'truth' and how we construct the world, and hence over our actions too. As such they provide the mechanism for rendering reality amenable to certain kinds of actions (Miller and Rose, 1993), and by the same token, they exclude alternative ways of understanding and interpreting the world.

Foucault also calls these dominant discourses *regimes of truth*. In a famous passage, he explains an important idea: that truth is not some objective reality, but what comes to be accepted as true at a particular time and in a particular place. We quote at length from this passage, since the field of minor politics could be thought of as working for regime change by making the regime visible and contestable, revealing it as *a* truth, not *the* truth, and as such lessening its ability to dominate and govern:

> We are subjected to the production of truth through power and we cannot exercise power except through the production of truth. This is the case of every society, but I believe that in ours the relationship between power, right and truth is organised in a highly specific fashion . . . [W]e must speak the truth; we are constrained or condemned to confess to or discover the truth. Power never ceases its interrogation, its inquisition, its registration of truth; it

institutionalises, professionalises and rewards its pursuit. In the last resort, we must produce truth as we must produce wealth . . .

Truth isn't outside power, or lacking in power . . . Truth is a thing of this world: it is produced only by virtue of multiple forms of constraint. And it induces regular effects of power. *Each society has its regime of truth, its 'general politics' of truth: that is the type of discourse which it accepts and makes function as true; the mechanisms and instances which enable one to distinguish true and false statements, the means by which each is sanctioned; the techniques and procedures accorded value in the acquisition of truth; the status of those who are charged with saying what counts as true* . . . [Truth] is linked in a circular relationship with systems of power which produce and sustain it.

(Foucault, 1980: 93, 131; emphasis added)

Such regimes of truth make assumptions and values invisible; they turn subjective perspectives and understandings into apparently objective realities; and they determine some things to be self-evident and realistic while others appear to make no sense and are obviously impractical. In other words, they are means by which the ethical and political are transformed into the technical and managerial. Reverting to Levinas and the ethics of an encounter, we can see regimes of truth as personifying the 'will to know', through totalising discourses that force everything and everyone into the same way of thinking and acting.

Connecting with our earlier discussion of disciplinary power (see Chapter 1), such dominant discursive regimes or regimes of truth serve a disciplinary or regulatory function. They shape what we think, how we talk and in what ways we act. We can see this at work in what we have termed the Anglo-American discourse of 'early childhood education and care'. This increasingly dominant discourse – built around modern disciplines such as developmental psychology and concepts such as 'development', 'early intervention', 'outcomes' and 'quality' – can be seen as an emergent regime of truth. A whole swathe of people – parents, preschool workers, researchers, politicians – now speak of such disciplines and concepts as if they were self-evident and necessary, offering neutral and accurate representations of how the world is, rather than as value-laden and contestable perspectives.

But as we have already emphasised, we are not only or even mainly governed directly: dominant discourses do not primarily act coercively, forcing us into thinking and doing against our will. We also govern ourselves and we do so through dominant discourses, acting upon ourselves rather than being directly acted upon: we are willing converts to the truth, not forced to accept a creed to which in our souls we do not subscribe. In Chapter 1, we introduced the concept of government-ality for this idea of self-governing as an effect of dominant discourses – 'a pattern of power in which the self disciplines the self' (Fendler, 2001: 120).

One way in which this works is through the process of *subjectifica-tion*. Via dominating discourses and practices human beings construct themselves as subjects. We also introduced, in Chapter 1, a preschool example of this process: Fendler's analysis of 'developmentality' in con-temporary education, a term she deliberately creates as 'a way of allud-ing to Foucault's governmentality, and focusing on the self-governing effects of developmental discourse in curriculum debates'. Through tech-nologies such as 'developmental appropriate practice', Fendler argues, children learn to govern themselves and create themselves as subjects in relation to norms of development, flexibility, autonomy and problem solving. As we have already discussed, these norms define the ideal subject of modernity and liberalism.

In his analysis of processes of subjectification and self-government (what he refers to as 'a regime of the self'), Rose (1999) foregrounds further norms of freedom, choice and entrepreneurship. These, like Fendler's norms, can be understood as requirements of new forms of liberal economics and government, which strongly value markets, con-sumerism and autonomy as independence:

> Modern individuals are not merely 'free to choose', but *obliged to be free*, to understand and enact their lives in terms of choice. They must interpret their past and dream their future as outcomes of choices made or choices still to make . . . *They operate a regime of the self where competent personhood is thought to depend upon the continual exercise of freedom, and where one is encouraged to understand one's life, actually or potentially, not in terms of fate or social status, but in terms of one's success or failure in acquiring the skills and making the choices to actualise oneself* . . . Individuals act upon themselves and their families in terms of the languages, values and techniques made available to them by professions, disseminated through the apparatuses of the mass media or sought out by the troubled through the market. Thus, in a very significant sense, *it has become possible to govern without governing society – to govern through the 'responsibilized' and 'educated' anxieties and aspirations of individuals and their families.*
>
> (*ibid.*: 87–88; emphasis added)

In contemporary liberal societies, therefore, effective government, just as effective markets, depends on self-governing individuals, with 'appropriate' subjectivities. An important corollary of the process of self-government as described by Rose is how it leads to ever increasing, and more intensive, targeting of policy. As the 'new ethic of self-conduct disseminates', 'mechanisms of regulation through desire, consumption and the market . . . come to extend their sway over larger and larger sectors of the population' (*ibid.*: 87). In this context, government focuses its attention increasingly on 'marginalized individuals who through ill will, incompetence or misfortune are outside these webs of "consuming civility"'. More and more initiatives, projects, programmes sprout up, focused on those individuals and families who cannot or do not wish to govern themselves in the required way for many, with entry into the discipline of the labour market as a recurring theme (as in 'welfare to work' policies). The welfare state reduces its coverage, but brings increasingly powerful technologies to bear on the minorities it targets.

This talk of dominant discourses, regimes of truth, governmentality and subjectification may all seem rather depressing and hopeless, strongly suggesting that our lives are determined by powerful forces against which resistance is impossible. Worse still, as we described in Chapter 2, some would argue that regulation is increasing as part of a shift from societies of discipline to societies of control where new technologies and methods enable more continuous and effective processes of surveillance and governing. While Rose questions a simple shift from discipline to control, he acknowledges a 'multiplication of possibilities and strategies . . . the emergence of new control strategies and a reconfiguration of old ones' (*ibid.*: 240).

Such pessimism is not necessary. Power relations are always present, as the means by which individuals try to determine the behaviour of others. But resistance is possible. Foucault, for example, does not believe that dominant discourses and processes of subjectification are irresistible. Indeed, if this was the case, if resistance was impossible, we should need to speak of domination, not power relations. For power relations are not fixed, instead they are unstable, reversible and changeable (Foucault, 1987). Dominant discourses and subjectification can be subjected to what Foucault terms practices of freedom. So while we cannot free ourselves of power relations, 'we are not trapped – we always have possibilities of change' (Foucault in Rabinow, 2000: 167).

'Minor politics' in preschools might be viewed in this light. They might undermine the power exercised by dominant discourses through the way they govern what we see as the 'truth', what we accept as rational and how we construct the world – and hence our acting and doing. By enabling people to see from a different viewpoint, a necessity might become a possibility, the accepted wisdom just one way of seeing things. Picking up on themes from previous chapters, the introduction of 'minor politics' might, for example, move discussion from the application of 'developmentally appropriate practice' to the politics of developmentality; from the measurement of 'quality' to the politics of evaluating pedagogical work; or from speaking about targeting interventions on 'the child in need' to the politics of the image of the child. Such examples of minor politics might contribute to being governed less by dominant discourses.

Foucault's interest towards the end of his life moved towards more individual practices of freedom, in particular how we can be agents in shaping who we are – our subjectivity – through 'care of the self'. 'Care of the self' is not about being interested in ourselves or discovering our 'true' self. Rather it is a matter of whether and how we choose to constitute ourselves. It is about the possibility of the individual exerting power on himself/herself to create subjectivity, to 'invent, not discover, who we are' (Bernauer and Mahon, 1994: 147); and by so doing resist the forces of power and knowledge that otherwise fashion our subjectivity. Care of the self is the 'practice of an intellectual freedom that is transgression of modern knowledge–power–subjectivity relationships . . . which seeks to open the possibilities for new relations to self and events in the world' (*ibid.*: 152–153). It is a mode of self-formation and the way we fashion our freedom,

> the process in which the individual delimits that part of himself that will form the object of his moral practice, defines his position relative to the precept he will follow and decides on a certain mode of being that will serve as his moral goal. And this requires him to act upon himself, to monitor, test, improve and transform himself.
>
> (Foucault, 1986: 28)

Foucault refers to this idea of 'care of the self' as ethics. But it could also be seen as a political act. It provides a way of controlling and limiting power (Foucault, 1987) by challenging the effects of dominant discourse on the self and disturbing governmentality. As such, 'care of the self' is an individual practice related to the idea of minor politics as collective confrontation of dominant discourse. Put another way, care of the self might be viewed as yet another level of politics, practised by the individual below major and minor levels, but connected to them since care of the self could make one a better practitioner of politics with others: Foucault argued that care of the self 'renders one competent to occupy a place in the city, in the community or in interindividual relationships'. At the same time, 'minor politics' may create a supportive environment for practising 'care of the self', making space for critical thinking and democratic discussion about subjectification.

. . . and injustice, too

We have talked about the conduct of minor politics in preschools as a possible way of resisting connected forces: dominant discourses, governmentality and subjectification. Another possibility (and we do not suggest that this exhausts the possibilities) is minor politics as a confrontation of injustice. It will not come as a surprise to readers that the meaning of the concept of justice is not generally agreed, or rather is open to various interpretations from various perspectives.

One line of thought views justice as about *relations with the Other*. For Readings (1996), whom we quote at the start of this book, justice is a matter of respect for otherness, of listening to thought. For Derrida, influenced like Readings by Levinas, justice 'arises in a particular relationship to the Other, as a response to suffering that demands an infinite responsibility' (Critchley, 1999: 99). Justice here is closely connected to the practice of an ethics of an encounter: the part that the preschool might play in the pursuit of justice so understood has been discussed earlier.

An other perspective views the main concern of justice as the *distribution of material resources and social positions* (I. Young, 1990), a matter of 'fairness concerning the distribution of goods in society' (Gray, 2000: 15). While we believe preschools to be social institutions of the greatest potential importance, we see only a limited place for them in addressing distributional justice, and indeed are sceptical of some of the expectations of preschools as solutions to poverty, underpinning policies in countries like the USA and Britain. Material and positional inequalities are generated by powerful structural forces and power relations, and preschools are not the best means to counter these forces. True, preschools may contribute to raising family incomes through enabling maternal employment, but not necessarily; for example, a recent randomised controlled trial in London found that access to a preschool increased maternal employment but did not raise household income since most mothers ended up in low-paid employment (Toroyan *et al.*,

2003). Meanwhile preschools do nothing to reverse the growing income inequality occurring in most countries (Esping-Andersen *et al.*, 2001). Investing in preschools in the belief that they can cure poverty provides one example of a failure by many governments, not least those espousing a 'third way' approach, to 'grasp the systemic connections between global market forces and the variety of problems – from exclusion to environmental risk – that [the third way approach] pretends to tackle' (Mouffe, 2000b: 111). As well as not working, strategies of 'early intervention' may distract attention from structural analysis of the causes of inequality, including the current state of capitalism, and from taking action that addresses the results of such analysis.

More relevant to our discussion of 'minor politics' and the preschool are other conceptions of injustice that have attracted more recent attention, going beyond the 'distributive paradigm'. Fraser (1997) suggests justice has more than one dimension, distinguishing between material redistribution and recognition of difference. The struggle for recognition, she argues, is 'fast becoming the paradigmatic form of political conflict in the late twentieth century' (*ibid.*: 11). She 'assumes that justice today requires both redistribution and recognition' (*ibid.*: 12).

I. Young (1990) also sees justice as multi-faceted. Rather than focusing on distribution, she argues that 'a conception of justice should begin with the concepts of *domination and oppression* [which] brings out issues of decision-making, division of labor and culture that bear on social justice but are often ignored in philosophical discussions' (*ibid.*: 3). Oppression and domination overlap. But they are also different. Domination entails institutional constraints on self-determination. Oppression involves the institutional constraint on self-development, including violence, exploitation, marginalisation, powerlessness, and cultural imperialism. It is about 'how dominant meanings of society render particular perspectives of one's own group invisible and stereotype one's group' (*ibid.*: 59).

Young also criticises the 'distributional justice' paradigm for its static approach. It focuses on patterns of distribution at any one time, rather than the reproduction of patterns over time, the latter implying the need for a focus on 'procedural issues of participation in deliberation and decision-making' (*ibid.*: 34). This does not mean that justice is divorced from distribution; it requires certain distributional outcomes. But other issues, including decision-making, are as important. Justice 'requires participation in public discussion and processes of democratic decision-making. Democracy is an element and condition of social justice' (*ibid.*: 91). Hence, she argues, justice coincides with the concept of the political, politics referring to 'all aspects of institutional organisation, public action, social practices and habits and cultural meanings in so far as they are subject to collective evaluation and decision-making' (*ibid*.: 34).

Politics depends on spaces, 'forums to which everyone has access . . . where people encounter other people, meanings and issues they may not understand or identify with' (*ibid*.: 240). This, it seems to us, is a description of how preschools might be – if they are understood and constituted as public spaces, open to all children and families. They can then become one of many spaces where issues of social justice as oppression and domination can be confronted.

Power and empowerment

The possibilities for minor politics that we have just outlined – resisting dominant discourses, subjectification and injustice – share a common theme of disrupting power relations. What does power mean in this context and how does the disruption of power relations relate to the notion of 'empowerment', which has become a very popular idea in contemporary politics? We need to start by recapping and reviewing Foucault's ideas about power and power relations, which for us provide a complex and important understanding of these concepts.

Foucault sought to move discussion of power away from a sovereignty model, in which powerful bodies (e.g. the state) used coercive instruments (e.g. law) to force others to do their bidding. While not denying the existence of sovereign power, he was more interested in the pervasiveness and complexities of power, and the techniques by which it was practised, often without those involved being aware of the involvement of power – hence his exploration of disciplinary techniques, dominant discourses and governmentality. He talked about power relations, and about how no one can stand outside them. While some persons may have more power than others, power is ever present and everywhere. It both surrounds people and is wielded by them – we may be subjected to power, but we also exercise power. So while there are structural disparities in power as a resource, all of us are implicated in relations of power: 'in human relations, whatever they are – whether it be a question of communicating verbally . . . or a question of a love relationship, an institutional or economic relationship – *power is always present: I mean the relationship in which one wishes to direct the behaviour of another*' (Foucault, 1987: 11; emphasis added).

From a Foucauldian perspective, the concept of 'empowerment' is problematic in two ways. First, its view of power is simplistic.

It understands power as a commodity, some kind of stuff, which is unequally distributed and which can be redistributed: those who have less power can be given more by those who have more power, who by so doing reduce the amount of power they have. 'Empowerment' is another story of progress, on the road to emancipation. But, following Foucault, power is not stuff to be redistributed: power is relations, not a thing, and power relations constantly re-configure and seek to govern in new ways. Nor is power a dyadic relationship, but rather a complex network involving mediating agents and third parties.

There is no end point when power will have been equally distributed, nor is it possible to step outside power by giving it away. 'Empowerment' is not progress, but the creation of new relations of power. So when researchers, policy makers and practitioners talk about empowerment, for children or parents, at the same time they are still seeking to govern or regulate behaviour, not overtly through diktat ('You *must* do this or else you will be punished') but covertly through dominant discourses ('We should do this as this child is "in need" because her development is impaired'). The risk of empowerment is that by giving the impression of reducing power, it makes the workings of power relations more invisible and harder to resist.

Second, 'empowerment' contributes to governing through subjectification. It is about giving entry into the dominant discourse, enabling the individual to become the subject of liberalism, which, we would suggest, is why we talk about it so much now. Empowerment is a concept of inclusion and normalisation, drawing on the importance attached to autonomy and self-determination in liberalism. Empowerment starts with an 'excluded subject' and treats exclusion as

> lack of self-esteem, self-worth and the skills of self-management necessary to steer oneself as an active individual in the empire of choice. The relations that humans have with themselves are to be the target of professional reconstruction, often backed with the power of law. The beauty of empowerment is that it appears to reject the logics of patronizing dependency that infused earlier welfare modes of expertise. Subjects are to do the work on themselves, not in the name of conformity, but to make themselves free.
> (Rose, 1999: 268)

'Minor politics' would treat 'empowerment' sceptically and critically, in particular given the frequency of its use by government, professionals and others. It would ask why empowerment becomes so prominent in public discourse here and now, and treat empowerment as a contestable concept located within a dominant discourse of liberal politics, replete with unspoken assumptions and values. In other words, it would consider empowerment as an active part of power relations, contributing to the construction of the normal subject as an autonomous agent actively participating in the transformation of their conditions, being an entrepreneur of their own life. 'Minor politics' offers examples of politicising more territory; 'empowerment' programmes, by contrast, are examples of 'contemporary liberal rationalities of government that endeavour to operationalise the self-governing capacities of the governed in pursuit of governmental objectives' (Dean, 1999: 67). In a nutshell, minor politics is for a less governed subject, empowerment for a more self-governed subject.

We find Foucault's ideas very important for understanding a whole dimension of power, which is often invisible yet has great significance for how we think and act. But we do not want to leave the impression that there is no unequal distribution of power, that there is no overt coercion of the less powerful by the more powerful, that sovereign power is not an issue. These are all issues that have immense consequences for our societies and the lives we lead, and which at a global level are literally matters of life and death. The fact that, for example, every year 10 million children die of preventable diseases or that 1.2 billion people (one in five of the Earth's population) survive on less than $1 a day (United Nations Development Programme, 2003) has little to do with dominant discourses and everything to do with massive inequalities in economic, military and political power.

Nor should these blatant issues of power and inequality be entirely excluded from 'minor politics'. It is possible for preschools to be forums for the discussion of such issues and other major political questions; for example the state of the environment, matters of war and peace, global inequalities, the conditions of family life and the impact of increasing neoliberalism in the workplace. However, the ability to influence events, create a sense of crisis, effect change will depend more on the ability of such instances of minor politics, in Rose's words, '[to connect] up with a whole series of other circuits and [cause] them to fluctuate, waver and reconfigure in wholly unexpected ways'.

What do minor politics look like?

We have sketched out an idea of minor politics as the contesting, in 'cramped spaces', of dominant discourses, subjectification and injustice.

We will turn in the next chapter to consider some examples – actual or possible – of minor politics in the preschool. But before doing so, we conclude this chapter by pulling together some of the main ingredients of minor politics.

Minor politics involves a *constant critique* and takes a reflective attitude. It is questioning and induces stuttering, disrupting discourses and destabilising accepted meanings, denaturalising the taken-for-granted, opening up issues to confrontation and contestation. It makes us aware that our constructions are constructions, which are produced in particular contexts and shaped by particular discourses.

Minor politics has *a place for experts* – but keeps them in that place. This means the 'demonopolisation of expertise', saying 'farewell to the notion that administrations and experts always know exactly, or at least better, what is right and good for everyone' (Beck, 1994: 29). This includes recognising two types of science and knowledge: what Beck terms 'laboratory science' which 'penetrates and opens up the world mathematically and technically but [is] devoid of experience and encapsulated in a myth of precision'; and a 'public discursivity of experience' (*ibid.*: 30). These different sciences can be played off against each other, without one being privileged against the other. 'Laboratory scientific' knowledge is therefore not dismissed. But it is treated as perspectival knowledge that provides a partial and contestable account of the world.

Minor politics is premised on *irreducible alterity* and the *inevitability of conflict*, indeed the crucial role these have to play in a pluralist democracy. For such a democracy needs the idea of multiplicity or diversity, rather than totality or unity; while conflict is not just the result of competing interests, but arises due to diverse concepts of the good and because of competing interpretations. Minor politics is *antirational*, too, in that it does not assume or envisage 'the creation of a rational consensus reached through appropriate deliberative procedures whose aim is to produce decisions that represent an impartial standpoint equally in the interests of all' (Mouffe, 2000a: 86). Not only difference but passions cannot be eliminated or confined to the private sphere, but they can be mobilised towards democratic designs.

In adopting this view of minor politics, we align ourselves with a model of politics that Mouffe (2000a, 2000b) has called 'agonistic pluralism', in contrast to two other models: antagonistic politics and deliberative democracy. Both of these are inscribed with rationalistic individualism. The former – 'antagonistic politics' – treats holders of opposing views as enemies to be overcome. The latter – 'deliberative democracy' – is closely linked to the ideas of the German thinker Jürgen Habermas (1929–), and has become influential in politics and policy in many countries in recent years. It seeks to avoid confrontation and efface the antagonistic dimension in politics, believing instead in the possibility of rational consensus arrived at through free, unconstrained public deliberation between free and equal citizens, brought about by the application of certain procedures summed up as Ideal Speech.

Mouffe criticises these models on various grounds, taking particular issue with deliberative democracy. She argues that it seeks to deny conflict and passions, different interests and alterity:

> The prime task of democratic politics is not, as deliberative demo-crats argue, to eliminate passions or to relegate them to the private sphere in order to establish a rational consensus in the public sphere. It is to mobilise those passions towards democratic designs . . . To deny that there ever could be a free and unconstrained public deliberation of all about matters of common concern is therefore crucial for democratic politics. When we accept that every con-sensus exists as a temporary result of a provisional hegemony, as a stabilisation of power, and that it always entails some form of exclusion, we can begin to envisage the nature of a democratic public sphere in a different way. Modern democracy's specificity lies in the recognition and legitimisation of conflict and the refusal to suppress it by imposing authoritian order.
>
> (Mouffe, 2000a: 92)

Agonistic pluralism does not believe it is possible to eradicate differ-ence, or even desirable to try. Ineradicable pluralism is at total odds with the idea of rational consensus (Mouffe, 2000a). But the inevitable conflict should not be a conflict between out-and-out enemies, as in 'antagonistic politics', but a struggle between opponents or adversaries: adversaries, or 'friendly enemies', with whom we share the common ground of 'adhesion to the ethico-political principles of liberal demo-cracy [liberty and equality, but with whom] we disagree concerning the meaning and implementation of those principles, and such a disagree-ment is not one that can be resolved through deliberation and rational discussion' (Mouffe, 2000b: 102).

According to an agonistic struggle one should not erase passions and send them away to the private sphere in order to bring about a rational consensus in the public. The task is rather to tame the passions in order to mobilise them for democratic goals, through collective forms of identification around democratic goals. 'A functioning democracy calls for confrontation between political positions' (Mouffe, 2000a: 90), so too much focus on consensus leads to apathy and a reluctance to participate in politics.

This idea of agonistic pluralism shares much in common with an approach to politics termed 'perspectival dialogism' (Yeatman, 1994). Both assume and value conflict and confrontation, and both recognise irreducible difference and no privileged position. Rather than consensus, the ambition is the possibility that agreement or compromise between different perspectives may be negotiated. This represents a provisional settlement that may serve for a period, but which is always liable to re-examination and re-negotiation: 'compromises are, of course, also possible; they are part and parcel of politics; but they should be seen as temporary respites in an ongoing confrontation' (Mouffe, 2000b: 102).

Minor politics, without the traditions and structures of major politics, offers possibilities for *creativity and experimentation*, in the form that politics take, in the questions that are identified and in the answers that are produced. At its best, minor politics should stimulate original and creative solutions, produce new knowledges, and open the way for new possibilities for thought, reasoning and practice. It is part of a metamorphosis of the modern state and its democratic practice. Beck (1994) argues that the 'authoritarian decision and action state gives way to the negotiation state', and quotes Hans Ensensberger: the 'core of today's politics is the ability of self-organisation . . . that begins with the most ordinary things: school issues, tenants' problems or traffic regulations' (39, 38). Self-organisation, says Beck, 'means (reflexive) sub-politicization of society' (*ibid.*: 38–39), and sub-politics means 'shaping society from below' with increasing opportunities for participation for 'groups hitherto uninvolved in the substantive technification and industrialization process' (*ibid.*: 23).

Minor politics, according to Rose, is conducted in *'cramped spaces' and engages with small everyday concerns*. We take it that preschools, and other institutions for children, would constitute 'cramped spaces', and that Rose's references to 'small concerns' and 'little territories of the everyday', could refer to a range of issues that arise in these spaces, issues that are not trivial or unimportant but which have been treated as such by major politics and its (mainly male) practitioners – just as Beck explicitly cites 'school issues' as an example of those 'most ordinary things' that he says are at the 'core of today's politics'. In fact, the issues that might form the content of minor politics in the preschool, some of which we shall discuss in the next chapter, are of great moment – to the individual, to the institution and to the wider community. 'Minor politics' presents the possibility of rescuing them from the depoliticised territory of the private sphere of the family, or the technical sphere of service delivery.

Chapter 7

The preschool as a site for democratic politics

From Beyond Quality in Early Childhood Education and Care *by Dahlberg et al. (1999)*:

[The preschools in Reggio Emilia have] a pedagogical practice located in a profound understanding of young children in relation to the world and a philosophical perspective, which in many respects seems to us postmodern ... [Some of the elements] of that practice, understanding and perspective [are]: choosing to adopt a social constructionist approach; challenging and deconstructing dominant discourses; realising the power of these discourses in shaping and governing our thoughts and actions, including the field of early childhood pedagogy; rejecting the prescription of rules, goals, methods and standards, and in so doing risking uncertainty and complexity; having the courage to think for themselves in constructing new discourses, and in so doing daring to make the choice of understanding the child as a rich child, a child of infinite capabilities, a child born with a hundred languages; building a new pedagogical project, foregrounding relationships and encounters, dialogue and negotiation, reflection and critical thinking; border-crossing disciplines and perspectives, replacing either/or positions with an and/also openness; and understanding the contextualised and dynamic nature of pedagogical practice ...

Pedagogical documentation [is] a vital tool for the creation of a reflective and democratic pedagogical practice. But pedagogical documentation is important for other reasons. It has a central role in the discourse of meaning making. Rather than rely on some standardised measure of quality, as in the discourse of quality, pedagogical documentation enables us to take responsibility for making our meanings and coming to our own decisions about what is going on ...

Pedagogical documentation also contributes to the democratic project of the early childhood institution by providing the means for

> pedagogues and others to engage in dialogue and negotiation about pedagogical work.
>
> (122, 145)

In this chapter we offer some examples of how preschools and their practices can become sites for democratic minor politics. The examples described are just a few of many that exist: we do not claim to offer anything like a comprehensive review. They include only some possibilities, for one hallmark of 'minor politics' is its creativity: the potential is almost limitless.

Nor would the examples we offer necessarily identify themselves as practising minor politics, and some might 'even refuse their designation as politics at all'. 'Politics' is our reading of what they are doing. But what they all have in common is that they exemplify the possibility of confronting and resisting power relations – dominant discourses or subjectification or injustice – and having 'the courage to think for themselves'.

By their attention to practice and thinking for themselves, the examples in this chapter might be said to be engaged in a 'politics of emancipation'. By 'emancipation', we are not speaking of freeing the self from obligation and responsibility; nor do we refer to some process of revealing and freeing one's 'true self'. Rather we refer to a tradition which links emancipation to praxis – 'our historically and culturally embedded life as finite selves in a world that is of our own making' – and to a critique of praxis:

> critique is a critique of existing praxis because it is felt to be unjust, unfree and untrue, or whatever. Furthermore, it is a critique that aims towards an emancipation from that unjust praxis towards another individual or collective praxis, a different way of conceiving of human life.
>
> (Critchley, 2001: 74)

Pedagogical documentation: the minor politics of pedagogical work

The municipal preschools in Reggio Emilia offer a good example of the way that major and minor politics can work together. Major politics (at the local authority level) provides space for minor politics in individual preschools. It also creates opportunities for connecting up minor politics through strong networks of association between individual municipal preschools operating within a framework of shared political values and pedagogical theories. Indeed Reggio illustrates the potential importance of the group of preschools (and other institutions); and, by so doing, also provokes questioning of the value attached by advanced liberalism to the autonomous individual institution (the mirror image of the autonomous individual subject) competing as an enterprise with other autonomous institutions/enterprises for a share of the market.

One of the results of a 'local cultural project on childhood' – a continuing project now in its fortieth year (in 2004) – has been the creation in Reggio of a new pedagogical project. This project, as the quotation starting the chapter suggests, consists of a rich amalgam of theories, understandings and practices, produced through a process of deconstructing dominant discourses and constructing new ones, rejecting normalising practices and being open to a multitude of influences. An important part of this process has been played by pedagogical documentation, our first example of how the preschool can be made a site for minor politics but which we have already introduced and described in earlier chapters in relation to evaluation (Chapter 4) and learning (Chapter 5).

If the preschool can be the site or locus for minor and democratic politics, then pedagogical documentation is a process for practising these politics, including the many groups, interests and perspectives involved with preschools. But this is possible only when the process of documentation is understood and undertaken as an exercise in critical thinking and agonistic pluralism, where conflict and dissensus, passion and alterity are not only tolerated but welcomed. Pedagogical documentation makes learning visible: but it goes beyond this and by so doing enters the political sphere, making what is visible subject to interpretation, critique and argumentation. By taking this vital second step, by becoming minor politics, pedagogical documentation can enable dominant discourses to be challenged rather than reinforced, normative frameworks to be transgressed rather than more tightly drawn, governmentality to be undermined rather than applied.

Pedagogical documentation is a tool for evaluation as meaning making, an approach we discussed in Chapter 4. This, we might say, is evaluation as minor politics, whereas quality (or excellence) is evaluation as technical practice. By making pedagogical work visible and subject to interpretation and argumentation within a community of participants (what Santos referred to in Chapter 5 as an 'interpretive community'), pedagogical documentation provides one means for making judgements of value – so different to the normalising judgements associated with evaluation as quality. Evaluation becomes a democratic process, and a (provisional) decision in which people are active participants and for which they must take responsibility – not delegating responsibility to the expert, the legislator and the inspector.

Pedagogical documentation illustrates the potentially close relationship between ethics and democratic politics. We could say that pedagogical documentation is a tool both for ethics – understood as the sphere of the undecidable – and for the political – understood as the search, through negotiation and compromise, for what is acceptable and for the negotiation of provisional agreements (for example between a diverse group of pedagogues or parents, or pedagogues and parents). We could also say that pedagogical documentation with meaning making is a form of evaluation that constitutes a practice of what Rose terms 'ethico-politics'. This, as we discussed in Chapter 6, strives to avoid closure by opening up 'the evaluation of forms of life and self-conduct to the difficult and interminable business of debate and contestation' (Rose, 1999: 192). In sharp contrast, the concept of evaluation as quality is an example of technical practice which 'seeks to close off ethical debate by appealing to the authority of a true discourse and, hence, inescapably to the authority of those who are experts of this truth' (*ibid.*).

Pedagogical documentation – through making practice subject to reflection, argumentation and interpretation, without appealing to authority – can serve many purposes: learning through co-constructing what Santos calls local and emancipatory knowledge; evaluation as meaning making; and a minor politics through opening up dialogue and difference, deconstructing and reconstructing discourses. What all of these have in common is children and adults being governed less and opening up to new possibilities.

The Mosaic Approach: the minor politics of children's participation

The Mosaic Approach owes a lot to the theory and practice of pedagogical documentation, involving a process for assembling, reflecting upon and interpreting diverse types of material that document facets of the preschool. But whereas the attention of pedagogical documentation has been focused on learning processes and the relationship between child and educator, the Mosaic Approach has emerged from a different interest: children's experience of and views about preschools coming from an interest in the concept of children's participation.

There has been a burgeoning interest in children's participation in recent years. There is evidence of this interest at international, national and local levels. The UN Convention on the Rights of the Child, agreed in 1989, has increased awareness of the importance of children's participation, including recognising the importance of their views. Article 12 specifies that

> parties shall assure to the child who is capable of forming his or her own views the right to express those views freely in all matters affecting the child, the views of the child being given due weight in accordance with the age and maturity of the child

while Article 13 says that

> the child shall have the right to freedom of expression; this right shall include freedom to seek, receive and impart information and ideas of all kinds, regardless of frontiers, either orally, in writing or in print, in the form of art, or through any other media of the child's choice.

There have been moves at governmental level to introduce mechanisms for listening to the views and experiences of children. An increasing number of countries have appointed a Children's Commissioner, or Ombudsman (Scottish Parliament, 2002): at least 18 countries at the end of 2002 (including Sweden) with more announced since (including Scotland and England). In England, to give another example, the government has produced 'Core Principles of Participation', with supporting guidance to government departments on participation by children and young people: 'the Principles provide a framework that government departments have to work to in order to increase the effective involvement of children and young people in the design and provision of policies and services' (English Children and Young Persons Unit, 2001). At a service level, there has been a growth over the past 15 years in organisations seeking the views of 'users'. This has begun to include children and young people, where children's views are in some instances gathered about health and welfare services, but less frequently about education. The language of consumerism, too, has had an impact in this area, with children increasingly viewed as consumers not only of products like clothing but also of services, consumers whose preferences can be sought.

This growing discourse of children's participation provokes what might be termed general questions about the concept and practice of participation, in that these questions apply to all ages and settings. For example, some of the potential problems with participation raised in discussions of 'participatory approaches' in the field of development studies could equally be applied to children's participation:

> The proponents of participatory development have generally been naïve about the complexities of power and power relations. This is the case not only 'on the ground', between 'facilitators' and 'participants', between 'participants' and more widely between 'donors' and 'beneficiaries', but also historically and discursively in the construction of what constitutes knowledge and social norms. While analyses of power in participation are not new, what is evident here is that there are multiple and diverse ways in which this power is expressed; furthermore, articulations of power in participation are very often less visible, being as they are embedded in social and cultural practices.
>
> (Cooke and Kothari, 2001: 14)

The underlying question here is whether participation is understood as a process of improving communication and better articulating preferences – empowering the individual as practitioner of choice – or whether participation is seen as part of a practice of minor politics, concerned as such with confronting manifestations of power relations such as dominant discourses and governmentality. Or put another way, to what extent are knowledge, values, assumptions and outcomes treated as givens; or how far are these viewed as open to question and infinite possibilities? Is participation intended to make for smoother governing, or to being governed less? Is participation a tactic or programme to be applied from time to time, or is it 'a value, an identifying feature of the entire experience' (Cagliari *et al.*, 2004)? We return to these questions in the next section on parents, only noting here that such questions apply as much to children as they do to adults.

There are also issues more specifically related to age. Within this expanding area of policy and practice, less attention has been given to the participation of young children (i.e. those below the age of 6 or 7 years). One reason relates to the methods necessary for listening to and responding to the views and experiences of young children, including those who are pre-verbal. There are also ethical considerations in considering young children's abilities to participate together with their need for protection.

But there has been some work. In the late 1980s, as part of the BASUN Project (a study of Modern Childhood in the Nordic Countries), groups of 5-year-olds across the five Nordic countries were interviewed about their daily lives both at home and in preschool (Langsted, 1994). Subsequently, a body of work involving listening to young children has developed in some of these countries. More recently, innovative work has been undertaken elsewhere. (For a review of work in England see Clark *et al.*, 2003, which includes a review of Danish work in this area by Hanne Warming.)

Young children (from infancy through to school age) and their participation in the preschools they attend were the subjects of a study conducted in London between 1999 and 2001. A framework was developed by a researcher for better understanding young children's experiences and perspectives about the preschools they attend (for fuller details, see Clark and Moss, 2001). The focus was on children's lived experiences and the framework – named the *Mosaic Approach* – had a number of distinctive features. It was adaptable, making it applicable across a wide range of provisions for young children. It was participatory, starting from the point of view that children are experts in their own lives (Langsted, 1994). It was multi-method, recognising the multiple languages of childhood, and using a range of different ways of documenting children's views and everyday experience; not only can this range expand over time, but the actual assemblage of methods can be chosen to suit particular children or settings.

Finally, it was reflective, recognising (following the ideas about listening from Reggio, see Chapter 5) that listening is an active process, which involves not just receiving but also interpretation and the constructing of meaning. Bartlett (1999) uses the phrase a 'mosaic of perspectives' for the process of listening to young children. The Mosaic Approach takes this further by adding a reflexive and interpretive dimension, able to include children and adults, both family members and preschool workers. The Mosaic Approach therefore, like pedagogical documentation, involves both the gathering of materials and dialogue, reflection and interpretation of these documents.

In the study in which the Mosaic Approach was developed, the multiple methods used with children under 5 years, attending a London preschool, included: observation based around the two questions 'What is it like to be here?' and 'Do you listen to me?'; child conferencing, a method for interviewing children covering, for example, favourite and disliked activities; cameras with which the children themselves took photographs, enabling them to represent visually their perspective of the preschool; tours of the preschool, an exploration of the institution led and recorded by children, making an audiotape, drawing and taking photographs; mapping the preschool, after the tour and with the help of photographs taken during the tour; and role playing, using play figures and play equipment. The methods used varied somewhat according to the age of the children. For example, role playing was used with children under 2 years, while photography was used by 3- and 4-year-olds, although these children also used cameras to record the lives of younger children in the preschool – a 'children about children' approach. Parents' and practitioners' perspectives on children's lives were also sought, mostly through interviews: for example, parents were asked what they thought would constitute a good or bad day for their children.

This varied documentation was then brought together to stimulate dialogue, reflection and interpretation. Dialogue took place between children, between practitioners and the researcher, between older preschool children and the researcher, between parents, children and the researcher, and between practitioner groups and the researcher. An example of working with the Mosaic Approach – with one child, Gary – is given below, to show how it works in practice and to give some indication of its possibilities.

Gary at preschool

Gary attended the preschool in central London where the Mosaic Approach was developed. The researcher first worked with Gary when he was three and a half years old, then again five months later. The methods used in working with Gary included: drawing; photography, Gary using a disposable camera; child conferencing; observation; Gary making a tour of the preschool; Gary making a map of the preschool with his friends; and interviews with a parent and worker. These different pieces of the mosaic, which Gary had been active in gathering, were brought together to provide documentation from which interpretations could be made of the important parts of his life at preschool. What seemed to emerge from the documentation were certain themes, priorities for Gary in his preschool: places to hide; outside space for imaginative games; time to play with his friend; the bikes; grown-ups keeping order; and having time for places, family and friends outside the preschool.

For example, the child conferencing provided an interesting starting-point for discussion. In July, Gary had named the slide as 'what he liked best' about the preschool. In November this had changed to 'going in my cave and working in the desert and listening to my music in my cave. It's very dark so I need my torch. It's a magic torch.' This response was echoed in Gary's answer to where his favourite place was in the preschool: 'In my cave listening to music. It's magic music from my magic radio.' Gary had then shown the researcher where the cave was during the tour he gave her of the site. It was a circular bench on a small piece of grass in the outside play area. He took a photograph of the cave and also included it on his map.

These themes became the focus for dialogue, reflection and interpretation with Gary, his friends, his mother and his key worker. Dialogue with Gary's mother and key worker made some of these impressions clearer, whilst in other instances it revealed differences of perspective. Gary's key worker, for example, also commented on the importance of the outside space to Gary and his friends, but was surprised to find out about a child that Gary was adamant he did not like.

The material gathered in this study, about the experience and views of Gary and other children who participated in the Mosaic Approach, was additionally used as part of an evaluative dialogue with the staff of the preschool, looking at what it is like for children to be in this place. First, the researcher discussed with staff the materials gathered by the children, including documentation about the babies who participated. These in turn formed questions for further reflection and action, beginning with discussion of questions the researcher had formed from working with Gary and reflecting on the documentation:

> Do you give me space to hide?
> Do you let me play on the grass?
> Do you give me time to make up my own games?
> Do you let me play on the bikes?
> Do you allow me to see my brother?
> Do you ask me what I think before changing the garden?

Two particular issues were taken as points for future action: wider consultation with children about the use of outside spaces; and possibilities within the preschool for siblings to play together. Discussions also considered the more fundamental question of how listening to young children can increase, among so many other agendas.

The Mosaic Approach opens up a space for listening to young children, and a creative methodology for their inclusion in minor politics. Children's perspectives – their perspectives on the institutions created for them by adults – can place a stutter in adult narratives about preschools and pedagogical work, and offer other more local narratives spoken by children. They can be a provocation to an outcome-focused instrumental rationality, by reminding us that preschools are places where children increasingly live their childhoods, and which may be valued by children for social, emotional, aesthetic and many other reasons, not all necessarily defined by adults as desirable out-comes. On a more specific note, methods such as the Mosaic Approach offer opportunities for children to shape the environment (inside and out), the practices and other aspects of their preschools, informing decision making.

Little narratives: the minor politics of parent involvement

Hughes and MacNaughton (2000) have examined the recent attention – we might say regime of truth – given to parents' becoming involved in their children's preschools. They conclude that most of the burgeon-ing literature places parents in a subordinate position to preschool workers, especially with respect to knowledge where scientific (and universal) knowledge trumps experiential (and local) knowledge: 'pro-fessional knowledge of the child is "developmental" (scientific), object-ive, norm-referenced and applicable to all children . . . [while] parental knowledge of the child is anecdotal, subjective, ad hoc, individualised and applicable only to specific children' (ibid.: 243). In the literature, parental knowledge is mainly treated as unimportant (i.e. parents are absent), as inadequate (i.e. parents are ignorant and need pro-grammes to educate them), or as supplementary (i.e. parents are spoken of as collaborators, but in reality their knowledge is treated as merely secondary).

Hughes and MacNaughton question the commonly proffered solu-tion – improving communications between parents and staff. Instead, they argue that 'communication cannot improve relationships between staff and parents unless it addresses the politics of knowledge underpin-ning them' (ibid.: 247). Or viewed from our perspective, without making relations between staff and parents a subject of minor politics, and defining minor politics in this case as a contested politics of epistemo-logy. Defining the subject as 'improving communications' risks slippage into the discourse of 'empowerment'. Instead, from a minor politics perspective the subject becomes contesting power relations, including resisting dominant discourses and forms of injustice.

How might 'minor politics' in this case be practised? The authors examine two possibilities. The first relates to deliberative democracy, a concept introduced in Chapter 6. Staff and parents could seek consensus about their knowledge of young children and design programmes that reflect this consensus. Using this approach would be informed by the work of Habermas, in particular his notion that public negotiation of difference and the formation of consensus can be achieved through the use of Ideal Speech.

The possibility of rational consensus created through Ideal Speech has been subject to wide-ranging criticism, both for the supposition underlying it (that it is possible to create conditions where in practice everyone can be included in deliberation on a free and equal basis) and for its goal of consensus. Mouffe, a firm believer in 'agonistic pluralism', as we also saw in Chapter 6, argues that Habermas, by envisaging a well-ordered democratic society without exclusions or antagonisms, cannot grasp the crucial role of conflict and its integrative function in a pluralist democracy: 'taking pluralism seriously requires that we give up on the dream of a rational consensus which entails the fantasy that we could escape from our human form of life' (Mouffe, 2000b: 98). While relating this general critique to the 'cramped space' of early childhood education, Hughes and MacNaughton conclude that

> the attainment of absolute, 'undistorted' truth in and through Ideal Speech necessarily implies the end of philosophy, the end of critical thinking. In that sense, if staff and parents reach consensus about the child and how best to care for and educate her/him, early childhood education as a discipline will disappear, rendered irrelevant by the coincidence of parental and professional knowledge.
> (2000: 251)

An other possibility for forming a new relationship between parents and staff is not based on a consensus view of the child but on many views, and opens up to exploring the power–knowledge relations around each one. In this case, Hughes and MacNaughton turn to the work of the French thinker Jean-François Lyotard (1907–1998) and his idea of 'little narratives'. Lyotard argued for the virtues of disagreement or dissensus for creating change and emancipation: for from his perspective 'consensus is the end of freedom and of thought . . . [since]

emancipation depends on the perpetuation of dissensus, that is, on a permanent crisis of representation, on an ever greater awareness of the contingent and localized – the unstable – nature of all norms for representing the world' (Bertens, 1995: 127).

Challenging the privileged status given to scientific knowledge, as a true representation of the world, Lyotard proposed that our descriptions of the world have no direct connection with it. They are language games taking the form of narratives. We describe the world about us by telling stories about it: but those within such narratives often cannot see them for what they are – stories. Hughes and MacNaughton argue that, from Lyotard's perspective, early childhood education is a 'local' culture that has come to be dominated by a narrative game called developmentalism, a meta-narrative which claims to tell universal truth about children based on scientific knowledge (note here the similarity of 'developmentalism' to Fendler's concept of 'developmentality', discussed in Chapter 1).

> Early childhood staff legitimise their work with young children within the narrative language game that constitutes that work – they refer to it as 'developmentally appropriate practice'... [D]evelopmentalism presents itself as a 'science' and is, accordingly, regarded as the 'universal truth'. When, however, developmentalism is redefined as a narrative language game, it becomes a 'local truth' valid only in specific socio-historical circumstances.
>
> (Hughes and MacNaughton, 2000: 252)

Hughes and MacNaughton suggest that early childhood staff seeking equitable communication with parents are likely to find Lyotard more helpful than Habermas. They use the example of a parents' meeting in an Australian preschool about a gender equality programme, a subject that evokes very differing responses. They describe this as a 'little narrative' about gender which captures various understandings, desires and feelings about gender, generates new questions and ideas about gender and generates new rules about how to discuss gender in the preschool (e.g. there are several equally valid ways to discuss an issue). Such 'little narratives', as described below, can become instances of minor politics:

> [The head of the preschool] and the parents could share their little narrative with other parents and staff via newsletters and noticeboards, inviting others to express their views about gender. In doing so, these other people would add to the narrative and

create a continuing dialogue about gender within the centre. As staff and parents co-author such 'little narratives' about issues that arise in and through staff and parents' daily contacts with children – for example, gender – the knowledge–power relationship would shift. From hierarchies of expertise, in which staff (the experts) instruct parents (the non-experts) about the issue, the relationship can become partnerships in which staff and parents co-author 'little narratives' and the questions, ideas and rules that they generate.

(*ibid.*: 255)

Hughes and MacNaughton show how parental involvement can be reconceptualised in terms of building local democracy rather than, as often presented, as an instrumental means to improve outcomes and performance through more effective governing. They also show how there are choices about the practice of 'minor politics' in preschools serving as sites of democratic practice. One such choice is between a Habermasian search for communicative procedures that will lead to consensus and Lyotard's enthusiasm for dissensus, 'revelling in the diverse ideas emerging from uncertainty . . . [and challenging] the "traditional" view that expertise is neutral, independent and external to social relations' (*ibid.*: 256).

This idea of parental involvement as democratic practice and dissensus as a necessary condition of minor politics also permeates the work in Reggio Emilia. It is indeed regarded as a fundamental value, 'an identifying feature of the entire experience, a way of viewing those involved in the educational process and the role of the school' (Cagliari *et al.*, 2004: 29). It is the expression of a deep commitment to democracy, making the preschool a place where democracy is lived out on a daily basis.

Writing about the centrality of participation to the Reggio Emilian project, and what they mean by participation, three *pedagogistas* (pedagogical advisors, each working with a small group of preschools) describe participation (of children, staff and others, as well as parents) as based on a number of shared concepts:

the idea that reality is not objective, that culture is a constantly evolving product of society, that individual knowledge is only partial and that in order to construct a project, especially an educational project, everyone's point of view is relevant in dialogue with those of others within a framework of shared values. The idea of participation is founded on these concepts and in our opinion so, too, is democracy itself.

(ibid.: 29)

Democracy, in short, is impossible where some claim *the* truth and privileged access to knowledge. Participation also means understanding the preschool in a particular way, as 'a social and political place and thus an educational place in the fullest sense'. But this understanding is not inevitable, self-evident, a given: 'it is a philosophical choice, a choice based on values'. It is just as possible to understand preschools as technical sites providing good opportunities for transmitting a certain body of uncontested knowledge (e.g. child development) to parents.

Another condition of participation as minor politics is a respect for others as competent participants. Many schools, the *pedagogistas* argue, are unable to see parents in this light. This is partly because they do not see themselves as social and political places and therefore fail to see the competency of parents as citizens; and partly because they prioritise specialised subject knowledge that, mostly, parents do not have. Taking a different perspective, Reggio preschools view everyone – parents, children, staff – as competent and able to become more so:

> [Competency] is a recognition of value that schools must give to parents, as well as to children and teachers. This recognition – again a choice based on values – is an acknowledgement of the citizen's right to engage in the discussion of social issues that concern everyone. Parents are therefore competent because they have and develop their own experience, points of view, interpretations and ideas, which are articulated in implicit and explicit theories and are the fruit of their experience as both parents and citizens. In another sense, competency is a process that is nurtured and enriched precisely by the participation process.

(ibid.: 30)

Given these conditions, given this paradigmatic mindset and its attendant choices, parental involvement can form an important part of minor politics in preschools (or schools). It can take place in many ways, including formal participation in management structures, pedagogical documentation and a wide range of 'little narratives'. But it cannot be formalised or programmed. Participation, the *pedagogistas* conclude, 'is not a model that can be reproduced and above all it is not a series of sequential events. It is an experience and a process whose contents and strategies are interconnected and interdependent and which generate unique and original paths' (*ibid*.: 30).

Reading critically

The increasing technologising of preschool policy and practice brings with it an increasing weight of paper, advising, guiding or insisting on what should be done and how – policy documents, research reports, curricula, standards, guidance on best practice, and so on. This growing mountain of official or expert paper becomes a prime means of governing preschool practitioners, laying down norms to which they must conform and contributing to a dominant discourse that smothers contestability and advances conformity. At the same time it crowds out other types of reading which might provide other perspectives. Reading thus becomes a means of closure and regulation rather than opening up to new possibilities and emancipation.

In such circumstances, one way to practise minor politics is to make some space, however difficult and limited this may be, to read non-prescribed texts that might provoke questioning. Another is to read at least some official/expert documents critically. Sevenhuijsen provides an example of applying such practice to an important Dutch policy document intended to provide the basis for decision making about the availability of and access to health care services. Her starting-point is the absence of a feminist approach to health care in the document, and she describes her critical approach as 'an exercise in the gender-reading of a public policy document' (Sevenhuijsen, 1998: 123). However, documents can be read critically from many perspectives.

She argues that policy documents can be analysed as vehicles of normative paradigms, a paradigm understood here as a means of regulation, a 'configuration of knowledge which orders the description of social problems'. These policy texts therefore are sites of power, because they govern what it is possible to think and say.

> Their modes of speaking structure the way individuals and social groups (in this case women and their political representatives) can formulate legitimate speaking positions and acceptable considerations, thus creating a distinct profile for themselves in the public sphere. By establishing narrative conventions, authoritative repertoires of interpretation and frameworks of argumentation and communication, *[these texts] confer power upon preferred modes of speaking and judging and upon certain ways of expressing moral and political subjectivity.*

Through examining official documents in this way it becomes possible to trace both the overt and hidden gender-load contained in the vocabulary. And it can help us to analyse the inclusionary and exclusionary effects of texts with regard to gender by examining the degree to which they are able to speak about women and issues of gender.

(*ibid*.: 123: emphasis added)

However, it is not just official policy documents that require critical reading by all concerned with preschools. So too does research, which is often offered as legitimation for particular technologies and can become a means for depoliticising policy and practice through scientifically based truth claims. Cherryholmes (1993) has shown how research can be read and interpreted in many ways, depending on the perspective with which the reader approaches the research – another case of minor politics in practice.

As an example he uses a well-known piece of American educational research, which he reads from three different perspectives: feminist, critical and deconstructive. This perspectival approach means rejecting 'fundamentalist tendencies to view texts as autonomous . . . [and recognising] that truth (capital T) and grounded meaning in any final or transcendental sense are not within our grasp' (*ibid*.: 3): facts about objects and events may be one thing, what they mean something else altogether. This leads Cherryholmes to argue that research findings 'tell stories' (a similar metaphor to Lyotard's 'narratives'), so that 'scientific texts cannot be decisively separated from those that are non-scientific', nor can literary texts 'be definitely and sharply set apart from non-literary texts' (*ibid*.: 5).

The conclusion drawn from this exercise in reading from different perspectives is that reading, and therefore research, cannot be neutral:

Interpretation requires choices and choices cannot be made without reference to values and preferences . . . [But] questions about 'getting things right' dominate contemporary research while questions of aesthetics and ethics and culture and language and community are shunned. Ethical questions are rarely posed by empiricists and then are usually limited to issues of treating research subjects (objects?) fairly . . . The emperor or empress, as you wish, of educational action and knowledge is not clothed with privileged knowledge, with empirical certainties, with grounded meaning, or with truth, protestations to the contrary notwithstanding. The positions that have been called positivism and empiricism were always problematic . . . We have been and are choosing community and a way of life and not simply generating knowledge with our research and reading. We are responsible for the stories we find within, upon and against the texts of research . . . [but] an inability to accept the obligations of reading always resided within us and remains difficult to resist.

(ibid.: 27, 28)

Cherryholmes's message is an important one at a time when research is increasingly offered to us as providing secure evidential foundations on which policy and practice can be built with certainty and universality. From a technological perspective, research on preschools makes truth claims which tell policy makers and practitioners what to do: it is the 'what works' part of the dominant Anglo-American discourse of early childhood education and care. But viewed from the perspective of 'minor politics', research (like other expert prescriptions) offers a story that can be read, interpreted and used in many different ways, and proposes *a* truth not *the* truth. The reader, therefore, has a choice to make about the stories and the truths she finds in the text, and bears a responsibility for that choice.

A politics of difference

Many preschools in many countries have begun to address diversity among children, parents and staff, and by so doing have opened up difference as a subject for minor politics. One of the most striking examples is the Sheffield Children's Centre in the north of England (this section draws heavily on Meleady and Broadhead, 2002, as well as an interview by one of the authors [PM] with Chrissy Meleady, the chair of the Centre, and Pat Broadhead, a researcher who has evaluated the work of the Centre). The Centre started in the early 1980s as a local community initiative in a materially poor inner city area. It now provides services in Sheffield for 700 children and young people from infancy to 18 years, as well as for their families. There are a range of 'core' services: early childhood education and care, free-time and play services (for school-age children outside school hours), and various forms of family support including a variety of health services, language workshops, a contact centre where children can meet parents from whom they are separated, provision for children with terminal illnesses, on-site and off-site access to a wide range of adult training opportunities, and an advocacy, welfare rights and legal support service. Then there is a plethora of other activity, which comes and goes depending on local demands and conditions: domestic violence work; work with gypsy and traveller families; a national support network for male childcare workers; advocacy work and many support groups for diverse minorities including victims of institutional child sexual abuse in Ireland, and for gay, lesbian, bi-sexual and trans-gender parents; running a credit union for staff, parents and members of the local community; race awareness training in schools; organising childcare for children whose mothers have been arrested; helping set up preschools for the local Chinese community and other groups; preparing a manual on hate crime for the local police force . . . the list stretches on.

In recent years the Centre has become increasingly involved in work with one of the most marginalised groups in English societies: refugees and asylum seekers. In addition to providing children and families with access to their 'core' services, services to meet the specific needs of refugees and asylum seekers have evolved: language translation; citizenship support to provide orientation and knowledge of the local context as well as help with money management; therapeutic support for children and parents often scarred by conflict, including art and play therapy; and advocacy work, supporting families in their dealings with authority.

But the Centre's work does not stop in Sheffield. Over the years, it has extended its work to 11 countries, including Ethiopia, Sri Lanka, Pakistan and Jordan. This overseas work supports and facilitates services for over 14,000 children.

How is the Centre open both to so many and so varied demands and how does it work? It is a complex entity, and no simple answers are possible: there are no formal planning systems or familiar management structures. Rather, its work is shaped by the intersection of three values, which find expression in its ways of working. First, there is a deep commitment to democratic participation and to including people even if you do not agree with them (an example is given of taking a child whose father was active in an extreme right racist group, but engaging with the father so that over time his views about minority ethnic groups moderated). Organisationally, the Centre is a co-operative run on egalitarian lines, with all staff, until very recently, paid the same. It is managed by a committee of staff and direct service users including parents and children. But around the formality of a committee is a network of informal democratic discussions, involving both staff and service users. An issue comes to the notice of the Centre or the Centre itself identifies a problem, there is discussion among staff members and service users about how to respond, sometimes nothing further materialises but more often a member of staff or of the Management Committee agrees to take a lead in developing new work, work begins and continues until no longer needed.

Second, a basic principle of the co-operative is to be open to the community, understood both as the geographical neighbourhood and as minority groups. There is a welcoming, a hospitality, a ready assumption of responsibility when individuals, families and minority groups come to seek help from the Centre. And this openness to community extends beyond Sheffield. Much of the overseas work has arisen from ethnic minority communities in Sheffield telling people in their home countries about the Centre's work in Sheffield, leading to invitations to come and support work in these countries.

Third, there is a deep, almost visceral, commitment to diversity 'as the norm not the exception' (the words of a report produced by children, parents and staff for an evaluation). The world, and its local community, are irreducibly plural, and the Centre expresses and celebrates that in every aspect of its work. The Centre is used by children and families from 75 ethnic groups. But diversity and its importance are recognised as extending well beyond ethnicity, to many other areas: religion, language, gender, class, age, sexuality, health and (dis)ability. This recognition is expressed in many ways.

There is a highly diverse and worldwide paid workforce, plus unpaid workers including solicitors, doctors and others with specialist skills. The workforce includes staff with a range of assessed disabilities who are supported by colleagues, parents and children. Like the service users, most staff are from minority ethnic backgrounds and speak many languages. Nearly 30 languages are spoken daily in the Centre, with others available. For example, in one group for 3- and 4-year-olds, Arabic, Spanish and English are spoken, while in another group Urdu, Spanish, English and Gaelic Irish are in regular use.

From its inception, the Centre has prioritised a mixed gender workforce – and, most unusually, has managed to achieve this for many years, recruiting roughly equal numbers of men and women workers. Thus in late 2000, of the 58 workers in Sheffield, 25 were men who worked across the age range of children, not just with older ones. Their commitment on this score goes beyond the Centre itself. Through housing a national Men in Childcare Support Network, the Centre has engaged with instances of repression in which individual male workers are treated stereotypically and otherwise repressively.

Practice, too, is inscribed with diversity. Gender is recognised as an important issue in all aspects of the Centre's life, to be addressed and included in all areas of policy and practice. The same applies to ethnic and linguistic diversity. Importance is attached to all children becoming multi-lingual, beginning as babies and continuing to learn in the pre-school, free-time service and the wide range of clubs and holiday activities. During each day, children will hear and use multiple languages. The diversity of spoken languages is encouraged in many other ways: there are resources (such as tapes) for children and adults to use in the Centre or to take home; language workshops for parents; visitors from minority communities invited into the Centre; family exchanges with other countries, most recently Spain, Cuba and Portugal. Recognition is given to other forms of communication: all children learn sign-language, encounter a range of scripts and learn about the rules for reading them. Quite young children become proficient in reading Braille.

Many festivals are celebrated. Visitors often come to talk about their cultures and re-affirm their children's culture. 'The Shack' provides an international centre for arts and culture

> encouraging children and young people to express themselves and be creative in a globalised world. Children experience the interaction of the arts with the environment, multi-culturalism, science, language and history ... The Shack supports children in focusing on children's rights, locally, nationally and internationally. Advocacy initiatives have encompassed conditions for street children, child soldiers, children exploited in the international sex industry and, more locally, children's inclusion in democracy, child workers in Britain and children's rights in education.
>
> (Meleady and Broadhead, 2002: 15)

Age is addressed through providing services for adults, not only parents but also older people. There are lunch clubs and outreach services for retired people, advocacy work and support groups for grandparents with grandchildren in care. But there are also projects that span the generations, for example reading and computing workshops where children mentor older learners and an inter-generational project where older people share their experiences with children.

Issues of sexuality, too, are discussed. There are groups for gay and lesbian parents, and, responding to an important issue among certain communities, there is a female genital mutilation group, with 205 girls and women attending in late 2000.

The Centre acknowledges an overtly political dimension in its work: 'if you want to impact on people's lives, you can't divorce this from the political context; otherwise you may improve the position of the individual but you don't change the conditions that create the problems'. But this places the Centre and its staff at risk. By its strong commitment to diversity, it has incurred the anger of extreme right groups. There have been attacks on staff members and the Centre is repeatedly vandalised, costing it large sums of money to repair. At the same time, the Centre has been prepared to engage with local communities of poor white British families, a group it views as a repressed minority. In collaboration with local schools, racial equality agencies and police, Centre staff have worked with many children from these communities, for example running workshops on diversity and identity and challenging the targeting of schools by extreme right political groups.

But the Centre also engages with major politics:

> [We] work with some of the most marginalized groups in our society and regularly advocate on their behalf. This can bring the Centre staff into conflict with mainstream authorities, ideas and perspectives. But we consider it essential both in terms of support to marginalized groups and in challenging endemic inequalities and oppressions which manifest themselves in language used and positions taken.
>
> (*ibid.*: 16)

The Sheffield Children's Centre provides a vivid example of the political potential of preschools (and other institutions for children). In all aspects of their existence – organisation, workforce and practices – the Centre shows how a preschool can become a site for democratic 'minor politics', in particular around questions of difference and injustice. But it also shows in action the idea of preschools as children's (and families') spaces, full of possibilities – pedagogical certainly, but also social, cultural and political. In the relationship that the Centre and its workers seek with the Other – a relationship of respect and responsibility in which diversity is the norm – it seems to us that this institution exemplifies pedagogical work inscribed with the ethics of an encounter.

Chapter 8

In search of Utopia

From Towards a New Common Sense: Law, Science and Politics in the Paradigmatic Transition *by Boaventura de Sousa Santos (1995)*:

'The future is no longer what it used to be', says a graffito on a wall in Buenos Aires. To be sure the future promised by modernity has no future. The great majority of people in the periphery of the world system no longer believe in it, for in its name they have neglected or rejected other futures, perhaps less bright and closer to the past, but at least capable of guaranteeing the communitarian subsistence and balanced relationship with nature that seems so precarious today. Nor do large sectors of people in core countries believe in the future either because the risks the future involves begin to appear more unlimited even than the future itself...

We must, therefore, reinvent the future by opening up a new horizon of possibilities mapped out by new radical alternatives. Merely to criticize the dominant paradigm, though crucial, is not enough. We must also define the emergent paradigm, this being the really important and difficult task... The only route, it seems to me, is utopia. *By utopia I mean the exploration by imagination of new modes of human possibility and styles of will, and the confrontation by imagination of the necessity of whatever exists – just because it exists – of something radically better that is worth fighting for*... The two conditions of utopia are a new epistemology and a new psychology. As a new epistemology, utopia refuses the closure of the horizons of expectations and possibilities, and offers new alternatives; as a new psychology, utopia refuses the subjectivity of conformity and creates the will to struggle for alternatives.

(479, 481; emphasis added)

We live in a period of great change, some would even say of paradigmatic transition or movement from one epoch to another. Technology

and science move at ever faster rates, personified by genetics and computing. Economically, many affluent countries of the North are moving
into post-industrialism; materially poor countries of the South with vast
populations, like China and India, are entering a phase of rapid and
massive industrialisation and economic growth; while all countries are
affected by changes in production, capital and employment. Markets
are opened up and competition intensifies. Cities in the Majority World
are growing rapidly, as people flood to them in search of work and a
better life. Politically, the Soviet empire has crumbled leaving the United
States as the only world super-power; while the European Union, which
in Europe at least has revolutionised relationships between nation states,
is at the time of writing about to make a great and peaceful expansion
east and south.

Yet, as we suggested in Chapter 2, this change arouses deep feelings
of ambivalence and disenchantment. Poverty, inequality and the HIV/
AIDS pandemic blight the global landscape, as do burgeoning urban
slums which are now home to a billion people. Widespread violence is
practised both by states and by groups (whether called terrorists or
freedom fighters) challenging these states. An almost palpable weariness
and insecurity hang over many workers doing their best to be flexible
and competitive in an increasingly uncertain world. The grave damage
mankind has done to its home, the Earth, has become vividly apparent
as global warming manifests itself in extreme weather conditions, while
many essential resources including water show signs of severe stress.
International organisations – the United Nations, the WTO, the European Union – stagger under the impact of national self-interests, the
decay of earlier idealism and a loss of confidence in their potential for
good among the population at large.

Equally telling, it is so difficult to see a future that holds out hope.
Frederick Jameson, the American cultural theorist, spoke of this in a
recent interview (Jonsson, 2003). If human beings, he observed, can
conceptualise the future except as a continuance of the present, then
they do so as a catastrophe, while to conceptualise society beyond
capitalism has become more difficult than to conceptualise life after
death. Santos, in the quotation that begins this chapter, expresses the
same feeling, summed up in the Argentinean graffito 'The future is no
longer what it used to be'. The future, in short, is unimaginable or
catastrophic or just plain depressing promising only more of the same.

Jameson and Santos both describe this situation in terms of an
absence of Utopian thought. Jameson says it is very typical of the West
that politics has been emptied of all Utopian energies. Santos recognises

a strong tradition of Utopian thinking, but dates its decline to the nineteenth century:

> Modernity has produced many utopias, starting in 1516 with Thomas More's, which gave it a name, and ending with the socialist utopias of the nineteenth century. But the fact of the matter is that the development of scientific rationality and scientific ideology since the nineteenth century, and their spilling over from the study of nature on to the study of society, gradually created an intellectual milieu that became increasingly hostile to Utopian thinking.
>
> (Santos, 1995: 480)

Yet though Utopia may be ailing, it is not dead. Levinas, in Chapter 3, readily acknowledges the Utopian nature of his ethics, but does not dismiss it: Utopia, he argues, provides us with guidance, something to strive for, and the possibility of occasional achievement. In Chapter 6, we referred to a concept of 'agonistic pluralism', under development by Mouffe. This concept, she says, assumes elements of Utopian thought – 'possible alternatives to the existing hegemonic order', whose current absence contributes to 'the growing dissatisfaction with liberal political institutions'.

In the same way, this book is an unapologetic exercise in Utopian thinking. Confronted by what we argue is a highly instrumental and impoverished discourse about preschools, which privileges technical practice in the interest of achieving predetermined outcomes, we have tried to imagine a different possibility: the preschool first and foremost as a public space for ethical and democratic political practice, where education takes the form of a pedagogy of listening related to the ethics of an encounter, and a lively minor politics confronts dominant discourses and injustice. In doing so, we have challenged instrumentality and technical practice; or rather, we have challenged the priority given to them today, but not their right to exist and find some place in preschools and, more widely, in education. In doing so we have tried to offer, in the words of Santos with which we start this chapter, 'a new horizon of possibilities mapped out by new radical alternatives'. What we are trying to offer is an alternative, an idea of a future that is neither a continuance of the present nor a catastrophe.

We are unapologetically Utopian, because we believe such thinking has a vital role to play in bringing about radical and transformative change. Without Utopian thinking linked to action, change is reduced to what Santos refers to as 'conformist action', defined as 'routinized, reproductive, repetitive practice which reduces realism to what exists and just because it exists' (Santos, 1998: 107). Conformist action describes much of our condition today. Its aim is how better to order things as they are, for example how to normalise policy, provision and practice around some expert-defined 'best practice', 'benchmark' or rating of quality or excellence.

In this context, too, politics is reduced to arguments about the best way to manage the status quo. Governments of whatever party label adapt to neoliberalism and govern in this direction, subordinating any other purposes to this task. Education suffers this same stifling fate. Politics in education, shorn of any argument about meaning, becomes a thin narrative of 'modernisation'. Instead of a continuous and critical relationship between traditions and change – 'critical modernisation' – we are offered a 'vulgar modernisation', dogmatic and ahistorical reform, involving marketisation and new modes of management in unholy alliance with a focus on education in its narrowest and most conservative sense, simply reduced to the acquisition of certain skills.

Utopian thought both provokes and enables radical critique of the status quo – through 'confrontation by imagination of whatever exists'. And it gives direction for future change, by 'the exploration by imagination of new modes of human possibility' that enable us to reinvent the future. It both deconstructs the present and reconstructs the future. It provides a provocation to politics, both major and minor, through the act of thinking differently.

Utopian thinking is not enough by itself to bring about radical change. That needs also a willingness to act. Both Utopian thought and action are more likely to occur and flourish when certain conditions are present. Utopian thought, we would argue, is most likely to thrive in spaces which enable thought to take place both beside each other and beside ourselves, listening, and keeping open the question of meaning as a subject of debate – in short, spaces which practise a concept of listening espoused by thinkers such as Readings and Rinaldi. This means spaces where there is an openness to experimentation, research and continuous reflection, critique and argumentation. In this way Utopian thought and action can be in constant relationship, and subject to revision in the light of experience, learning and discussion.

Such spaces, and the collectivities that occupy them, can take various forms. They can be individual preschools (and/or schools) with an active group of children and adults (both workers and parents), perhaps joined by others (for example other pedagogical workers such as *pedagogistas*; politicians; and local citizens) who want to participate with them in Utopian thinking and action. Sheffield Children's Centre, described in the previous chapter, is a case in point.

They can be networks of some or all preschools (and/or schools) located within the same area. This is how we can think of the municipal preschools in Reggio Emilia and in some other Italian cities, and indeed this is how they think of themselves, at least in Reggio. Each municipal preschool in Reggio 'is a network and the schools form a network with each other [which] has created a strong culture of exchange and change . . . [T]he importance of being perceived as schools that operate within a network should be underscored' (Rinaldi, forthcoming b: 12).

Examples of local networks, such as in Reggio and in some other Italian cities, are engaged in a process of Utopian thought and action, a process which might be termed a local 'cultural project on childhood'. In such cases, this process has now run over several decades as thought and action have grown, rhizome-like, through relationships of reciprocity and new perspectives acquired from border crossing. Such experience shows how Utopian thinking and action can be a long-term process with regular changes of direction, and need not become a single-minded striving after some immutable vision of a New Jerusalem. Rather networks require a desire to explore 'new modes of human possibility', and that means being open to new ideas and new knowledges.

But collective thought and action, especially given technologies for communication, can also nowadays be geographically dispersed: space for Utopian thought and action can be conceptualised in ways other than the purely territorial. Space can be looser networks of individuals or institutions spread across a region or a country, sharing Utopian thinking by various means and wanting to draw ideas and inspiration from each other about Utopian action. It can also be an international, even global, network or alliance, focused on Utopian visions for the preschool based on values shared by network members. There are numerous examples of such networks, inspired by particular ideals of pedagogical work, for example Montessori, Steiner, Freinet, High Scope and Reggio Emilia.

In the case of Reggio, the municipal preschools in Reggio are linked in a complex network with many other preschools in almost every part of the world. There are 'Reggio networks' in 13 countries: Italy itself, Australia, the United States, Korea, Japan, the United Kingdom, Germany, the Netherlands and all five Nordic countries. Membership of this global network represents a commitment to shared values and possibilities, not a requirement to follow slavishly a model or programme. It creates, in Rinaldi's vivid expression, a 'new cultural geography':

Those who are part of it [the worldwide Reggio-inspired network] already feel tied to something which is now symbolic, something more than a geographical reality. This is the new cultural geography of people who share, who accept the fate of sharing values, which goes beyond geographical borders and creates a network of people who share a common sensitivity and common ideals . . .

What we've absolutely wanted to oppose is the temptation to start off by putting on display and circulating some kind of pre-packaged boxes, using a doubtful method of applying business to pedagogy . . . We think rather that [the network] can be the source of exchanges and reflections, therefore today the argument is that every culture has to develop its own strategy in the field of school education. *Together*, we can try to share values which are universal, but at the local level, all the different actors – in Sweden, just as in Japan or Australia – will have to try to develop them for themselves.

(Rinaldi, forthcoming b)

But we could think more broadly still about networks and alliances. They could involve preschools and schools border crossing, to make connections with other types of institution, other groups, other areas of Utopian thinking. Preschools (or schools) could be inserted into wider Utopian thinking about alternative futures, exploring the connections between alternative futures for education and alternative futures for economy, environment, technology and so on. Rather than being part of a 'specialist' network, some preschools might prefer to contribute to another type of space, gaining support and inspiration from more general networks – which in turn might learn from including an educational perspective.

An example of a broad-based emergent network is the annual World Social Forum (WSF), first held in the Brazilian city of Porto Allegro in 2001, and initiated 'to discuss strategies of resistance to the model for globalisation formulated at the annual World Economic Forum at Davos by large multinational corporations, national governments, IMF, World Bank and the WTO' (World Social Forum, 2003). The WSF speaks the language of Utopian thinking with its slogan: 'Another world is possible'. In the words of its Charter of Principles, the WSF 'is an open meeting place for reflective thinking, democratic debate of ideas, formulation of proposals, free exchange of experiences and interlinking for effective action, by groups and movements of civil society that are opposed to neo-liberalism and to domination of the world by capital and any form of imperialism' (World Social Forum, 2001).

The idea of innovative preschools and local projects, with a strong ethical and political commitment, entering into a global civil society seems to us particularly interesting as a possibility for change. Indeed, more than interesting because, if our analysis in Chapter 2 is at all relevant, we need to see preschools as always in relationship to wider economic, social, cultural and technological processes. Utopian thought and action, therefore, must start from an analysis of how preschools are currently governed by wider discourses as well as what alternative wider discourses Utopian action presumes.

A certain kind of subject will facilitate Utopian thought and action, what Santos calls a 'destabilizing subjectivity' (Santos, 1998: 107) in contrast to a 'conformist subjectivity that takes as inevitable whatever exists, just because it exists' (Santos, 1995: 480). A destabilising subjectivity combines a sceptical capacity for critical thinking with an imaginative flair for alternative possibilities, a habit of mind that loves experimentation and new possibilities. It may refuse 'the subjectivity of conformity and creates the will to struggle for alternatives'. It is open to indignation but also surprise and wonder; committed yet with a recurrent sense of unease and self-questioning; passionate, but also alive with humour and laughter. A destabilising subjectivity, and Utopian thought, is nourished by border crossing, driven by an insatiable curiosity and a desire for new perspectives, different ways of thinking, alternative possibilities.

Preschools, and the many people who work in or with preschools, have mostly not border crossed. Too often, thought and practice have been constrained by remaining within the confines of a narrow field, centred on developmental psychology. But as we have tried to indicate in the book, it is possible to draw inspiration from many fields, and from thinkers who have never written about preschools: Foucault, Derrida, Levinas, Mouffe, Deleuze, Rose and Tronto to name but a few. And there are exceptions, preschool workers who have journeyed more widely. Loris Malaguzzi, for example, was a committed border crosser:

> [He] was extremely familiar with the [early childhood] field and its traditions; but he also had the courage and originality to choreograph his own thinking. By placing himself and the Reggio practice in continuous dialogue with different scientific and philosophical perspectives, not to mention the world of poetry, architecture, art etc., he succeeded in exposing our cultural heritage and opening up new possibilities.
>
> (Dahlberg, 2000: 178)

Reference to Malaguzzi is a reminder that Utopian thought and action can arise serendipitously, from a unique combination of people and place. Nor is Reggio alone – there are other examples of individual preschools or groups of preschools whose work has been inspired by some form of Utopian thinking. But are there ways in which Utopian thought and action can be stimulated, encouraged and supported?

We may have given the impression that Utopian thinking and action must take place apart from, even in opposition to, the state and majority, mainstream politics. That may often be so: in which case, individuals and groups engaged together in a search for alternatives will need to be particularly strong and inventive, and solidarity will be a particularly important resource. But it is not necessarily so, depending on how the state defines its purpose and practises democracy.

In his Utopian thinking around a paradigmatic transition arising from the inability of modernity to regenerate itself, Santos imagines 'the emergent paradigm [constructing] itself through a triple transformation: power becomes shared authority; despotic law becomes democratic law; knowledge-as-regulation becomes knowledge-as-emancipation'. Within this broad framework, he further imagines a new purpose for the state, to create the conditions for social experimentation: more specifically, 'in the paradigmatic transition, the welfare state is the state form that guarantees social experimentation' (Santos, 1995: 483). It is not, he argues, up to the state to evaluate the performance of these alternatives, evaluation of social experimentation being 'undertaken by the social forces inside interpretive communities with recourse to dialogic rhetoric' (*ibid.*: 488). D. Held (1995) expresses a similar idea, of a state which enables experimentation, when he proposes that 'a society in which Utopian *experimentation* can be tried should be thought of as a utopia. Utopia is a framework for utopias' (239; author's emphasis).

But this may be some way off yet. While we can see examples of Utopian action emerging despite the state, even in reaction to the perceived failings of the state (which is one reading of the 'city projects' in northern Italy), it is harder to think of current examples of the state as a guarantor of social experimentation. Indeed, following Santos's line of argument, this is not surprising, with the conditions for such a possibility some way off yet. Perhaps the Nordic countries, with their strong decentralisation from national government to local and institutional levels and their strong democratic traditions, are moving closest to being able to adopt this role.

But is it possible to envisage the role of the state going even further, beyond guarantor to a more active relationship with social experimentation? We think it is, but it means the state coming into a new relationship to change. In traditional major politics, the state develops a policy, which is then defined and implemented; this is an act of governing, foregrounding uniformity and viewing implementation as a managerial and time-limited act of change from one system to another. General guidelines including timetables may be issued, large-scale programmes of training activated, consultants or advisors sent forth, evaluations and reviews conducted in order to assess conformity to the new norm.

Such major politics with their general change processes will continue. But they could be accompanied by encouragement and support for more local processes of social experimentation – local Utopian thought and practice. Such processes might have a close relationship to public policy, exploring the possibilities and potentialities in that policy. But they might also be more distanced from policy, more experimental, more provocative.

Such experimentation requires, we think, a number of conditions that the state might help provide. First, a recognition that deep change involving transformations of thought and practice is a long-term process – indeed may prove to be a continuous process. The preschools in Reggio Emilia have, as we have seen, been engaged in social experimentation for 40 years with no end in sight since the idea of closure is radically at odds with their search for new knowledge and thought; while even to understand and use their tools, such as project work or pedagogical documentation, takes many years (see, for example, the discussion of the Stockholm Project in Dahlberg *et al.*, 1999). The time frame and open-endedness of experimentation are radically at odds with the short-term search for closure of most policy implementation.

Second, a willingness to be selective, to support experimentation in those preschools or other institutions where there is a desire to experiment and a commitment to the work, time and thought that experimentation requires. This does not mean ignoring other institutions, which may come into various relationships with these 'centres of experimentation'. But it does mean abandoning the idea that all must be treated the same and all must follow the same path. Third, making available people to work in the long term with these institutions and networks that we have termed centres of experimentation, people who can work and think alongside the teachers over time, share their desire to experiment, are accustomed to border crossing, and can bring important experience and critical thinking to the process of change.

This prospect of the state actively supporting social experimentation, however distant, provokes a number of questions that need further reflection and discussion. Can the mentality of the nation state change, so it can view experimentation as a continuous and diversifying process (singularities that provoke ever more new ideas), rather than as a pre-cursor to establishing new totalising systems (a prototype or pilot project for a new 'best practice', leading on to mass production)? Can or should the state entirely absent itself from evaluation or, indeed, limit itself to a political role of guarantor or promoter of experimentation? For ex-ample, are there certain forms of experimentation that the state would and should say were ethically and politically unacceptable (for example projects promoted by fascist or racist organisations)?

This possibility – however remote it may seem – of the state taking an active role in experimentation connects back to our earlier discus-sions, in Chapter 5, of the importance of experimentation as part of a pedagogy of listening, an ethics of an encounter and a philosophy of difference. To the possibilities of an experimenting pedagogue, an experimenting preschool and an experimenting local community, we can add the possibility of an experimenting state. We could even imagine going one step further.

If there is a potential enabling role for government in relation to Utopian thought and action, as an active supporter of experimentation, then this role need not be limited to the nation state. The European Union (EU) could contribute to pedagogical experimentation, creating a sort of 'European Utopian Area' that encouraged Utopian thought and action and the creation of cross-national networks and other con-nections. Diversity within Europe is not just a matter of recognising what is distinctive about national identities and systems. It can also involve a recognition of how thought and practice can and do cross borders to create connections and alliances between people and institu-tions in many different countries. Reggio is but one of the latest of a long line of examples of Utopian pedagogical thinking and practice, each of which has sprung up in one very local part of Europe – north-ern Italy in the case of Reggio – but has been welcomed in many other places in (and beyond) Europe (other examples include the work of Owen, Montessori, Froebel and Freinet).

The EU has already achieved the extraordinary feat of laying to rest thousands of years of war between the peoples and states of Western Europe. That achievement is itself the result of Utopian thought and action, in this case by the statesmen who founded the Union (or the European Economic Community, as it was originally called) after the

Second World War, and who were brave enough to imagine an alternative to endless fighting. Another Utopian vision, largely achieved, was the creation of a space for the free movement of goods, capital and people. Now the time has come for a reinvigoration of European Utopian thinking, applied to a range of institutions and practices including, but not only, preschools. This should not offer a pale copy of an Anglo-American neoliberalism, with its attendant preschool discourse, but instead should be inspired by a vivid idea of experimentation, difference and border crossing, combining the promotion of diversity with the fostering of connections between those who share common values and hopes. Some other international organisations have become a means of grasping others into dominant and totalising global discourses; the EU, unique as a *democratic* international institution, albeit far from perfect, can explore an alternative idea of 'glocalisation', encouraging and linking local experiences across national borders, valuing the provocation of difference.

Bringing about change through Utopian thought and action cannot be legislated from above, through some law or regulation requiring all preschools to be Utopian! Government, at most, can create conditions that favour experimentation, and then encourage the emergence of groups and networks. But the results are likely to be patchy – some will flourish, others fade quickly and yet more never get started in the first place. This seems unavoidable. But it also raises the recurring dilemma of the relationship between diversity and equality.

The issue of equality can best be met by opening up to all the opportunity to experiment. At the same time, walking on two legs, we suggest that the chance for experimentation, only likely to be taken by some, is combined with some form of framework that encompasses all preschools, which could cover areas such as funding, access, staffing and curriculum. The detail and extent of that framework will be a political subject to be resolved in each country: in England, for example, 3- and 4-year-olds are entitled to part-time publicly funded preschool attendance, while in Sweden entitlement is for children from 12 months of age and for longer hours. The common principle though is that the state retains some responsibility to ensure certain basic conditions and entitlements, providing a modicum of equality, irrespective of the presence and vigour of local social experimentation.

But, over and above the role of the state, what conditions might favour Utopian thought and the experimentation of Utopian action? We have mentioned the virtues of networks, as modes of solidarity and exchange. There may be value too in 'outside project workers', not consultants offering a time-limited input of expertise, more like critical but caring friends, offering a permanent provocation to new thinking and practice, who enter into a long-term commitment to become a part of the preschool group or community of preschools. *Pedagogistas* occupy this role in Reggio and some other places in Italy, but there could be other possibilities. Evaluation of work, through processes such as pedagogical documentation, can also play an important part, as we have seen, in deconstructing current practice and reconstructing a new one. But the use of evaluation here is very specific: not to judge the conformity of practice to a current norm (such as happens when the concept of quality is used); rather to deepen understanding and further experimentation, an evaluation that forms part of a professional and political debate (what might happen when working with the concept of meaning making).

Utopian thought and action also require time – as do all the ethical and political practices we have discussed. Time to read widely and look into different areas, time to listen and discuss, time to think, time to do pedagogical documentation. Time for workers in preschools to do these things, but also for others who should be involved in Utopian politics – politicians themselves, but also parents and the elusive but potentially important 'concerned citizen'. Yet time today is at a premium, an increasingly scarce and costly commodity. Preschool workers have little or no time free from their daily work with children, usually considerably less than school teachers. Parents spend longer hours in the labour market, and at the same time are expected to undertake an increasing amount of work to meet their personal and family responsibilities, manage their risks and upgrade their competencies: being a practitioner of freedom and an entrepreneur of the self is a never-ending and time-consuming business, leaving little time free for critical thinking or Utopian action.

These possible participants in Utopian thinking and action, and in ethical and political practice, face ever more demands on their time. Some of those demands assume the capacity of people to be increasingly productive, for example through better management of their lives, the application of technology or out-sourcing various tasks of private life. Following this way of thinking, more can simply be squeezed into the time available through increased personal productivity and doing more and more things at the same time. On other occasions new demands simply ignore the time dimension or underestimate the time required. The consequence is populations of harassed, tired people, trying to juggle too many balls, surviving (mostly) but not flourishing.

We cannot go on in this way. Especially not if we want to engage people in creating new possibilities for education, with (pre)schools as spaces for ethical and democratic practice, which might be thought of as one important direction for Utopian thought and experimentation. Thought and listening, border crossing and diversity, reading and reflecting, deconstruction and reconstruction, innovation and experimentation, all require time. They are relational activities that cannot be reduced to technical practices whose productivity can be gradually increased.

We have to think differently about time, in a Utopian way. People working in any preschool (and school) need, as a matter of course, time for doing a range of routine activities not involving direct contact with children, from preparing future work to meeting parents. But those involved in Utopian thought and action need additional time for this work and this requires funding for this purpose: this is one practical way that government (or other funding bodies) can support experimentation.

But for parents and others to participate fully if they so choose requires more radical thinking. If paid work increasingly absorbs our time and energies, then we have less for other things. The hegemony of formal paid work has to be challenged, its stranglehold on time loosened. We need to experiment with new projects on time; for example an entitlement for men and women to take a certain period of paid leave from employment over a working lifetime for reasons other than childcare. One reason might be to participate in various democratic fora, another in various forms of social experimentation. Put another way, we might extend an exemplary system of parental leave, such as in Sweden, adding an entitlement to time away from work of, say, 5 years between the ages of 20 and 65. We call Swedish parental leave exemplary, and a good basis for a broader entitlement (a 'time account') because it combines a high level of payment to leave takers (80 per cent of normal earnings for most of the leave period) with many options for how leave is taken: it can be taken full time, half time, quarter time, or even one hour a day; and it can be used as one block of time or several shorter periods (for further information see Haas and Hwang, 1999; and Deven and Moss, 2002).

When we come to payment, this leave period could be paid at a proportion of earnings, being conditional on a previous employment record. Or we could explore another idea, the social wage or citizen's salary, a basic income to which everyone over a certain age would be entitled, an old idea most recently proposed by Hardt and Negri:

'the social wage extends well beyond the family to the entire multitude, even those who are unemployed, because the whole multitude produces and its production is necessary from the standpoint of total social capital . . . [W]e could call this guaranteed income a citizenship income, due each as a member of society' (2001: 403). The German sociologist Ulrich Beck pursues the same principle but relates it to a more specific concept of 'public work', 'a new focus of activity and identity that will revitalize the democratic way of life' and implying 'active compassion', 'practical critique' and 'active democracy':

> In the future what will probably win out is a blending of formal work and voluntary organization, the dismantling of legal and mobility barriers between the two sectors, the creation of opportunities for leaving or changing one's principal occupation . . . Two things would thus become possible. First, the equation of public activity with remunerated employment would be broken. Second, public work would create new foci of political action and identity formation within and opposed to a fragmented society.
>
> (Beck, 1998: 60)

Beck goes on to look at various ways of paying for 'public work', offering three models: a tax-financed basic support payment, a sort of 'public stipend' for all participating in voluntary organisations, and a 'citizen's support for all'.

Mouffe, arguing that there is a crisis of work and exhaustion of the wage society, similarly draws a connection between making more space for activity that falls in neither the public nor the private sector and introducing a system of democratic income distribution, adding a third measure, the reduction of hours spent in employment:

> Such measures [reduced working hours, massive development of non-profit activities by associations and an unconditional minimum income] would foment a plural economy where the associative sector would play an important role alongside the market and the state sector. Many activities of crucial social activity discarded by the logic of the market would, through public financing, be carried out in this solidaristic economy. A condition for the success of such initiatives is of course the third measure, the implementation of some form of citizen income that would guarantee a decent minimum for everybody.
>
> (Mouffe, 2000b: 126–127)

Mouffe sees these measures as forming the basis for what she describes as 'a post-social-democratic answer to neo-liberalism' (*ibid.*).

André Gorz (1989) proposes a 'guaranteed income' scheme that is a form of hybrid between extended leave and a guaranteed minimum income. His aim is to find a way 'to eliminate not only poverty and involuntary unemployment, but also the lack of time, harassing work conditions and the obligation to work full time throughout one's entire working life' (209). His principle is the redistribution of the 'economically necessary quantity of work', which within two decades, he argued, would have reduced to 1,000 hours per person per year. Citizens who average these annual working hours over a period would be entitled to a regular guaranteed income, and so could vary their working time, working more some periods and less others when they could use their time for other purposes:

> the possibility of periodically interrupting your working life for six months or two years at any age will enable anyone to study or resume their studies, to learn a new occupation, to set up a band, a theatre group, a neighbourhood cooperative, an enterprise or a work of art, to build a house, to make inventions, to raise your children, to campaign politically, to go to a Third World country as a voluntary worker, to look after a dying relative or friend, and so on.
>
> (*ibid.*: 210)

The problem with Utopia is not that it is Utopian, in the sense of being 'unrealistic' or unrealisable. As we heard from Levinas in Chapter 3, Utopia provides us with guidance, something to strive for, and the possibility of occasional achievement. The problem with Utopia (and perhaps one reason why it has gone out of fashion) arises when it becomes totalitarian, allowing no space for or respect to other Utopian thought. The greatest danger for democracy, it seems to us, is totalising Utopian thought, which denies or grasps every alternative, and where meaning is not kept open and the object of debate. Such totalitarian and repressive utopias offer closure and no possibility for future change, only a realisation of one grand design.

This is Utopian thinking without any possibility of alternatives, an idea of linear progress leading to a singular Utopia, the final solution. And in the process such thinking can crush important experiences, often built up over many years through a mix of local Utopian thought and minor politics. In the preschool field today, we are concerned that neo-liberalism, a current example of totalising Utopian thought, may ruin much important pedagogical work developed within a framework of decommodified public responsibility, in its obsession with markets and privatisation.

In his discussion of 'public works', Beck (1998) is struggling with a central question in post-industrial societies – how can individualism be connected with solidarity? In many ways that too has been a question we have been struggling with in this book. Or, put another way, how can we create new relationships of inter-dependency, when identities are increasingly complex, multiple and fluid? How can we make common cause over those matters that affect us all, in a way that does not require the denial of difference and conflict? Answers to such questions must be couched in terms of ethics and politics, for these are two of the most important arenas in which relations in society are formed and reformed. For example, we would suggest that a 'pedagogy of listening', inscribed with the ethics of an encounter, offers an example of what might be termed solidarity in learning, combining as it does a recognition of the profound importance of relationships *and* a deep respect for otherness. Similarly, 'agonistic pluralism' provides a concept for the conduct of minor politics which encompasses connectedness *and* difference.

They must also, in our view, involve problematising the ideal subject of current liberalism, which foregrounds autonomy as independence, self-governing and flexibility. But with the decline of major politics and the breakdown of institutions and identities that forged mass relationships of solidarity, it seems obvious that we should pay more attention to those expanding institutions in society which are used for long periods of time by the great majority of the population: preschools, schools and free-time services. These institutions have the potential for becoming spaces for ethical and political practices that can engage many people, of all ages.

The importance of these institutions in the forging of new relationships of solidarity rests not just in their wide recognition and use. They are more than just convenient meeting points, important though this is. Their importance rests as much if not more in their potential purposes and the choices with which these confront us: as sites for governing or for emancipation, for conformist or transformative action, for transmitting or constructing knowledge, for reinforcing or reconstructing discourses. Returning to our starting-point, the words of Bill Readings, for us the Utopian possibility, a possibility so full of hope and excitement, a prize almost beyond measure, is that more preschools and schools might become loci of ethical practices, and by so doing contribute to relationships, with each other as well as our environment, which are founded on a profound respect for otherness and a deep sense of responsibility for the Other.

References

Ball, S. (1994) *Education Reform: A Critical and Poststructural Approach*. Buckingham: Open University Press.

Bartlett, K. (1999) 'Real engagement by children', *Early Childhood Matters*, 9 (February 1999), 112–118.

Bauman, Z. (1991) *Modernity and Ambivalence*. Cambridge: Polity Press.

Bauman, Z. (1992) *Intimations of Postmodernity*. London: Routledge.

Bauman, Z. (1993) *Postmodern Ethics*. Oxford: Blackwell.

Bauman, Z. (1995) *Life in Fragments*. Oxford: Blackwell.

Bauman, Z. (1999) *In Search of Politics*. Cambridge: Polity Press.

Bauman, Z. (2000) *Liquid Modernity*. Cambridge: Polity Press.

Beck, U. (1994) 'Reinvention of politics: towards a theory of reflexive modernisation', in U. Beck, A. Giddens and S. Lash, *Reflexive Modernity*. Cambridge: Polity Press.

Beck, U. (1998) *Democracy without Enemies*. Cambridge: Polity Press.

Becker, G. (1976) *The Economic Approach to Human Behaviour*. Chicago: University of Chicago Press.

Beilharz, P. (2000) *Zygmunt Bauman: Dialectic of Modernity*. London: Sage.

Bernauer, J. and Mahon, M. (1994) 'The ethics of Michel Foucault', in G. Gutting (ed.) *The Cambridge Companion to Foucault*. Cambridge: Cambridge University Press.

Bernstein, B. (1977) *Class, Codes and Control*, Volume 3: *Towards a Theory of Educational Transmissions*. London: Routledge & Kegan Paul.

Bertens, H. (1995) *The Idea of the Postmodern*. London: Routledge.

Borgnon, L. (forthcoming) *A Virtual Child*, manuscript for a forthcoming doctoral thesis, Stockholm Institute of Education.

Burman, E. (2001) 'Beyond the baby and the bathwater: postdualistic developmental psychologies for diverse childhoods', *European Early Childhood Education Research Journal*, *9(1)*, 5–22.

Butler, J. (1993) *Bodies that Matter: on the Discursive Limits of Sex*. London: Routledge.

Cabinet Office Strategy Unit (2002) *Delivering for Children and Families: Interdepartmental Childcare Review*. London: Cabinet Office Strategy Unit.

Cagliari, P., Barozzi, A. and Giudici, C. (2004) 'Thoughts, theories and experiences for an educational project with participation', *Children in Europe*, 6, 28–30.

Caputo, J. D. (1997) *Deconstruction in a Nutshell: A Conversation with Jacques Derrida*. New York: Fordham University Press.

Catarsi, E. (2004) 'Malaguzzi and the municipal school revolution', *Children in Europe*, 6.

Ceppi, G. and Zini, M. (1998) (eds) *Children, Spaces and Relations – Metaproject for an Environment for Young Children*. Reggio Emilia: Reggio Children.

Cerny, P. and Evans, M. (1999) *New Labour, Globalisation and the Competition State* (CES Working Papers no. 70). Berlin: Harvard University Center for European Studies.

Cherryholmes, C. H. (1988) *Power and Criticism: Post-structural Investigations in Education*. New York: Teachers College Press.

Cherryholmes, C. H. (1993) 'Reading research', *Journal of Curriculum Studies*, 25(1), 1–32.

Clark, A., McQuail, S. and Moss, P. (2003) *Exploring the Field of Listening to and Consulting with Young Children* (Research Report 445). London: Department for Education and Skills.

Clark, A. and Moss, P. (2001) *Listening to Young Children: the Mosaic Approach*. London: National Children's Bureau.

Clark, T. (2002) *Martin Heidegger*. London: Routledge.

Clarke, J. (1998) 'Thriving on chaos? Managerialisation and the welfare state', in J. Carter (ed.) *Postmodernity and the Fragmentation of Welfare*. London: Routledge.

Cohen, B., Moss, P., Petrie, P. and Wallace, J. (2004) *A New Deal for Children?* Bristol: Policy Press.

Colebrook, C. (2002) *Gilles Deleuze*. London: Routledge.

Cooke, B. and Kothari, U. (2001) 'The case for participation as tyranny', in B. Cooke and U. Kothari (eds) *Participation: The New Tyranny*. London: Zed Books.

Council of Europe (1996) *Social Charter*, revised version. Online. Available HTTP: <http://www.coe.int>.

Critchley, S. (1999, 2nd edn) *The Ethics of Deconstruction: Derrida and Levinas*. Edinburgh: Edinburgh University Press.

Critchley, S. (2001) *Continental Philosophy: A Very Short Introduction*. Oxford: Oxford University Press.

Critchley, S. (2002) *The Ethics of Deconstruction: Derrida and Levinas*. Oxford: Blackwell.

Crouch, C. (2001) *Coping with Post-democracy*. London: Fabian Society.

Dahlberg, G. (2000) 'Everything is a beginning and everything is dangerous: some reflections on the Reggio Emilia experience', in H. Penn (ed.) *Early Childhood Services: Theory, Policy and Practice*. Buckingham: Open University Press.

Dahlberg, G. (2003) 'Pedagogy as a loci of an ethics of an encounter', in M. Bloch, K. Holmlund, I. Moqvist and T. Popkewitz (eds) *Governing Children, Families and Education: Restructuring the Welfare State*. New York: Palgrave McMillan.

Dahlberg, G. (2004) 'Making connections', *Children in Europe*, 6, 22–23.

Dahlberg, G. and Åsen, G. (1994) 'Evaluation and regulation: a question of empowerment', in P. Moss and A. Pence (eds) *Valuing Quality in Early Childhood Services*. London: Paul Chapman Publishing.

Dahlberg, G. and Lenz Taguchi, H. (1994) *Förskola och skola – om två skilda traditioner och om visionen om en mötesplats* ('Preschool and school – two different traditions and a vision of an encounter'). Stockholm: HLS Förlag.

Dahlberg, G., Moss, P. and Pence, A. (1999) *Beyond Quality in Early Childhood Education and Care: Postmodern Perspectives*. London: Falmer Press.

Dean, M. (1999) *Governmentality: Power and Rule in Modern Society*. London: Sage.

Deleuze, G. (1988) *Foucault*. Minneapolis: University of Minnesota Press.

Deleuze, G. (1992) 'Postscript on the societies of control', *October*, 59, 3–7.

Deleuze, G. (1994) *Difference and Repetition*. New York: Columbia University Press.

Deleuze, G. (1995) *Negotiations, 1972–1990*. New York: Columbia University Press.

Deleuze, G. and Guattari, F. (1999) *A Thousand Plateaus: Capitalism and Schizophrenia*. London: Athlone Press.

Deleuze, G. and Parnet, C. (1989) *Dialogues*. London: Athlone Press.

Derrida, J. (1999) *Adieu to Emmanual Levinas*. Stanford, CA: Stanford University Press.

Deven, F. and Moss, P. (2002) 'Leave arrangements for parents: overview and future outlook', *Community, Work & Family*, 5(3), 237–255.

Dobrowolsky, A. (2002) 'Rhetoric versus reality: the figure of the child and New Labour's strategic "social-investment state"', *Studies in Political Economy*, (Autumn), 43–73.

Dreyfus, H. and Rabinow, P. (1982) *Michel Foucault: Beyond Structuralism and Hermeneutics*. Brighton: Harvester Press.

English Children and Young Persons Unit (2001) *Core Principles of Participation*. Online. Available HTTP: <http://www.cypu.gov.uk>.

English Department for Education and Employment (1998) *Meeting the Childcare Challenge*. London: Stationery Office.

English Qualifications and Curriculum Authority (2000) *Curriculum Guidance for the Foundation Stage*. London: EQCA.

Esping-Andersen, G. (1999) *Social Foundations of Postindustrial Economies*. Oxford: Oxford University Press.

Esping-Andersen, G., Gallie, D., Hemerijk, A. and Myles, J. (2001) *Why We Need a New Welfare State*. Oxford: Oxford University Press.

Fendler, L. (2001) 'Educating flexible souls', in K. Hultqvist and G. Dahlberg (eds) *Governing the Child in the New Millennium*. London: Routledge Falmer.

Fink, D. (2001) 'The two solitudes: policy makers and policy implementers', in M. Fielding (ed.) *Taking Education Really Seriously: Four Years Hard Labour*. London: Routledge Falmer.

Foerster, H. von (1991) 'Through the eyes of the other', in F. Steier (ed.) *Research and Reflexivity*. London: Sage.

Foucault, M. (1977) *Discipline and Power: The Birth of the Prison*. Harmondsworth: Penguin Books.

Foucault, M. (1980) *Power/Knowledge: Selected Interviews and Other Writings, 1972– 1977*, ed. C. Gordon. London: Harvester Wheatsheaf.

Foucault, M. (1983) 'On the genealogy of ethics', in H. Dreyfus and P. Rabinow (eds) *Michel Foucault: Beyond Structuralism and Hermeneutics*, 2nd edn. Chicago: University of Chicago Press.

Foucault, M. (1986) *The Care of the Self*. New York: Pantheon.

Foucault, M. (1987) 'The ethic of care for the self as a practice of freedom: an interview with Michel Foucault', in J. Bernauer and D. Rasmussen (eds) *The Final Foucault*. Cambridge, MA: MIT Press.

Foucault, M. (1988) *Politics, Philosophy, Culture: Interviews and Other Writings, 1977– 1984*, ed. L. Kritzman. New York: Routledge.

Fraser, N. (1997) *Justice Interruptus*. New York: Routledge.

Garber, M., Hanssen, B. and Walkowitz, R. (2000) 'Introduction: the turn to ethics', in M. Garber, B. Hanssen and R. Walkowitz, *The Turn to Ethics*. London: Routledge.

Giudici, C., Rinaldi, C. and Krechevsky, M. (eds). (2001) *Making Learning Visible: Children as Individual and Group Learners*. Cambridge, MA: Project Zero and Reggio Emilia: Reggio Children.

Glasersfeld, E. von (1991) 'Knowing without metaphysics: aspects of the radical constructivist position', in F. Steier (ed.) *Research and Reflexivity*. London: Sage.

Gore, J. (1998) 'Disciplinary bodies: on the continuity of power relations in pedagogy', in T. Popkewitz and M. Brennan (eds) *Foucault's Challenge: Discourse, Knowledge and Power in Education*. New York: Teachers College Press.

Gorz, A. (1989) *Critique of Economic Reason*. London: Verso.

Gray, J. (1995) *Enlightenment's Wake: Politics and Culture at the Close of the Modern Age*. London: Routledge.

Gray, J. (1999) *False Dawn: the Delusions of Global Capitalism*. London: Granta Books.

Gray, J. (2000) *Two Faces of Liberalism*. Cambridge: Polity Press.

Green, A. (2003) 'Globalisation and the role of comparative research', *London Review of Education*, 1(2), 83–98.

Grosz, E. (ed.) (1999) *Becomings: Explorations in Time, Memory and Futures*. Ithaca, NY: Cornell University Press.

Haas, L. and Hwang, P. (1999) 'Parental leave in Sweden', in P. Moss and F. Deven (eds) *Parental Leave: Progress or Pitfall?* The Hague and Brussels: NIDI CBGS Publications.

Hanssen, B. (2000) 'Ethics of the Other', in M. Garber, B. Hanssen and R. L. Walkowitz (eds) *The Turn to Ethics*. London: Routledge.

Hardt, M. and Negri, A. (2001) *Empire*. Cambridge, MA: Harvard University Press.

Hatch, J. A. (1995) 'Studying children as a cultural invention: a rationale and a framework', in J. A. Hatch (ed.) *Qualitative Research in Early Childhood Settings*. Westport, CT: Praeger.

Held, D. (1995) *Democracy and the Global Order*. Cambridge: Polity Press.

Held, V. (2002) 'Care and the Extension of Markets', *Hypatia, 17(2)*, 19–33.

Hughes, P. and MacNaughton, G. (2000) 'Consensus, dissensus or community: the politics of parental involvement in early childhood education', *Contemporary Issues in Early Childhood, 1(3)*, 241–257.

Hutton, W. (1995) *The State We're in*. London: Jonathan Cape.

Ignatieff, M. (2000) 'Human rights as idolatry', the Tanner Lectures delivered at Princeton University, 4–7 April 2000. Available at: www.tannerlectures.utch.eds/lectures/ignatieff_os.pdf.

Jonsson, S. (2003) 'Operation rädda utopin' ('Operation save utopia'), *Dagens Nyheter*, 12 May.

Kemp, P. (1992) *Emmanuel Levinas: En Introduktion* ('Emmanuel Levinas: An Introduction'). Göteburg: Daidolos.

Khosravi, S. (1998) 'Efter Lasermannen' ('After the Laserman'), *Moderna Tider*, (October), 28–29.

King, M. (1997) *A Better World for Children: Explorations in Morality and Authority*. London: Routledge.

Kjørholt, A. T. (2001) 'The participating child – a vital pillar in this century?', *Nordic Educational Research, 21(2)*, 65–81.

Knowles, C. (1999) 'Cultural perspectives and welfare regimes', in P. Chamberlayne, A. Cooper, R. Freeman and M. Rustin (eds) *Welfare and Culture in Europe: Towards a New Paradigm in Social Policy*. London: Jessica Kingsley.

Laing & Buisson (2002) programme for Third Annual Children's Nurseries Conference, London, 4 February 2003.

Laing & Buisson (2003) *Children's Nurseries UK Market Sector Report 2003*. London: Laing & Buisson.

Langsted, O. (1994) 'Looking at quality from the child's perspective', in P. Moss and A. Pence (eds) *Valuing Quality in Early Childhood Services*. London: Paul Chapman Publishing.

Lather, P. (1991) *Getting Smart: Feminist Research and Pedagogy with/in the Postmodern*. London: Routledge.

Le Métais, J. (2003) 'Where are we going? International trends in primary education', *NfER News, Autumn/Winter*, 9.

Lenz Taguchi, H. (2000) *Emancipation och motstånd: Dokumentation och kooperativa läroprocesser i förskolan* ('Emancipation and resistance: Documentation and co-operative learning processes in the preschool'). Doctoral thesis. Stockholm: LHS Förlag.

Lenz Taguchi, H. and Munkhammar, I. (2003) *Consolidating Governmental Early Childhood Education and Care Services under the Ministry of Education and Care: a Swedish Case Study* (UNESCO Early Childhood and Family Policy Series No. 6). Available at www.unesco.org.

Levinas, E. (1987) *Time and the Other*. Pittsburgh, PA: Duquesne University Press.

Levinas, E. (1988) 'The paradox of morality', in R. Bernasconi and D. Wood (eds) *The Provocation of Levinas: Rethinking the Other*. London: Routledge.

Levinas, E. (1989) 'Ethics as first philosophy', in S. Hand (ed.) *The Levinas Reader*. Oxford: Blackwell.

Levinas, E. and Kearney, R. (1986) 'Dialogue with Emmanuel Levinas', in R. A. Cohen (ed.) *Face to Face with Levinas*. Albany, NY: State University of New York Press.

Liedman, S.-E. (2001) *Ett oändligt äventyr: Om människans kunskaper*. Falun: Albert Bonnier Förlag.

Lind, U. (2003) 'Postmodern reconceptualisation of aesthetics for education', paper given at NFPF/NERA Congress 'Education as a Critical Force: Myth or Reality?'. Copenhagen, 6–9 March.

Lister, R. (2003) 'Investing in the citizen-workers of the future: transformations in citizenship and the state under New Labour', *Social Policy and Administration*, *37(5)*, 427–443.

Lyotard, J.-F. (1984) *The Postmodern Condition: A Report on Knowledge*. Minneapolis, MN: University of Minneapolis Press.

Malaguzzi, L. (2004) 'Walking on threads of silk: interview with Loris Malaguzzi', *Children in Europe*, *6*, 10–15.

Meleady, C. and Broadhead, P. (2002) 'A curriculum for diversity', *Children in Europe*, *3*, 14–18.

Miller, P. and Rose, N. (1993) 'Governing economic life', in M. Gane and T. Johnston (eds) *Foucault's New Domains*. London: Routledge.

Ministry of Education and Science (Sweden) (1998: English language edn) *Curriculum for Preschool*. Stockholm: Ministry of Education and Science.

Moss, P., Dahlberg, G. and Pence, A. (2000) 'Getting beyond the Problem with Quality', *European Early Childhood Education Research Journal*, *8(2)*, 103–120.

Moss, P. and Pence, A. (eds) (1994) *Valuing Quality in Early Childhood Services*. London: Paul Chapman Publishing.

Moss, P. and Petrie, P. (2002) *From Children's Services to Children's Spaces: Public Policy, Children and Childhood*. London: Routledge Falmer.

Mouffe, C. (2000a) 'Which ethics for democracy?', in M. Garber, B. Hanssen and R. L. Walkowitz (eds) *The Turn to Ethics*. London: Routledge.

Mouffe, C. (2000b) *The Democratic Paradox*. London: Verso.

Nordin-Hultmann, E. (2004) *Pedagogiska miljöer och barns subjektskapande* ('Pedagogical environments and children's construction of subjectivity'). Doctoral thesis. Stockholm: Liber.

Organisation for Economic Cooperation and Development (OECD) (1999) *OECD Country Note: Early Childhood Education and Care Policy in Sweden*. Online. Available HTTP: <http://www.oecd.org>.

Organisation for Economic Cooperation and Development (OECD) (2001) *Starting Strong: Early Childhood Education and Care*. Paris: OECD.

Organisation for Economic Cooperation and Development (OECD) (2002) *OECD in Figures: Statistics of the Member Countries* (2002/Supplement 1). Online. Available HTTP: <http://www.oecd.org>.

Osgood, J. (2004) 'Time to get down to business? The response of early years practitioners to entrepreneurial approaches to professionalism', *Journal of Early Childhood Research*, *2(1)*, 5–24.

Penn, H. (2002) 'The World Bank's view of early childhood', *Childhood*, *9(1)*, 118–132.

Peperzak, A. T. (1998) *Beyond the Philosophy of Emmanuel Levinas*. Evanston, IL: Northwestern University Press.

Polanyi, K. (1957) *The Great Transformation*. Boston, MA: Beacon Press.

Popkewitz, T. (1998) *Struggling for the Soul: The Politics of Schooling and the Construction of the Teacher*. New York: Teachers College Press.

Popkewitz, T. and Block, M. (2001) 'Administering freedom: a history of the present – rescuing the parent to rescue the child for society', in K. Hultqvist and G. Dahlberg (eds) *Governing the Child in the New Millennium*. London: Routledge Falmer.

Power, M. (1997) *The Audit Society*. Oxford: Oxford University Press.

Prout, A. (2000) 'Children's participation: control and self-realisation in British late modernity', *Children & Society*, *14*, 304–331.

Rabinow, P. (2000) *The Essential Works of Foucault 1954–84*, Volume 1: *Ethics*. London: Penguin Books.

Radin, M. J. (1996) *Contested Commodities: The Trouble with Sex, Children, Body Parts, and Other Things*. Cambridge, MA: Harvard University Press.

Rancière, J. (1991) *The Ignorant Schoolmaster: Five Lessons in Intellectual Emancipation*. Stanford, CA: Stanford University Press.

Ransom, J. (1997) *Foucault's Discipline*. Durham, NC: Duke University Press.

Readings, B. (1996) *The University in Ruins*. Cambridge, MA: Harvard University Press.

Rinaldi, C. (1998) 'The space of childhood', in *Children, Spaces, Relations*. Reggio Emilia: Reggio Children.

Rinaldi, C. (1999) untitled paper given to a British study tour to Reggio Emilia, April.

Rinaldi, C. (forthcoming a) 'The construction of the educational project', in *In Dialogue with Reggio Emilia*. London: Routledge.

Rinaldi, C. (forthcoming b) 'The organisation, the method: conversation with Carlina Rinaldi by Ettore Borghi', in *In Dialogue with Reggio Emilia*. London: Routledge.

Rinaldi, C. (forthcoming c) 'Formation and professional development in a school of education', in *In Dialogue with Reggio Emilia*. London: Routledge.

Rinaldi, C. (forthcoming d) 'Documentation and research', in *In Dialogue with Reggio Emilia*. London: Routledge.

Rinaldi, C. (2001a) 'The courage of Utopia', in C. Giudici, C. Rinaldi and M. Krechevsky (eds) *Making Learning Visible: Children as Individual and Group Learners*. Cambridge, MA: Project Zero and Reggio Emilia: Reggio Children.

Rinaldi, C. (2001b) 'Documentation and assessment: what is the relationship?', in C. Giudici, C. Rinaldi and M. Krechevsky (eds), *Making Learning Visible: Children as Individual and Group Learners*. Cambridge, MA: Project Zero and Reggio Emilia: Reggio Children.

Rinaldi, C. (2001c) 'The image of the child', presentation given at the World Forum, May 2001.

Rose, N. (1999) *Powers of Freedom: Reframing Political Thought*. Cambridge: Cambridge University Press.

Santos, B. de S. (1995) *Towards a New Common Sense: Law, Science and Politics in the Paradigmatic Transition*. London: Routledge.

Santos, B. de S. (1998) 'The fall of the *Angelus Novus:* beyond the modern game of roots and options', *Current Sociology, 46(2)*, 81–118.

Scottish Parliament (2002) *Children's Commissioner Bill: Q & A Briefing*. Available at www.scottish.parliament.uk.

Seidman, S. (1998, 2nd edn) *Contested Knowledge*. Oxford: Blackwell.

Sennett, R. (1998) *The Corrosion of Character: the Personal Consequences of Work in the New Capitalism*. London: Norton.

Sevenhuijsen, S. (1998) *Citizenship and the Ethics of Care: Feminist Considerations on Justice, Morality and Politics*. London: Routledge.

Sevenhuijsen, S. and Williams, F. (2003) 'Recent parenting policies: an analysis through the ethic of care', paper given at a seminar 'Employment and Care', Cumberland Lodge, 27–28 October.

Smart, B. (1999) *Facing Modernity: Ambivalence, Reflexivity and Morality*. London: Sage.

St Pierre, E. A. (2000) 'The call for intelligibility in postmodern educational research', *Educational Researcher, 29(5)*, 25–29.

Stiglitz, J. (2002) *Globalisation and its Discontents*. London: Allen Lane, Penguin Press.

Swedish Ministry of Education and Science (1998) *Curriculum for Preschool* (English translation of *Läroplan för förskolan, Lpfö-98*). Stockholm: Swedish Ministry of Education and Science.

Swedish National Agency for Education (2000) *Descriptive Data on Childcare and Schools in Sweden* (Report No. 192). Available at www.skolverket.se.

Taylor, M. C. (1987) *Alterity*. Chicago: University of Chicago Press.

Taylor, M. C. (1991) *The Ethics of Authenticity*. Cambridge, MA: Harvard University Press.

Toroyan, T., Roberts, I., Oakley, A., Laing, G., Mugford, M. and Frost, C. (2003) 'Effectiveness of Out-of-home Day Care for Disadvantaged Families: Randomised Controlled Trial', *British Medical Journal, 327*: 906–909.

Toulmin, S. (1990) *Cosmopolis: the Hidden Agenda of Modernity*. Chicago: University of Chicago Press.

Tronto, J. (1993) *Moral Boundaries: A Political Argument for the Ethics of Care*. London: Routledge.

United Nations Development Programme (2002) *Human Development Report 2002*. Online. Available HTTP: <http://www.un.org>.

United Nations Development Programme (2003) *Human Development Report 2003*. Online. Available HTTP: <http://www.un.org>.

UNICEF (2000) *A League Table of Child Poverty in Rich Countries* (Innocenti Report Card, Issue No. 1). Florence: Innocenti Research Centre (UNICEF).

UNICEF (2002) *A League Table of Educational Disadvantage in Rich Nations* (Innocenti Report Card, Issue No. 4). Florence: Innocenti Research Centre (UNICEF).

Walkerdine, V. (1984) 'Developmental psychology and the child-centred pedagogy: the insertion of Piaget into early childhood education', in J. Henriques, W. Holloway, C. Irwin, C. Venn and V.Walkerdine (eds) *Changing the Subject: Psychology, Social Regulation and Subjectivity*. London: Methuen.

White House, the (2002) *Good Start, Grow Smart: The Bush Administration's Early Childhood Initiative*. Online. Available HTTP: <http://www.whitehouse.gov>.

White, S. (1991) *Political Theory and Postmodernity*. Cambridge: Cambridge University Press.

Whitty, G., Power, S. and Halpin, D. (1998) *Devolution and Choice in Education*. Buckingham: Open University Press.

World Social Forum (2001) *Charter of Principles*. Online. Available HTTP: <http://www.wsfindia.org>.

World Social Forum (2003) *Who Are We?* Online. Available HTTP: <http://www.wsfindia.org>.

Wragg, T. (2003) 'Wise words', *Guardian Education*, March 4.

Yeatman, A. (1994) *Postmodern Revisionings of the Political*. London: Routledge.

Young, I. (1990) *Justice and the Politics of Difference*. Princeton, NJ: Princeton University Press.

Young, R. (1990) *White Mythologies: Writing History and the West*. London: Routledge.

Index